SHROUDED TRUTH

BIBLICAL REVELATIONS THROUGH PAST LIFE JOURNEYS

BOOK ONE OF THE RADIANT LIGHT SERIES

REENA KUMARASINGHAM

from the
heart press

Publication by From the Heart Press; First Publication March 2018
Website; http://www.fromtheheartpress.com/

Text and front cover copyright: Reena Kumarasingham
ISBN: 978-0-9567887-5-7

A CIP catalogue record for this book is available from the British Library.

Design: Ashleigh Hanson, Email; hansonashleigh@hotmail.com

Front cover artwork: Sanja Jovic, Website; www.sanjajovicart.com

To find out more about Reena Kumarasingham, visit the website;
http://www.divineaspect.com

REVIEWS

Shrouded Truth walks the path of enlightenment through Biblical references that follow the lives and messages of James, Paul, Mary Magdalene, Thomas, and others; and is a highly recommended pick for Biblical scholars from novices to advanced thinkers.

By reviewing these lives and their impact and messages on spiritual thinking, Reena Kumarasingham provides a direct connection between how and why these people evolved as they did and God's greater purpose.

If this was the only approach supporting *Shrouded Truth*'s contentions, it would be effective in and of itself. There's a lot more going on than biographical reflection alone. The information presented herein has been obtained not through studying Biblical events but by including information received from sessions of past life regression. Therapist/author Kumarasingham has become an expert in the field, training Regression Therapists around the world in the techniques and possibilities of working with past life information.

The story of Jesus Christ, when viewed from the typical scholarly and religious angles, is already notable; but when imbibed with insights gained from past life regression work, it is particularly insightful: especially, here, where eight different people unrelated to one another contribute their versions of Biblical events and their meaning.

By now it should be evident that one prerequisite for appreciation of *Shrouded Truth*'s focus and contents is an acceptance of past life regression. The memories presented herein popped up over a four-year period in different parts of the world and were experienced by common people who had no prior connection with each other or with Biblical scholarship.

This fact is, perhaps, one of *Shrouded Truth*'s greatest strengths, because it's hard to refute or ignore the kinds of insights and connections that dovetail so neatly and explicitly in this coverage. Through serendipity and possibly determined spiritual effort, these disparate individuals came to Kumarasingham's attention: thus, this book.

A second big plus to Kumarasingham's approach is his attention to blending known, proven facts about the times with these past live experiences. This makes for far more than a collection of impressions and ideas, linking historical fact to the new information: *"…it is not far-fetched to think that James had a commercial network and a small fleet of trading boats that travelled to England. Although the area was not called 'England' during the Biblical period, the memories were being filtered through Mia's current-life vocabulary, hence her use of terms from the current times. As is mentioned by Isabel Hill Elder, 'It is not by mere chance that Arimathean Joseph became acquainted with Cornish tin and Somerset lead mining, for as a Prince of the House of David, Joseph was aware that his kinsmen of the tribe of Asher had made Cornwall famous for the prized metal.' Again, this implies that the family of Jesus was an important, well-to-do family."*

The result is a unique blend of historical fact, verbatim chronicles from past life regression narratives, and new perspectives on Biblical events that intrigues and invites debate from Biblical scholars.

Shrouded Truth is a unique, highly recommended Biblical study that should be included in any serious historical and cultural examination of Jesus' life and times.

D. Donovan, Senior Reviewer - Mid West Book Reviews

CONTENTS

FOREWORD

Culture shapes our thinking and actions far more than we realise. More obvious examples are from our friends and workplace and less obvious ones are the ways we think and behave that were passed down the generations and conditioned into us when we were children. Newspapers have different political positions, and depending on what we read will subtly change our thinking. Our religious views may close us to other perspectives. Some psychologists argue that we are simply the product of the culture we live in. If we are born white into a western, Christian family, we will be totally different from a Hindu living in India, even if at birth we possessed the same DNA. I would argue that we can be unique and not possessed by whatever culture we live in. We need to stand back and have an open mind about new ideas and use our intuition if the idea feels right.

When people bring new information to the world that goes against the prevailing culture, it calls for great courage. In the twelfth century, Cathars living in Southern France introduced the ideas of reincarnation at a time when the prevailing Roman Catholic religion had different views. They were hunted down and burnt at the stake in the tens of thousands by soldiers sent by the Pope. In medieval Europe we have had hundreds of years when people who did not comply with the culture of those times were accused of heresy and tortured. Extreme violence creates fear and this energy can stay in our common psyche and affect us all. But it is only when people are prepared to express different views and provide evidence to support it that the world moves forward in a positive way.

This book will provide new information about the biblical time that was obtained through past life regression. Of course, there are many debates about the truth of past lives. Sceptics often point at some factual inaccuracies in a narrative and feel that this is proof that it must have been created from the imagination. But how many of us can recall early life experiences and details such as the names of our friends at a birthday party without some gaps in recall occurring? And when the information is accurate, sceptics suggest that the information may come from something the person had read or watched on the media and it was buried below the level of conscious awareness. However, professor Ian Stevenson and his successor professor Jim Tucker at the University of Virginia have investigated and documented thousands of cases in which children's reports of past lives cannot be explained away except for reincarnation.

I have followed the work of Reena over the three to four years the book has developed. Reena is a highly talented therapist working with past lives. She also goes around the world from Australia, to Europe and the USA training Regression Therapists to work with past lives and has become an expert in this area. I have been amazed at Reena's ability to pull reference information from numerous sources about the biblical period. This is such a complex subject to research, given that much information has either been lost or distorted over time. Yet Reena draws this all together in a way that is easy to follow and understand.

In summary when you read this book all you need to do is have an open mind and know that the integrity of the author is intact, and enjoy the magical journey she takes you on.

Andy Tomlinson, March 2018

INTRODUCTION

One of the most prolific and thoroughly researched stories ever told, the life story of Jesus Christ, has seen so many different variations. From his birth to his death, what's known of his life has been dissected, told and retold through different perspectives. Without a shadow of a doubt, Jesus is one of the most inspiring and enigmatic people to have ever existed.

Shrouded Truth tells the story of Jesus Christ through the eyes of eight different souls, through memories of their past lives. The people who participated in this book had very little, if any, connection to one another. These memories popped up spontaneously, at different points in the space of four years, in different parts of the world, by ordinary people who were experiencing sessions for different intents and purposes. They had varying degrees of prior knowledge of the biblical stories – some none at all, and some rather in depth. Synchronicity played a big part in bringing these individual souls to me, as though it was a deliberate attempt by the souls themselves to get their message across. Through serendipitous and synchronous events, all their sessions were recorded, and by their good grace and permission *Shrouded Truth* was born.

Before we delve into the story, it is prudent to first address the elephant in the room: reincarnation, past lives and regression – are they real?

The immortal soul is an important part of all religions. The Egyptians had such elaborate beliefs about death and the afterlife, that they performed complex rituals around preserving the 'ka' and 'ba' (soul) of the person after death. Many modern-day Christians and Muslims believe in heaven and hell; souls will be judged based on their deeds on earth

3

and will spend all of eternity in one or the other as a result. Nearly 350 million Buddhists and 800 million Hindus believe that the immortal soul incarnates over and over again until they reach the state of Nirvana.

The Quran and the Zohar, the mystical texts of Islam and Judaism respectively, both mention reincarnation:

'And you were dead, and He brought you back to life. And He shall cause you to die, and shall bring you back to life, and in the end shall gather you unto Himself.' – Quran (2:28)

'All souls are subject to reincarnation; and people do not know the ways of the Holy One, blessed be He! They do not know that they are brought before the tribunal both before they enter into this world and after they leave it; they are ignorant of the many reincarnations and secret works which they have to undergo, and of the number of naked souls, and how many naked spirits roam about in the other world without being able to enter within the veil of the King's Palace. Men do not know how the souls revolve like a stone that is thrown from a sling. But the time is at hand when these mysteries will be disclosed.' – Zohar (II 99b)

Even the early Christians, including some of the first Popes of the Church, believed in reincarnation. St Gregory of Nyssa believed that 'it is absolutely necessary that the soul be healed and purified; and if that did not occur during life on earth, it should be done in future lives'.[1]

St Clement of Alexandria supported this belief; but perhaps the person most associated with the principle of reincarnation

4

was his pupil, Origen, who included the reincarnation doctrine in his book *On First Principles*: 'Each soul comes into this world strengthened by the victories or weakened by the defeats of its previous life ... Your actions in that world determine your place in this world (on earth) which must determine the next one ...'[2]

The Fifth Ecumenical Council of Constantinople in AD553, three centuries after his death, reportedly decided against Origen and declared the reincarnation doctrine heretical. Some believe that the Emperor Constantine removed all these references from the Bible at the Council of Nicaea in AD325, and that the only evidence is under the ashes of the Alexandrian library, which was destroyed.[3]

Saying that, there are surreptitious references to reincarnation in the Bible including John 9:1–2, which states: 'As Jesus was walking along, he saw a man who had been blind from birth. "Rabbi," his disciples asked him, "why was this man born blind? Was it because of his own sins or his parents' sins?"' The only way that this man's sins could have caused him to be born blind is for him to have sinned before he was born in his current body.

Furthermore, a 2009 survey by the Pew Forum on Religion and Public Life, a non-partisan American think tank based in Washington D.C. found that 51 per cent of the world's population believes in reincarnation, as do 24 per cent of American Christians.[4]

Let's not forget that respected academicians in the twentieth century too believed in reincarnation. Carl Jung, in a lecture that he presented in 1939, said, 'This concept of rebirth necessarily implies the continuity of personality. Here the human personality is regarded as continuous and accessible to memory, so that, when one is incarnated or born, one is able, at least potentially, to remember that one has lived through previous existences. As a rule, reincarnation means rebirth in a human body.'[5]

Dr Ian Stevenson, a Canadian psychiatrist who worked for the University of Virginia School of Medicine for fifty years, as chair of the Department of Psychiatry from 1957 to 1967, Carlson Professor of Psychiatry from 1967 to 2001, and Research Professor of Psychiatry from 2002 until his death, spent forty years of his life researching 3,000 children from Africa to Alaska, who claimed to remember past lives spontaneously. Some of the anecdotes came from children who live in rural areas, who had no access to mass media, and are so detailed and personal that the account could not have been imagined but only recalled. His work was collated and written up in around 300 papers and 14 books on reincarnation, including *Twenty Cases Suggestive of Reincarnation* published in 1966. His work, plus his successor, Jim Tucker's and that of many others since who have documented past lives of children, is a strong indication of the existence and authenticity of reincarnation and past lives.

The first known writings that mention past-life regression – to access memories in past lives – is in ancient Indian literature, the Upanishads, but the Yoga Sutras of Patañjali (written in the second century BC) discuss the concept in greater detail. The Hindu scholar Patañjali discussed the idea of the soul becoming burdened with an accumulation of impressions as part of the karma from previous lives. Patañjali called the process of discovering these impressions past-life regression, or *prati-prasav* (literally 'reverse birthing'), and saw it as a means of addressing current problems through memories of past lives.

Past-life regression rose to prominence in the West in the late nineteenth century, through the works of mediums and spiritual practitioners. However, in around the mid-twentieth century, psychologists, psychotherapists and academics started to conduct research into past lives and past-life regression, use it in a therapeutic setting, and also developed a more standardised framework that most practitioners work with now. Noted experts in this field include Dr Brian Weiss (psychiatrist), Andy Tomlinson (psychotherapist) and Dr Roger Woolger (Jungian therapist).

A popular misconception of those who are sceptical is that people who experience past-life regression always experience lives of people who are well known – monarchs, celebrities, authors, artists. However, this is an inaccurate presumption. In my experience of practising and training therapists in regression therapy, I have only encountered a handful of people who have experienced what is known as a high-profile life. Most of the experiences are those of peasants, soldiers and everyday people going through everyday trials and tribulations.

Shrouded Truth offers an insight into Jesus Christ the person – and also the people around him. As the inspiration that he was, and still is, most writings about the life of Jesus do not focus on his human aspect, but perpetuate his Divinity. It is therefore incredibly fascinating to delve into the lives of the people around him, and to witness a story emerge that is really quite unexpected.

Shrouded Truth is not intended to be contentious or offensive. It merely offers a different perspective of one of the most famous stories of our time. Historical records, written or spoken, cannot always be regarded as provable facts. The picture can change with new discoveries and archaeological relics. No matter how detailed or fascinating that original account was, pulling together the pieces of the different accounts provides deeper meaning to the story.

For those of you who have picked up *Shrouded Truth*, I ask that you have an open heart and mind, put preconceived notions on the backburner and decide for yourself which version resonates with you most once you have finished reading it.

A difficulty with the subjects in trance is that they sometimes repeat themselves, and their grammar can be poor, particularly for those who do not have English as their first language. So some minor adjustments have been made to improve the readability. For clarification I have occasionally added some of my own comments in square brackets. The overriding intent is to present transcripts that are readable yet as accurate as possible to the original content.

I would like to thank and acknowledge everyone who has participated in this book. Firstly, to all the regressees who participated in this book – for your volunteered time, commitment and permission to use your sessions in creating this book. This was a real team effort and this book could not have been produced without all of you. Secondly, Andy Tomlinson, whose support, advice and expertise has been invaluable. Thirdly, Sanja Jovic, the talented Artist of Light who painted the beautiful cover for *Shrouded Truth*. She has intuitively captured the energy of this book, and I am forever grateful for her unconditional generosity. Fourthly, Sara Wright, who did a great job transcribing the recordings, and who provided me with objective and valuable feedback. Last but certainly not least, Julie Ann and Natasha Lyons, for holding me, and for their belief in me.

1

DUTIFUL

*You will never do anything in this world without courage. It is the
greatest quality of the mind, next to honour.*

– Aristotle

I first met Mia as a client, nearly five years ago, for a between-
lives spiritual regression session. This is a process propagated
by an American Psychiatrist, Dr Michael Newton, where
clients in deep trance are facilitated to go to a space in-
between lives, to discover plans and purpose for this, their
current life. (See end of Appendix 1 for more information.)

Mia is a mother and wife living in the south of Britain, so it
was by virtue of close proximity that she opted to come to me
as a client. During the between-lives session, we
spontaneously discovered that Mia had experienced a past life
during biblical times.

She went back to a life as a man in his late twenties with
bandages around his feet, wearing a smock that fell just below
his knees. It was dark and he was in a cave with friends. She
became visibly distressed – pale and tearful, and was feeling
scared. 'We have to get Jesus away … It feels like it has all
gone wrong,' she declared.

At that point, I, having grown up as a Hindu, had very little
knowledge of the New Testament. So while the information
was fascinating to me, the session was facilitated to maximise
the between-lives experience for Mia.

Two years later, after I'd had a few different clients who spontaneously regressed back to biblical times, Mia agreed to participate in the conception of this book with her past-life recollection of a man who turned out to be James the Lesser, the brother of Jesus.

Upon entry, Mia went back to a memory of being a man in his early twenties with straight, dark-brown hair and beard, wearing dusty, strappy sandals on his dusty feet. He was wearing a long beige robe with a strappy belt that hung down in tassels. The belt held his purse containing silver coins.

Mia: I'm a merchant ... Mm. It's part of the family business.
Reena: What sort of merchant are you?
Mia: We trade metals. And silks. And spices. The metals are new. This is something I want to trade.
Reena: Did you introduce this to the family business?
Mia: Mm. I introduced it.
Reena: And is it doing well?
Mia: We're only just starting. But the rest of it does very well.
Reena: Tell us about your family.
Mia: We are a merchant family.
Reena: Is your dad in the business with you?
Mia: Mm.
Reena: And what does he do?
Mia: He's the head of the family.
Reena: And how about your mum?
Mia: My mother is very special.
Reena: In what way is she special? Can you give us more information?
Mia: Like an angel.

Reena: Are you the only child? Or are there others there?

He went on to explain that he was the third child – with two older brothers, and a younger sister. He then went on to say that while both his mother and sister were never exactly involved in the family business, his two brothers were. At that point of the memory, they had stopped being involved.

Reena: What do they do now, your two brothers?
Mia: [pause] My brother's a holy man.
Reena: Both of them or one of them?
Mia: Both. One follows the other.
Reena: How do you address them?
Mia: Jesus and Mark.
Reena: OK. So Mark follows Jesus? [Mia nods.] And do you follow them? [Mia shakes head.]
Reena: OK. What happens next?
Mia: My father needs me.
Reena: How do you refer to your father?
Mia: He is my lord and master.
Reena: What is his name?
Mia: Joseph.

By this point, we had gathered evidence that Jesus' father was not a poor carpenter as is popularly believed. He was a merchant, whose reach stretched far and wide if he was trading silks and spices. Jesus, according to the Gospels of Matthew and Luke, was of the royal lineage of King David, via the generational descent in the male line through his father, Joseph.[1] It does make more sense for Jesus' family to have had some status within the community. So how did the tradition of Joseph being a carpenter start?

According to Laurence Gardner, in his book, *The Magdalene Legacy*, the true meaning of this tradition was lost in translation, when the Gospels were translated into English in the seventeenth century. The term used to describe Joseph, the ancient Greek term of *ho tekton* (which has been misconstrued as being a 'carpenter'), really defines him as a learned man and one who is the 'master of the craft'. Joseph, being a successful merchant in this regression, is in line with Gardner's thesis as well as being part of the Davidic bloodline.[2] The regression continues.

Reena: How was Joseph when Jesus and Mark left the business?
Mia: Cross.
Reena: Shall we go back to the time when Jesus left the business then? And just tell me what it is you are aware of?
Mia: I am younger. The first son was to go into the priesthood. This is our way. [pause]
Reena: Is it your family way or a cultural way or …?
Mia: Cultural. We are Jewish. But we are not traditional Jews. We are part of a sect.
Reena: And what is the name of the sect?
Mia: I think we are Essenes. Joseph is proud of this. My father is very proud. And proud his son will join the priesthood. He goes at puberty. Jesus goes at puberty to be trained in the priesthood.
Reena: And how old are you?
Mia: Five or six. I am sad … [Mia's voice gets softer and trails off]
Reena: What's making you sad?
Mia: He is my big brother. I love him.
Reena: Are you close to Jesus?

Mia: I really look up to him. He's got big eyes. He is so gentle. My other brother is a bit tougher. We fight.
Reena: You and Mark?
Mia: Mm. Jesus never fights. He's like my mother. [big sigh]
Reena: How about your sister? Does she fight?
Mia: No.
Reena: Is she like Jesus?
Mia: No.
Reena: What is your sister like?
Mia: She is very sweet but very naughty. She is rebellious.
Reena: How do you address your sister?
Mia: Sarah.
Reena: And what is your mother's name?
Mia: Mary.

The next significant event takes us forward to the time when Mark wanted to leave the family business.

Mia: I'm older. This is where Mark wants to leave. He wants to follow Jesus.
Reena: He wants to go into the priesthood?
Mia: No. Jesus has left the priesthood.
Reena: And what does your dad say to Mark?
Mia: He says that's not the way. He is supposed to come into the business.
Reena: How old are you at this point?
Mia: Seventeen. Mark has been in the business, as have I. But now he wants to leave. He wants to become a disciple.
Reena: A disciple of Jesus?

Mia: Mm. He is saying this is The Way and my father is saying this is not The Way. But he is going to go anyway.

Reena: How are you feeling about all this?

Mia: A bit scared.

Reena: What is scaring you?

Mia: Now it's up to me. My father is old. It's up to me to run the business. Without any help apart from my father, who is very old now.

Reena: What does your father say to you? Do you assume that you have to run the business or does your father tell you?

Mia: He tells me but I know.

Reena: How does your father address you?

Mia: 'You are my only son.'

Reena: 'You are my *only* son,' he says?

Mia: This is what he says now.

Reena: Is he unhappy with Jesus or …?

Mia: No. But he gave his son to God. So he is no longer his son.

Reena: And with Mark walking away, did Joseph kind of disown Mark, then?

Mia: He has left. He has chosen a path.

In the next significant event, Mia finds her past-life name.

Mia: I am James. I have found my identity now.

Reena: How did you find your identity?

Mia: I became a man.

Reena: Oh? Is that like a naming ceremony or did you just find your identity internally?

Mia: We do have a ceremony but it took some time for me to feel myself.

Reena: OK. So what's happening in this significant event, James?
Mia: I have gone to see my brothers. And my mother and my sister are there.
Reena: Did they go with Jesus as well?
Mia: Mm.
Reena: So the only ones left in the business are you and your father?
Mia: My father is now dead.
Reena: How old are you now?
Mia: I am in my early twenties.
Reena: How long has your father been dead for?
Mia: Not long.

Historical speculation is that Joseph died in AD29, before Jesus started his ministry.[3] By Mia's account, this would mean that James was born sometime between AD6–8, and Jesus around 7BC, which is in line with historical records.[4]

When asked about his emotions around the death of his father, James said that he was sad but free of his father's expectations of always doing as he was told.

Reena: So you go off and see your brothers and your mum and your sister. Tell us what's happening.
Mia: There is a huge crowd. I haven't seen him for a long time. He looks older.
Reena: Jesus?
Mia: Mm. But still so kind.
Reena: And what happens next?
Mia: [sighs deeply after long pause] I just weep at his feet.
Reena: What's made you do that?

Mia: I don't know – it's so strange. [sighs] I just felt so lost and now I feel found.

Reena: Is this the first time you have seen your brother since he left?

Mia: Not since he left but for a long time.

Reena: What happens next?

Mia: I'm talking to my brothers … We're talking about his [Jesus'] beliefs … He left our more traditional priests. He's got his own ideas. And he's quite vocal and forthcoming with them.

Reena: What happens next?

Mia: He lifts me and hugs me and calls me his brother … He says, 'Come be my brother now in life - not just with past ties.'

Reena: And what do you say in response?

Mia: I feel I have obligations but [sighs] – oh, gosh – in my heart I have to … I have to be with him … I say I'll join but I need to continue to work. My mother is pleased. She is with my sister and she says this is how it's meant to be. This is how it's meant to be now.

Reena: So what happens to your business?

Mia: I can take time and run part of it. There are ways. My position is to also be in the world, not to be with Jesus all of the time. And to travel. I travel on business and also then, within the travelling … There's a network, it's to carry messages within that network.

Reena: Tell us more about this network and what sort of messages are being carried.

Mia: Part of it is about freedom for the Jews, for the Jewish people. This is a turbulent time. It's to carry messages of uprisings.

Reena: How are you feeling now?

Mia: I wonder what I've got myself involved with. [sighs deeply] ... This is a freedom movement. It's a mass freedom movement. But Jesus is different. While others call for war and violence, Jesus says that freedom comes from a freedom of the heart and through love and that's how we gain our freedom. It's different. *Very* different. He's talking really about, it's very different, the spiritual freeness from the priests as well that are very revolutionary. Being true to God. Being closer to God and that it's God's love and God is the only master, not the Romans and not the priests.

When asked if James understood the essence of the message, he replied: 'Much of it. But I feel I don't understand all of it. Certainly not in the way Jesus does. Jesus has an understanding that I don't think any of us truly grasp, apart from maybe my mother.'

When asked how the message is received in the wider public he gave a big sigh. 'Many don't want to fight but they want to feel a respect for themselves. They want a new message: they are thirsty for it, thirsty for change. They are fed up with being dictated to by the Romans and by the priests. It's received well because of who he is. Because of the love, the energy. The love is ... He just settles everybody. And in his presence there is a knowing that all will be well. Just to sit in his presence ...'

James then went on to describe a little of their lifestyle. According to him, he, Jesus and his followers travelled together often. Sometimes they were joined by their mother Mary and sister Sarah. Sometimes they stayed in James' and Jesus' family home, but when they travelled, they relied on the generosity of their supporters for shelter and lodging.

When asked for a name or title for the people who follow Jesus' teachings, James responds: 'He calls them his children. And his family. They are his brothers and sisters, his children, his family. They are his family. It's a very big family.'

James is then asked about the political environment around him. 'It's more the priests. The priests are not happy – not happy at all. [They] are afraid of an uprising. They are afraid they will lose their power. They are afraid they will lose their power by the Romans smashing all the Jewish establishments. All the infrastructure. And they are afraid they'll lose their power from beneath. From the people. That people will no longer respect them. So they are being squeezed by the power above and the power below. And they are not happy … So, they spread rumours. They are very angry. They have meetings and are very angry. I have said Jesus is not the troublemaker. He talks of peace. But he is the most charismatic. He is the one they are most afraid of, even though there are others. The Romans are more unhappy with others. But the priests …'

When asked how Jesus responded to the priests' unhappiness and their rumours, James laughs and responds, 'We are all children of God,' and then, 'God is my Father and when it's my time, He will receive me. I will return to Him.'

Reena: Are these the same priests that Jesus went to when he was a teenage boy, when he hit puberty?
Mia: Some of them, yes. They feel betrayed.
Reena: What are they betrayed by?
Mia: Because Jesus is cleverer than them and he is teaching things different to how they taught it to him. And he has a different understanding of their teachings. Different meanings that they have never seen before

and they don't want to accept this. They don't want to change from the old ways.

This account is consistent with not just that of the New Testament but also historical accounts of the environment of Judea during the days of Christ. The first century AD saw Judea in heaving political turmoil and religious unrest. From 150BC to AD100, Galilee, the birthplace of Jesus, was also the birthplace of revolts against the Romans, and their crushing taxes and land regulation. There were three broad levels to the socio-hierarchy of the Judean populace:[5]

- The Pharisees – devoutly orthodox, they were keen on maintaining the rigorous Jewish faith that Jesus was against.
- The Sadducees – predominantly the Jewish aristocrats, wealthy and in collaboration with Roman rule – they had some theological differences with the Pharisees.
- The Essenes – who saw that Judea was getting corrupt and who withdrew into the caves and the wilderness and were spearheading the change in regime. Ascetic in outlook, they were reputed to be the most cultured and learned religious order.

It was also interesting to note that though Jesus was sent to study with the Pharisees, he disagreed with their teachings and held the ideologies that the Essene community had. The Essenes were free of the contamination of politics or orthodox religion, and wanted a change for Judea.[6] Again, this is in line with what Mia was recounting.

The next significant event found James eating with a group of people, who he identified as Jesus' disciples and wife.

Reena: Who is his wife?

Mia: Mary.

Reena: Isn't Mary the mother?

Mia: Yes.

Reena: It's a different Mary then?

Mia: Mm.

[Later, in the debrief, Mia says that during the regression, she was sure that this was Mary Magdalene, although she was not known or addressed as 'Mary Magdalene' during that time.]

Reena: And where is Sarah?

Mia: Sarah is helping to prepare the food.

Reena: How many disciples are there?

Mia: Many disciples.

Reena: How many are there at the meal?

Mia: Fifteen.

Reena: Is Mark there? [Mia nods]

Reena: Are you a disciple?

Mia: I am a disciple but my role is different. I am not with the Master all the time.

Reena: What is your role?

Mia: I go between the inner circle and the outer world.

Reena: So who are the fifteen who are there? Mark ...

Mia: Jesus, John, Sarah, my mother, Mary, James ...

Reena: Aren't you James?

Mia: There's another James. [long pause] Peter. I don't like Peter.

Reena: What about Peter don't you like?

Mia: I don't trust him. He loves Jesus but he cannot see ... He just cannot see the truth. He still has anger in his heart.

Reena: Can Jesus see this?

Mia: Mm. Jesus loves him, though. He laughs. Jesus laughs and tells me not to worry. [pause] I really don't like him.

Reena: Have you told Jesus your feelings?

Mia: Mm. He [Peter] is rude.

Reena: Who else is there?

Mia: ... the rest of his inner circle. I don't spend so much time with them. The time I spend, I spend with Jesus and then I continue with my work outside. I am not really part of their circle. And this is the problem. This is where Peter thinks he's the boss of the circle. This is what I do not like.

Reena: Who do *you* think is the boss of the circle? Or is there a boss of the circle?

Mia: Jesus is the Master.

It is worth pointing out here that there is historical speculation that the term 'Jesus of Nazareth' is not a reference to the town that Jesus was born in. In the Old Testament, Nazareth was not listed as a town in Jerusalem. Instead 'Jesus of Nazareth' could be a misinterpretation of 'Yesus Nazarene' from the New Testament. Nazarene is the term given to the spiritual leadership of the Essenes.[7] So, Jesus being the Master fits in quite nicely with the speculation of biblical historical scholars. The regression continues.

Reena: Does Peter think he is the Master as opposed to Jesus?

Mia: No, but he sees that Jesus is concerned with spiritual things and that he must run the more mundane.

Next, James relays a memory of arguing with Peter before the meal, thinking that Peter is trying to take over and enforce his will – which, in James' opinion, is not the will of God. In response, Peter tells James patronisingly to stop being a spoilt child.

Then James talks about sitting down to eat and describes the meal. He sits as far away from Peter as possible. They dine on stew, with goat meat. They also have olives, fruit and dates, cuisine that is consistent with what was commonly eaten during that time in that part of the world. Goat's meat was the most common meat, and stewed meat was considered to be a dish given to honoured guests. Olives, dates and fruit are also recorded to be an important source of food consumed by Israelites in those times.[8]

At the mention of the fruit, James smiles.

Reena: Do you like dates?

Mia: Mm. I like sweet things. And we have wine. And a type of bread. It's a very special occasion.

Reena: What's special about it?

Mia: Jesus is explaining the planning. He's explaining that he must leave and go into hiding and how things should be run in his absence.

Reena: What's makes Jesus want to go into hiding?

Mia: That it's getting too dangerous for him. We aim to continue his teachings there..... But he is fighting with this idea. Fighting with the idea of going into hiding or facing the priests and so there is a discussion. [pause] He now decides he wants to face the priests. ... He decides he wants to travel ... to where the priests are holding a meeting. He wants to face them.

Reena: How do you feel about this?

Mia: I'm not happy. I think it's too dangerous.

Reena: How do the others feel about this? Your mum, Mary, Peter, Sarah, Mark?

Mia: Everyone feels it's too dangerous. But his mind is made up.

[It is interesting to note that this could be an account of the Last Supper.]

Reena: And what happens next?

Mia: He prepares to travel ... I go on ahead of them. ... I have to do some business and sort some things. And so I arrive later.

In the next scene, James says that he is always on the outside – not part of the inner circle.

Reena: And how does that make you feel?

Mia: It's OK. This is my position.

Then he explains that he is not with Jesus, but in the capital that he eventually identifies as the Holy City. James is with Mary, his mother, Sarah, his sister, and Mary, Jesus' wife. Due to religious reasons, the ladies are unable to have contact with Jesus and the rest of the priests during the time of the meeting. So James stays with them to protect them. A little later, James gets a message from Mark that Jesus has been arrested.

Reena: How does this make you feel?

Mia: I knew. I knew something would happen.

Reena: What happens next?

Mia: My mother is quite calm but the other women are wailing.

Reena: Sarah and Mary?

Mia: Mm. I ask my brother to stay. I must go and try and bargain for him.

At this point, James did not know what the charges were for Jesus' arrest. Calmly but urgently, James decides to see Jesus and the city governor, as the next course of action, to offer a bribe for Jesus' release.

Reena: How do you address the city governor? Do you address him by name?

Mia: Pontius Pilate.

Reena: And what does Pontius Pilate say when you offer him a bribe?

Mia: He will accept but he will put it to the people and offer to free one of the prisoners. This is the best he can do.

Reena: How many prisoners are there besides Jesus?

Mia: There's many but they will execute three.

Reena: Tell me what happens next.

Mia: I go to the guards and I offer a bribe to the guards. They say they will accept the bribe but they must have someone in his place … [sighs] I accept this. I tell them I must find someone that looks like Jesus and that it will be OK because he will be released. The people are bound to want Jesus … One of the followers [sighs heavily] offers to take Jesus' place. Jesus is nearly dead anyway. They've tortured him. He is unconscious. We take him and we hide him.

Reena: [referring to the heavy sighs] Are you feeling emotional? [Mia nods] Are you feeling emotional that Jesus is nearly dead or that someone has offered to replace him?

Mia: The whole thing. And someone must take his place.

Reena: And you take Jesus and hide him …

Mia: We hide him in a cave, a burial cave where he won't be disturbed. But we have to heal him. [sighs heavily] Oh, gosh!

It was clear through this entire exchange that the weight of what James had orchestrated weighed heavily on him. This was startling to me, as the person conducting the regression, as it was the first time that I had heard of Jesus being substituted during his sentence.

Reena: What happened to this other person that is taking his place?
Mia: There's only me, my brother and the women that know this. It must be so secret. We leave the person that takes his place. [sighs heavily … pause] Jesus is safe. [long pause] And then we go to the trial and Pontius Pilate keeps his word. He offers it to the people and the people do not choose Jesus. And an innocent man will die. Is it right that it's a different innocent man? [sighs heavily]
Reena: Does Jesus know that this is happening?
Mia: No. Jesus is still too ill. [sighs] The only ones that know are me, my mother, Jesus' wife and my brother.
Reena: Does your sister know?
Mia: [shakes head] People will realise, though. His [the substitute's] face has had to be bloodied. He looks beaten. And I did that to him – I asked him to do that.
Reena: Did you ask or did he volunteer to do it?
Mia: He volunteered. But it was at my request.
Reena: This person … do you know him?
Mia: Yes. [long pause]
Reena: Can you tell us his name?
Mia: No.

During the account of the next few memories, Mia became increasingly distressed, holding her face and head in her hands, sighing repeatedly and even pulling on her hair.

Mia: He (the substitute) is killed.
Reena: How is he killed?
Mia: On the cross. We have to take his body, we have to dispose of the body, because it will be realised it's not Jesus. Oh, gosh, what a mess! What a mess! [sighs heavily] We take the body and we bury it. We must remove it [from the cross] so that when people come, they do not see the difference. I think some people have already guessed.
Reena: How did you get access to the body?
Mia: We are allowed to take it because we are the family. [sighs heavily] … Terrible. I feel sick.
Reena: Do you think it's your fault?
Mia: It's not my fault but I've played a part. And as [to] the part I have played, was it correct?

James then went on to explain the substitute was a follower who looked just like Jesus, though not an exact doppelgänger. The substitute had known exactly what he needed to do, and gave his life willingly for Jesus to survive.

While it was the first time I had heard of a substitute being crucified, the Koran has a verse that mentions a substitute – Surah An-Nisa' number 157 that says (interpreted), 'And (because of) their saying: "Surely we have killed the Massih – son of Maryam", the messenger of Allah, and they could not kill him nor could they crucify him, even though a likeness of that was made for them.'[9]

While most Western scholars, Jews and Christians, believe that it was Jesus who died, most Muslims believe he was raised to Heaven without being put on the cross and God transformed another person to appear exactly like Jesus, who was crucified instead of Jesus.

There are also Gnostic Gospels, like the Gospel of Basilides, that mention that Jesus survived the crucifixion and specifically say that Simon of Cyrene was the substitute. 'Thus he himself did not suffer. Rather, a certain Simon of Cyrene was compelled to carry his cross for him. It was he who was ignorantly and erroneously crucified, being transfigured by him, so that he might be thought to be Jesus.'[10]

This account of the crucifixion is also found in two second- and third-century Gnostic texts in the Nag Hammadi Library: the Apocalypse of Peter[11] and the Second Treatise of the Great Seth, in which Simon of Cyrene is also identified as being one of a succession of bodily substitutes for the spiritual Christ.[12] The regression continues.

Mia: So we take the body [to dispose of] and when the rest of the disciples come, the body's gone. They are all proclaiming it's a miracle and I know … [pause] I tell Jesus.
Reena: What is Jesus' reaction?
Mia: Angry. He is angry with me. He said that no one should die in his place. I did what I felt was right. Nobody should have died. He should have been released. Jesus kisses me and tells me he knows. He says he has to see his disciples one last time … to explain his message. He has to explain his message so it doesn't get misinterpreted …

James elaborated that, in his understanding, it was a message of love. Of equality. All men and women are equal in the eyes of God. We are all brothers and sisters. We are all family. We are all children of God.

> Reena: And tell me what happens next.
> Mia: I am preparing. We're going to leave. He must leave. He must recuperate in the mountains for some time before [sic], because it will be a very long journey.
> Reena: His wounds are quite extensive, then?
> Mia: Mm. He was beaten very badly.
> Reena: Who beat him?
> Mia: The guards. The guards were paid by the priests to beat him. [sighs heavily] He has many wounds. They marked him when they held him. They marked him as if he had been crucified. He was stabbed. And they tortured him.

This piece of detail is quite significant in the regression because even though Jesus was not crucified, he was marked as though he was. This would account for all the subsequent witnesses of Jesus feeling distraught at seeing his wounds, including the marks of crucifixion.

Next, James talks about Jesus meeting his disciples, telling them that he is not dead, and that he has to leave.

> Reena: Does he tell only the fifteen that were at the dinner?
> Mia: Not the fifteen. No, the fifteen had left. The fifteen was made up of me, his mother, his wife. He tells the remaining ones.
> Reena: What is their reaction?
> Mia: Disbelief. They are confused. I am waiting for him. He wanted to talk to them alone, though.

Next, James gives the account of travelling to a safe place, in hiding. At first, only James and Jesus went to the safe place – for Jesus to heal. Then, they continued on, with many travelling with them.

Eventually James left them to travel on by himself.

Mia: I need to go back and make sure everything is OK. I need to make sure they will not be followed.
Reena: It seems to me that you are taking care of all the mundane things in all this. Where is Peter in all this?
Mia: Peter is … [sighs] He takes some of the disciples and he teaches. They must all split up. They must all go in different directions. This is a very dangerous time.

The next significant event that James remembered was when he next met Jesus.

Mia: I travel. Yeah. He's in France. My mother's old now. It's her time.
Reena: Is she in France as well?
Mia: Mm. With Mary [his wife]. They have a child. They have two children now.
Reena: Jesus and Mary?
Mia: Mm. Jesus wants to travel. He says he must carry his message. He wants me to go with him. He must leave Mary. He needs to travel. He wants to go south.
Reena: South to where?
Mia: I think Crete.
[Laurence Gardner also names Crete as one of the islands that was Jesus' destinations.][13]
Reena: Do you go?
Mia: [nods] He wants to travel with me because I travel and … I have the ship! [laughs] So we travel. And Jesus

tells me he's afraid his time is coming. And he says his time has come to travel and carry [on] spreading his Gospel. He is afraid that on these travels he may not get back to [his mother] Mary and his wife, and he makes me promise to look after his son, to help his son, and I promise that whatever happens I will take care of his family.

I then asked a series of questions about his own family. James said he did have a wife and that it was a marriage of convenience. She passed away while he was not around. They did not have any children.

We drew this session to an end. What struck me while I was conducting this regression is that by James' account, Jesus was not the only son of Joseph, the poor carpenter. In fact, it seemed that Joseph was a merchant, and was fairly well-to-do by the standards of the civilisation that they lived in. A handful of Biblical historians are in agreement that Jesus was a true lineal descendant of the Shepherd King, David.[14] As such, this family would have had both means and some influence in the community in those times.

According to Laurence Gardner, by historical accounts, Jesus was the heir to the throne of David, the dynastic House of Judah. In this kingly line, the patriarchal title of 'Joseph' was applied to the next in succession. According to Mia, because James' second brother seemed to be disowned because he chose to discard his cultural familial role of assuming the responsibilities of the head of family including the running of the business, the duties of the second son fell on James' shoulders. Hence, James would have assumed the title Joseph.

Furthermore, despite his mother Mary's reputation as being a virgin, the New Testament makes it clear that Jesus is not the only son. Matthew 13:55 clarifies that Jesus had brothers, and in the New Testament epistles, St Paul refers to his meeting in Jerusalem with 'James, the Lord's brother'. First-century historian Flavius Josephus refers to 'James, the brother of Jesus, who was called Christ'.[15]

Another point to note is the role Mia's James played in making arrangements with the Romans about the crucifixion, and taking Jesus' body from the cross. Tradition holds that it was Joseph of Arimathea, a wealthy, influential relation, who did this. The fact that Pontius Pilate accepted his involvement in Jesus' affairs without question, and also accepted a rather large bribe from him, shows that Joseph of Arimathea did have familial ties with Jesus, and was rather well-to-do. However, records show that there was no such place called 'Arimathea'. 'Arimathea' is actually another title representing high status. So Joseph of Arimathea is in fact a title, not a name. Outside the scriptures he is presumed to be Jesus' mother's uncle. However, if he were, sources say he died in either AD63 or AD82, which would put him at between 100 and 125 years of age.[16] So, he could not be Jesus' granduncle, but someone younger.

Historically, it is much more feasible that the person who interceded on Jesus' behalf was his own brother, as Mia claims. James took on the role as the head of the family business, making him an influential merchant. He had familial ties with Jesus, therefore enabling him to intercede when he did. He would have been between 58 to 75 years of age, if he had died between AD63 and AD82.

This therefore could mean that James, Jesus' brother and Joseph of Arimathea, are indeed one and the same. This connection strengthens as the regression continues.

2

DEVOTED

It is not in the stars to hold our destiny, but in ourselves.
— William Shakespeare

Our session the following week picked up from where we left off at the previous session. James described the landscape as being different, green with trees, and colder. He gave the account of getting to France by boat. His companions in the boat were Jesus, Mary, the wife of Jesus, Sarah, Mary's sister and two of Jesus' followers who were there to protect them.

In the recollections of Clement, there is mention of Joseph of Arimathea being the leader of a band of people, including Martha, the three Marys, Salome, Lazarus, Zacharius and his servants.[1] While there is no mention of Jesus, it makes sense that if the existence of Jesus was to be kept quiet, great pains must have been taken to write him out of history post-crucifixion – for his safety and the safety of the spiritual mission he had.

Reena: Who made the decision to go to France? Was it you? [Mia nods] And what drew you to France?
Mia: It's far and out of the way.
Reena: Do you know anyone there?

Mia: I know of a settlement there. It's not just Jewish but there are friends of Jews. They're not hostile. There are some Jews but they are open in their thinking.

To the north of Marseilles was Vienne, which at that time housed the Herodian estate in Gaul – used as a place of exile by Herod Archelaus (brother of Herod Antipas).[2] Being of the Sanhedrin Council, which was the Supreme Court made up of seventy of the most influential men in ancient Israel, Joseph of Arimathea, or James, would have had knowledge of, and ties to, this potential safe refuge, and may have made arrangements to send his family members and their entourage there, which would tie up with what Mia is claiming.

There are also records, one especially from Cardinal Baronius, a curator of the Vatican Library, that mentioned that they sailed along the Mediterranean towards the coast of Gaul and landed at Marseilles. From there, Joseph of Arimathea, travelled to Britain in AD36.[3]

The regression continues. The next significant event saw James landing and letting everyone else off. However, James stayed long enough only to put more supplies on the boat. He felt an urgent need to go back to Jerusalem to continue trading, but more importantly to make sure that people thought that Jesus was dead.

Reena: What's so important about people thinking Jesus is dead?
Mia: Because Rome stretches throughout Europe.
Reena: And what does that have to do with everyone knowing Jesus is dead?
Mia: To protect him so they don't come after him. They see him as a troublemaker.
Reena: What happens next?

Mia: His disciples are confused. They're confused about ... that he's still alive and they want to tell everyone. I tell them they can't and they want to spread the message. I tell them they *can't* [desperately, emphatically]. They want to take his teachings ... He tells them to take his teachings and go into the world. And also they must go to the outer edges of the Roman Empire. All of them have to move to the edges to be safe.

Reena: What does Peter think of this?

Mia: I don't like Peter. I don't really talk to him. Peter was there but we don't get on.

In order to keep the charade going, James places urgency in getting back to his life as a merchant – to act as normally as possible. So he busies himself by working with the Romans in extending his trade routes throughout the Roman Empire. Though this keeps him safe, he is constantly asked about rumours surrounding his brother Jesus, which he denies.

Reena: What happened to Mark?

[long pause]

Mia: He travelled south. He couldn't stay with Jesus. It was too risky.

Reena: Did you see Mark again after he went south?

Mia: No, I haven't seen him.

Reena: So you extended your trade routes. Where did you extend them to? What are the two furthest points?

Mia: We wanted the ore. We went to England. That was the furthest. The first time, we knew there was good metal coming from England because of what was being traded. And so we took goods. We took spices and different things.

Reena: How did you travel to England?

Mia: Boat.

Reena: Was it the same boat you all travelled in to France?

Mia: No.

Reena: Have you got a fleet?

Mia: Maybe not a fleet but we have some boats.

According to Isabel Hill Elder, in her book *Joseph of Arimathea*, by the eleventh century BC the tribe of Asher, seafaring men from Israel, under the name Phoenicians, had coasted along Spain and Gaul, establishing a trade with the 'tin islands' – the Scilly Isles and Cornwall. Camden's *Britannia* volume 1 chronicles that the merchants of Asher worked or farmed the tin mines, not as slaves, but as masters and exporters. There is some evidence of their cultural residue left in Cornwall, namely the practice of burying their dead, as opposed to burning like the Romans; as well as the similarity of Welsh and Cornish words and whole sentences with the Hebrew language.[4]

Sir E.S. Creasy, in his *History of England*, writes, 'The British mines mainly supplied the glorious adornment of Solomon's temple,' thereby giving us another recorded anecdote of the tin being used by the Israelites.[5]

So, it is not far-fetched to think that James had a commercial network and a small fleet of trading boats that travelled to England. Although the area was not called 'England' during the Bibilical period, the memories were being filtered through Mia's current-life vocabulary, hence her use of terms from the current times. As is mentioned by Isabel Hill Elder, 'It is not by mere chance that Arimathean Joseph became acquainted with Cornish tin and Somerset lead mining, for as a Prince of the House of David, Joseph was aware that his kinsmen of the tribe of Asher had made Cornwall famous for the prized metal.' Again, this implies that the family of Jesus was an important, well-to-do family.[6] The regression continues.

> Reena: So you took your spices and other things and sailed to England.
> Mia: We met the king. A kind of tribal king.
> Reena: What was your reception like in England?
> Mia: I took an English person with me. There were people in France who were English. I took a trader and he spoke. They were very ... [long pause] They were very loud and ... they were friendly. They liked what we brought because they hadn't seen it before. But they were very different ... Not as refined as the Romans.

Then we went on to the topic of gifts. James rather smugly mentioned that the tribal king, whom he addressed as 'My Lord', wanted to bestow upon James his pretty daughter as a gift. James insisted that it would have been rude to have refused.

> Mia: [smiles coyly] Work must be done to form trade routes!
> Reena: And what happened next?
> Mia: I explained I'd have to travel. And he's agreed sometimes she would come with me and sometimes she would stay.
> Reena: Where did you and she stay? Did you take her back to Jerusalem or were you staying in England or somewhere else?
> Mia: I took her with me ... to France.
> Reena: Did she meet Jesus? And his family?

Mia: Yes. And I took her to … outside of Rome. To trade. It wasn't Rome. It was near. I don't like going to Rome.

Reena: What don't you like about it?

Mia: Too many Romans.

There is record of James (under the name of Joseph of Arimathea) being the guest of the Silurian King Caractacus and his brother Arviragus around the Isle of Avalon, known as Somerset in current times. It was recorded in the Domesday Book that Arviragus gifted James twelve hides of land, tax-free, each hide representing 160 acres.[7]

Laurence Gardner independently concluded that because James the Just first visited Siluria in AD35, his wife would appear to have been the daughter of King Cymbeline and the sister of Arviragus, Enygus, thus justifying the generous gift of the twelve hides of land to him.[8] Again, this is consistent with Mia's account.

The next memory saw James with Sarah, his daughter with his new wife.

Reena: And where do you set up home?

Mia: I like it in Britain. It's cold but where we are there's a freedom. I like it.

Reena: Where in Britain are you?

Mia: West.

Reena: Did Jesus and Mary and the kids ever come to see you in Britain?

Mia: I came to them.

Reena: What about your child? Did they come and visit your child?

Mia: No.

Reena: How did that make you feel?

Mia: Most people don't travel.
Reena: Did Jesus' children ever come to Britain?
Mia: Not when they were young.

At this point, James recalled that Jesus had three children: a daughter called Sarah, a son called Jesus and another son whose name James could not recall. There will be more about this detail in the coming chapters.

The next significant event saw James visiting his brother and his family. Jesus was not there, however. He'd gone south to Greece to see some disciples. James received an astonishing proposition from Mary, the wife of Jesus.

Mia: Mary wants me to take young Jesus … take him back to England.
Reena: Did Mary tell you why she wanted young Jesus to go to England with you?
Mia: We have a community there. And maybe for marriage.

So James takes Jesus Jr back to Britain with him and proposes that he marries his cousin Sarah – James' daughter. I ask what happened then, and James replied, 'Jesus [Jr] settled in Britain. We have a community there. So I could go home to Jerusalem.'

There is a strong tradition that Joseph of Arimathea had settled in Avalon and built not just a community of believers in Jesus, but also a wattle church, on the grounds of which Glastonbury Abbey stands today. The wattle church considered to be the first Christian church erected in Britain, and is chronicled in *The Church in These Islands before the Coming of Augustine*, written by Rev G.F. Browne, former Bishop of Bristol. The more researchers study Celtic Druidic religion, the more similarities they find with old Israel – and this is credited to Joseph of Arimathea and the integration of the first Christian communities with the Druidic tradition in Britain.[9]

Tradition in Britain holds that while Jesus was a boy, his mother Mary entrusted him to Joseph of Arimathea, her uncle, to travel to some major trading ports and ended up in Glastonbury and the Mendips. William Blake, a famous English poet and artist, was so moved by this tradition he wrote a poem about it – *Prelude to Milton*, better known as the hymn 'Jerusalem'.[10]

However, our regression is consistent with Laurence Gardner's version that actually it was Jesus *Jr* who travelled to Britain with *his* uncle, James aka Joseph of Arimathea, sent by Jesus' wife, Mary. Laurence Gardner goes on to give an account that the feet that indeed walked 'upon England's mountains green' were indeed those of the son of Jesus, who consecrated St Mary's chapel, in what's now known as Glastonbury Abbey, to his mother, Mary Magdalene.[11]

Gardner also mentions that while Jesus Sr was referred to as Yeshua, Jesus Jr was referred to as Gais or Gesu.[12] I find it interesting that within the strong Druidic priesthood, the name 'Yesu' was incorporated in the Druidic Trinity as a godhead.[13] The use of the term 'Yesu' is consistent with Mia's account and Laurence Gardner's independent finding that it was Jesus Jr who made the trip to Britain, and that eventually he does marry – but to whom is hazy.

The regression continues.

Mia: My wife has died.
Reena: How does that make you feel?
Mia: Sad. She was a very good woman. It's time for me to go home. I'm getting old.

Reena: At this point was Jesus your brother still alive?
Mia: No.
Reena: How about Mary, his wife?
Mia: Yes.
Reena: How did Jesus die?
Mia: In her arms.
[The following events took us through James' death.]
Mia: I'm too old for all this.
Reena: What is 'all this'?
Mia: All this nonsense. All these silly people.
Reena: Who are these people? Are you talking about the Romans?
Mia: No. Most of them are the Jews. They are so silly.
Reena: Are you in Jerusalem?
Mia: [nods] They want me to shut up but I am too old for that. It's not just the Jews but really it's the Jewish elders, which is funny because I am as old as some of them, or older.
Reena: How old are you roughly?
Mia: Three score years and ten [seventy]? I'm not quite there.

When asked to elaborate on what he was telling the Jewish elders that they did not like, James responded, 'I am telling them about Jesus and his message. And just that the world's a bigger place than just Jerusalem. They are so small … they are so small-minded. I am just an old man but they can't tell me what I should be saying. It doesn't matter to me. All they can do is kill me and I am going to die soon anyway. A body can only last so long. So I will just keep on saying what I am saying and if they don't like it …'

Reena: And what happens next?

Mia: I have a place of worship and they want me to shut it. I tell them I won't. We are arguing. And because I have money, I have a good building. This annoys them that I have the money and so I also have the power and, I like to think, the charisma. Well, I like to think so. I am arguing with the elders and with other people who are higher up. And we're pushing each other. [emphatically] I won't take their nonsense!

Reena: Are you physically pushing each other?

Mia: Physically pushing each other. One man pushes me and I fall.

Reena: Where do you fall?

Mia: I fall down to the ground. I'm still alive but I'm hurt. The building was not so high but I'm old.

Reena: Where were you when they pushed you off?

Mia: We were all on the roof of the building, where we often go for meetings. I was shouting. I was shouting to the people below. I don't know if it was an accident or if I was pushed on purpose. I like to think it was an accident.

Then, I navigated the soul of James/Mia to go the point just after his death, where Mia reported that she was floating above the physical body and was still aware of everything that was happening around her.

Mia: There's my people there and the other people. And I was badly hurt. And so one of them says they should stop the pain and beat me on the head.

Reena: Did they?

Mia: Yeah. [pause] They're all arguing and there's a fight.

Reena: What's the fight about?

Mia: Because of what's happened to me. Some are saying it's an accident and some are saying it was on purpose. It's all a bit chaotic. It was time, though.

This account of James' death is in line with records of James the Just, the brother of Jesus, being hurled from the pinnacle of the temple to his death and being stoned to death at Jerusalem by the Jews in AD62.[14] However, if the hypothesis is that James and Joseph of Arimathea are the same person, this contradicts the many accounts of Joseph of Arimathea being laid to rest in AD82 and his remains being in the Isle of Avalon.[15] However, when asked after her regression, Mia was sure that the trip to Jerusalem when James was nearing his seventies was indeed his last trip, and that he died in his homeland.

After his death, James became aware of what had happened to Mark.

Mia: He was killed.
Reena: Down south?
Mia: Mm.
Reena: Who killed him and how?
Mia: The Romans … I'm not sure [how]. He was killed shortly after Jesus' crucifixion.

This piece of information is especially pertinent in Thomas' chapter, later on in this book.

As it seemed to have been a long, tough life, I then navigated James' soul to a place of healing energy and light so that he might recharge and refresh before meeting his Spirit Guides to get some higher wisdom about that life.

Mia: They're telling me this was an information life. I gained a lot of knowledge and I gained a lot of love. It was a good life. It was not as hard as many at that point.

Reena: Can I just ask: the soul of Jesus – was he an evolved soul or was he just a soul that did amazing things in a physical body?

Mia: He was evolved and he came with a message.

Reena: OK. And what was the soul's plan behind the choice of being his brother? What did you want to achieve?

Mia: I feel quite separate from that life. It was not about my soul's evolution but being of service. But I went into that one with very little issues. I needed to be pure to get the job done ... There were so many jobs. And maintaining the purity of the bloodline.

Reena: Did you do that by marrying Jesus junior with your daughter as well?

Mia: Mm. Maintaining the bloodline keeps the knowledge. It's so the knowledge was kept alive in a physical way. The knowledge had to be kept alive not just as being written because that could be destroyed. There was the need for the physical manifestation.

Reena: Is the knowledge infused in the genes and the blueprint of the people and the souls that came after or is that completely off tangent?

Mia: We were able to maintain the purity of the message and not be corrupted or for the message not to be corrupted or destroyed.

Thus began the explosive conception of this book and the enlightening journey that it took us on. It was interesting how Mia's account was independently corroborated by historical accounts of the time, and yet was unique at the same time.

Based on Mia's regression, there is no doubt that Jesus had siblings, and that James was indeed his brother. It left very little doubt that James and Joseph of Arimathea were indeed the same person – Jesus' brother. What is more fascinating is that Jesus was indeed substituted on the cross, and did not actually die, but went on to father three children and continue his ministry in Crete and southern Greece, while Mary Magdalene and her entourage went to France.

More than the storyline, I was struck by how selflessly James devoted himself to his brother, his brother's family and the cause. James was a key player in this story, not so much spiritually, as that was Jesus' role, but practically. If James had not possessed the means, connections and wealth, the story of Jesus would have been very different indeed. Perhaps Jesus would have gone the way John the Baptist had – beheaded – and had his title of Messiah revoked. Who knows what would have happened to Mary Magdalene and her children. James, to me, is the practical, material balance to Jesus' spiritual, esoteric inspiration.

As we progress through the revelations of other regressed memories, the most fascinating discovery is that most other accounts continue to corroborate and add to Mia's memory of James.

3

ENTHUSIAST

A life spent making mistakes is not only more honourable, but
more useful than a life spent doing nothing
– George Bernard Shaw

Greg was one of my long-time clients, and we'd explored
many of his past and current life memories. Shortly after Mia's
between-lives session, Greg wanted a session to work on a
personal current life issue. To the surprise of both of us, he
regressed back to another biblical character – Paul the
Evangelist – as the source of his current life challenge.
Though his session was recorded, there was no intent to
collate it in a book until a couple of years later. Like Mia,
under the condition that his true identity was kept
confidential, Greg agreed to let his sessions be used in this
book.

In his first session, he immediately dropped into the life of
a bearded man, wearing a mucky cloth draped around his
shoulders, with a rope tied around his waist, and bare feet. His
first impression was seeing a man with white cloth draped
over his arms and body, who was standing with his arms out,
like a cross-type position. It was getting towards the end of
the day and they were outdoors, amongst a group of twenty or
thirty people, watching and listening.

Reena: And tell us more about this man with his arms out.

Greg: Seems to have this big glow around his head.

Reena: What colour is the glow?

Greg: It can't be said that it has a colour. I just get the feeling there's an energy or just a presence around him. There's almost like a saint-like quality that he has.

Reena: Who is this man?

Greg: Jesus.

Reena: Who is he in relation to you?

Greg: I don't know, but the thought that came into my head was 'brother'. He doesn't seem like a brother, he seems different.

Within the context of Jesus being part of the Essene community, this term would not seem so controversial. Within this community, a male member addresses another male member as 'Brother', thereby denoting equality, filiality and mutual respect for one another.

It is also interesting to note that, as you will see in later chapters, while the other people who were regressed perceived Jesus as a man with special qualities, Paul's first perception of Jesus was that he was almost like a saint – which is in line with his portrayal of Jesus as the Son of God.

The regression continues.

Greg: I'm just listening to him talking, we all are.

Reena: And how do you feel listening to him talking?

Greg: Really inspired. Almost like a feeling of reverence, it's like not being able to say anything in case it breaks the special magic of the moment of what he's saying – of the moment of where we are ... He's just talking about love. And needing to spread the message of love.

Reena: And how does this make you feel?
Greg: Quite inspired.

Wanting to know a little more about his younger years, to ascertain more details about his identity, Paul was taken back to his first significant memory in that life. He went back to the time when he was five or six, being in a small room running and playing with other children around. He felt happy and contented being in that 'lovely wonderful place'. He identified having three other brothers, a mother and a father, and this is where he names himself as Paul.

The next significant event saw Paul at fourteen, participating in a Jewish ceremony.

Greg: There's someone in front of me, a priest of some sort, holding like a kind of cup, no, more like a bowl, a goldish/light-coloured bowl. He is draped with different-coloured clothes and a scarf-type thing, a religious type of scarf. They are singing a song that I am having to join in with. I think this is a ceremony of my coming of age.

Reena: How does the song make you feel?

Greg: There's something about it that feels false. It's like I am going through this ceremony to keep everybody happy but it's not something I particularly enjoy ... It's about me embracing the Jewish religion and it doesn't quite work for me ...

Finally, it's over and I can come back again. My brothers are looking at me a bit distant now like I am not a child to play around with. They are treating me like an adult and I don't really like it. I don't feel any different to how I was before ... makes me feel a bit sad.

Reena: What's the age difference between you and your younger brothers?

Greg: I get the feeling that one of them is about eight and the other is about twelve.

This recollection is interesting because it clearly shows that though Paul was participating in a Jewish ceremony or ritual, he clearly did not feel comfortable with it. This goes against the tradition and common perception that Paul was in fact a Pharisee, who adhered strictly to Jewish rituals and traditions and persecuted the early Christians who went against the Jewish teachings.

Reena: What happens next?

Greg: I have to wear different clothes now ... like a loin cloth with a belt. But it's clean material so I have to be careful not to dirty it. I can see this bright light. It's like I am part of a bright light ... It's outside, I am by myself.

Reena: Is this after the ceremony?

Greg: It's a few days afterwards. I have been walking out in the desert, I think you'd call it a desert, it's quite barren in the area there. I have sat down and am reflecting on everything that happened in the ceremony and the changes at home. I have this feeling of a bright light all the way around me. It's like a very religious type of spiritual experience.

I just feel very serene. Almost like nothing else really matters ... I am just getting the feeling that there is something special that I have to do and this is what this experience is about ... I think it's some sort of teaching that I have to do. Not a lot of detail, just the experience of realising the contrast between [this and] the ceremony that I went through, that meant nothing inside, despite all the people and the fancy clothes they were wearing and the gold cup. All that they had and here I was in the middle of this desert area by the small tree and this amazing experience came through. Almost teaching me what's real and what isn't real.

Reena: Where in the body are you feeling this feeling?

Greg: It's an experience that I am feeling in my head ... it's almost like I have transcended out of the human body and I'm just having a spiritual experience of connecting with other spiritual bodies. It's like an experience of floating, almost like telepathic communication ... It's to remind me who I really am.

Reena: And can you share who you really are?

Greg: It's to remind me that there is a spiritual part, that the world is magnificent, and it's also to remind me that there is a world of ceremonies and physical things and that they have to coexist. Both ways are trying to represent spirituality but one is just experiencing and being whilst the other is doing things with traditions and process.

The common story about Paul is that he, or Saul as he is referenced in the Bible, discovered spirituality from Jesus, after the crucifixion, while he was on the road to Damascus. Interestingly, this recollection brings to light that Paul had his own spiritual awakening and experience at the age of fourteen, before meeting Jesus.

It gets even more fascinating as the following accounts take us back to when we first met Paul, listening to Jesus talk with a group of twenty to thirty people, and that their relationship seems to be a close one. This again contradicts the common story that he met Jesus after the crucifixion.

Greg: The things he says make so much sense. It kind of just feels right ... The talk's finished now so I go up to him and put my arm round him and we walk off together. There are lots of people wanting to talk to him and spend time with him. But it's almost like a family reunion with him ... He's full of excitement about all the places he's been to and the things he's learned. I just stay quiet and just listen ... a bit in awe.

Reena: What happens next?

Greg: We're discussing plans. He's telling me that he has to leave and go to another part of the country. I ask him if I can come and listen. He says of course. So I have to go back and tell everyone at home that I'm going to go.

Reena: And what was the response?

Greg: A lot of sadness. My other brothers want to come too but they are too young. I pack my things, not that I have many, and I go out and join him and we go off together. There's a group of about twelve or fourteen people walking with him. I've got something on my feet now, they are sandals.

Reena: These people following him ...?

Greg: They are just following him, listening to him. Doing things like sort out food and clothing and finding places to stay at night when they go to villages. Helping out.

Reena: Are there any woman or only the male gender?

Greg: No, there're women, two or three women. But there's no one in relationships. They are just all independent people.

Reena: OK, just tell us what happens next?

Greg: We are just going from place to place. Starting to know a lot of the things he's talking about. It's like I've heard it a few times and it makes sense ... and it's like, 'Oh, that's a different way in which he's telling that now,' and, 'Oh, that's interesting.' And I'm just doing a little bit of talking to others myself. I've got the general idea of how he does it so I am speaking to a few others. And if they don't understand what he just said I am going over the story again. A lot of it is stories, until they get it.

Reena: Does everyone do that in the group that is walking with him or just you?

Greg: Some do, some are just pleased to be there, some just like to be in the energy, some are doing practical things. It's almost like there aren't any rules about what they do or don't do.

Reena: It's whatever they want to do. Can you tell us what happens next?

Greg: It's an evening and a number of us are settling around a table ... I was going to say eight or nine but I think there're a few people who aren't quite at the table who are within earshot. But there're eight or nine people around the table that are actually eating.

He [Jesus] is talking about how things are going to get difficult in the future ... He's saying that there are a lot of people that don't like what he's saying, that he's too much of a threat. And whereas at the moment we've been more in the outskirts of things, it's been less of a problem. But as you start to go into some of the cities, and some of the towns, there's going to be more resistance. There's going to be more people who try to stop it from happening. He's just talking about what to do.

Reena: Whereabouts are you now? Which part of the world?

Greg: This is in Judea.

Reena: And so are you going to go into Judea, into the proper centre?

Greg: That's part of the discussion, who is going to go with him and who is going to leave ... I say I want to stay. A few of the others are going to stay in some of the places where we've been and reinforce some of the things that we have talked about. So the group is going to get quite small.

Reena: Do some of them leave?

Greg: Well, they're not planning to, when we leave in the morning, they're not planning to come. Not right away but they may come a little later. It's like we're all part of the same thing but we're doing it in different ways. Just, it's not like leaving in terms of going away forever, it's almost just like a parting.

Reena: Do you know who the other people that are gathered around this table are?

Greg: Hmm ... There's James.

Reena: Who is James?

Greg: I don't know; he's just called James.

Reena: Are there any women present?

Greg: Yeah.

Reena: Do you know who they are?

Greg: I'm not too sure of what their names are ... Sarah ... and ... I'm not getting any more.

Reena: Is there a meal involved here?

Greg: There is every evening we get together, it's part of the ritual. It's almost like during the day we're all working, giving information and help and teachings to others and in the evenings it's kind of like, not a pep talk but it's kind of like any concerns anyone has, they can raise them.

It's almost like getting a deeper motivation. Or just talking through potential problems of where we're going. It's just keeping everyone together as a group. So the evenings are very similar. There's not one evening that is greatly different than the other.

Reena: Is there anything else of significance this night?

Greg: I kind of get the feeling that things won't be quite the same afterwards and I think the others feel that too. There's not a sadness, more of an acceptance.

The next event sees Paul and the rest of the followers in a larger place with lots of buildings.

Greg: We're walking there and there's lots of people looking at us. It's almost like they're not sure who we are, or what we do. But there is a curiosity overall all the same. We're just passing messages on to come along to a talk.

So there's like a hill, a small way outside. I am quite amazed at how many people are coming. I've not seen as many people as this. It's quite surprised all of us 'cos there appeared to be a bit of, not quite hostility, but there was certainly no warm welcome. So it's quite surprising how many people are coming. We're all a bit surprised by this.

So I'm taking my place, near the front, just so I can keep an eye on things. I just don't really know what to do with so many people. When it's been smaller groups I've taken one or two people to one side and talked to them and help explain it but it's such a big group, almost a hundred people, I don't really know what to do. I can't count them there are just so many faces ... And there's like a quietness. You can hear that some of the people are moving about, settling down, sitting down. It's like there's no banter or arguing or anything of that nature; it's almost like they know what they are going to get almost before they come. Very unusual. So I sit at the front, just float about and see what happens.

Reena: And what happens next?

Greg: Well, Jesus starts doing one of his talks, really excelling this time. He's got lots [of ways] of telling his stories, which I always found interesting to listen to anyway ... When he's finished talking they [the crowd] all want to touch him or speak to him but I've got to try and keep them away just to kind of give him a bit of space. It's a bit dusty and we're all still over-thirsty because we haven't eaten or had much chance to drink. This has all caught us by surprise so we all try to break free from the crowd so we can have our evening meal and talk.

Jesus just wants to keep talking and talking to them all. Eventually they break free and we usher them away and get into the house where we're staying and close the doors. We wash our feet and hands and drink and there's a meal ready for us.

Reena: Who does this house belong to?

Greg: It's one of the people in the town that's allowed us to stay. Some of the others are staying in other houses and some of them are sleeping outside... people just sleep wherever they can.

We are just discussing the bigger crowds, and how to handle it. I make the suggestion that we encourage people at the next talk to bring food and water with them. So if they can go on for longer, they can even eat there rather than having to rush to come back.

Evening's the main meal of the day. You don't have much chance for the rest of the day so if you don't have a main meal you can get hungry.

Reena: Can you remember any of the stories that Jesus told during this?

Greg: He talked about the Pharisees I think. He thought of them as friends. He treated them differently, though they shun him. And that surprised a lot of people because they don't like the Pharisees ...

He explains how certain traditions get in the way of these acts of kindness and how it's important to understand that the traditions are just simply that, they are a guidance, but it's important that these acts of guidance should be done as people need them . And that surprised a lot of people too.

He talked about women too. He talked about a woman who cared for a man who had leprosy and instead of shunning him, she just cared and gave him water and food and eventually the leper went off. He went off with a smile on his face.

He's just explaining about these acts of kindness and they were forgotten and how anybody can do it, wherever they are. The leper went off to the leper colony but at least for that day he had a wonderful memory to take with him. So these are the sorts of stories that he tells.

It is interesting to note that of all the people who were regressed, Greg's Paul paid the most attention to how and what Jesus was teaching. It was the most prevalent in his memories. This is in line with his passion for evangelising and teaching Jesus' message.

The next event saw us moving forward four years … to the crucifixion.

Greg: And we are just at the point where Jesus is carrying the cross. I can't help being a bit frightened by it all even though I knew what was going to happen so I just kept quiet in the background … So it's all like a bit of [a] state of shock nevertheless.

It's still not easy to see it happening and what is hard is that all the people who are shouting and jeering at him, they are the very people who were listening to his stories and it's almost like they didn't get it. I wonder if they get this though, that despite all the things that have been done to him he's still showing kindness. So I've followed the procession that has taken him all the way there and he's put on the cross and left. I'm in the crowd so I just leave too … (feeling) very sad.

Reena: When he was put on the cross, where were you situated?

Greg: I was just in the crowd.

Reena: Was there anyone near him?

Greg: I couldn't see an awful lot. There were some soldiers there. I'm just so sad and overwhelmed by it all. The next event sees Paul being ushered into a small room the day after the crucifixion, where there are four or five people.

Reena: Who is ushering you?

Greg: James, I think. And there is Jesus, he's quite badly hurt so that he's resting. It's definitely him and he's alive.

Reena: Who is there?

Greg: There's Mary. That's his wife … There's James who has brought me in. I think there's Peter and Judas there. Judas is the one who … Well, he's saying he betrayed [him] but Jesus is saying that you did what I asked you to do. I asked you to do those things, someone had to do them and it was a really difficult job. But he's full of grief. He's full of grief because even though he did it, he thought there'd be a different outcome.

Judas is leaving, Jesus is explaining that Judas is going to kill himself and we're saying but why, you're alive, he's seen you're alive … I just can't understand it. Jesus is explaining that even though Judas was asked to do it and what the reason was, he feels guilty for all of the hurt and pain that Jesus has been through.

Jesus can't be around to teach, we all know that, 'cos if anyone sees him, then there won't be a chance to rescue him a second time.

It feels almost like Judas has betrayed the whole cause of trying to get this message out. Even though it's been explained to him that it's just going to happen in a different way, he just doesn't seem to understand it and Jesus is saying that things are just going to have to unfold as they unfold and don't try to force anything.

I am just confused by the whole thing, it's just too much. First of all, seeing him being killed and I didn't know that he was going to be taken down and I'm just asking him how it was done and he explains that another body was put in there. Someone had died and soldiers were bribed, and they were quite happy for that as long as there was a body there for people to look at. They looked very similar.

Reena: Who bribed the soldiers and masterminded the rescue?

Greg: The whole plan was Jesus', of course. He asked different people to do different tasks. It's almost like this was all known, like it was all pre-planned, completely, it was almost like everybody knew the part they had to play.

Paul was not involved in the inner circle of the plan that James had conspired – only James, Mary Magdalene, Mother Mary and, eventually, Jesus, were aware. So, it is interesting to note that Paul reflected the perception of knowledge received by the second tier – the disciples – which is why he thought it was Jesus who was carrying the cross and was crucified. It also makes sense that Jesus was to shoulder the responsibility as the main decision-maker, as opposed to James, who still had a reputation to protect as Joseph of Arimathea.

Reena: Can you describe Jesus' appearance [at] this time … is he badly wounded …?
Greg: Well, they did put nails in his hand, he has the wounds from that. He has the wounds around his head and where he was whipped, I think in quite a bad state, he's going to need a lot of nursing. I think the plan is to take him to a place … it's like a plank with wheels, a trolley, that can take him to a safe place and he'll just be nursed and looked after.

I think Mary Magdalene is going to be the one to look after him. They are going to keep it quite small to start with. The plan is we all go our different ways and then come back in a few months' time. I don't think there's any need, we've all made a note of where we're going. I've got a cousin I can stay with so I'm going there. They know where I am going.
Reena: Is this cousin in Judea?

Greg: [nods] … and then we regroup in two or three months' time and that is how we'll find out from Jesus what he wants to do next.

The next event finds Paul at a meeting of eight people over a meal in the evening. He sees Jesus standing there, with a smile on his face, like old times, with many of his wounds around his face healed.

Greg: Jesus is asking each of us what we'd like to do. I am saying that I'd like to go to the island of Cyprus. I've heard about this island and I'd like to take some of his teachings there. The others are talking about the other places that they'd like to go to.

… Someone wants to go to Turkey, someone wants to go to North Africa and someone wants to stay in the area and continue the teachings. It's almost like they don't know exactly where they want to go, it's like approximate directions, and then they'll just flow with things. Jesus and Mary and Joseph kind of go off together.

Reena: Is this Joseph his father?

Greg: This is another Joseph … But I think I get the feeling that he [Jesus] is going to just go off. He's got his own plan of where he's going to go off to, but he's going to have to stay in hiding certainly from the Romans.

The next significant event sees Paul in Cyprus.

Greg: I'm in Cyprus and I'm going from village to village trying to do the same as what Jesus was telling. I'm finding that some villages accept me and some villages don't, but that's exactly the same as what happened to Jesus. I think it's quite hard doing that. It seemed so easy following Jesus.

It's quite hard because it's almost like you have to be aware of everybody and everything and when you're saying things you are saying it to everybody. But I persevere. I've been there for a few years and I've got a small community going in one or two places to pass on the stories that they've been told.

I'm feeling a bit restless that there's no big towns in Cyprus. It's all like tiny villages and people are like … it's a bit like when we first started out with Jesus. It's almost like this is to just teach a little bit about 'how to teach things and do things'.

A lot of the times I am talking about what Jesus said and what he did. It's a lot easier to refer to him than say it's coming from me. It has much more of an effect; it's almost like he creates an eternal ring. A bit like a god, they're so used to having things that are really spiritually important that they can't see but they get told about. In those times I could say it would be my truths that I pass on as Jesus' truths, and that works really well and it honours him for the work that he did.

But I am getting a little restless because things aren't really flowing in the way that I thought they might do.

Reena: So what happens next?

Greg: I am catching a boat and I am going to a bigger place and I am going to the mainland. I'm going to Italy. I'm going to do things a little differently in Italy. In Cyprus everything was done quite casually, in other words. Everybody listens to the words but it's up to them how they interpret them or how they do things.

It was almost like they needed to have some sort of structure in place for the message to be retained. It's almost like it was too pure for them to understand and relate to. It's like they have to keep being reminded of it on a regular basis. So in Italy I'm going to take it a little bit differently to make it a bit more formal – going to get some of what he said written down. Try to create places where people can come to once a week, a little bit like how the Jewish religion works.

Reena: Now, you are going to Italy. How did going to Italy affect you in terms of the fact that there were some Romans who had issues with Jesus?

Greg: I can turn up. They think Jesus is dead.

Reena: How about your teaching?

Greg: Well, I have to be careful of that, but people are receptive to it out in the countryside. It's almost like out in Rome, there's lots of difference in Rome itself ... but when you get out in the countryside, it's almost like it's a different country. So you can be in Italy and it's a lot like being in a bigger version of Cyprus. But the Italians seem to be much more receptive to doing things in a structured way, whereas in Cyprus they were a slightly simpler people, simple fisherman or herders looking after goats. They were kind enough to listen to the words and I'm sure it helped them a little bit, but it didn't really make much impact at all.

So in Italy they seem to have more trade, more specialists in different areas, so that their ability to think and be able to relate to what they've been told ... it's not quite as simple as people in Cyprus. So that I'm spending time giving that message, the bit that really worked well, was to talk about Jesus and about Jesus' messages. So that's how I'm going to do it.

It works out quite well and the people come every week, so that you can reinforce the messages. That part works really well with that bit of structure in place … and I got similar things written down in a formal way. But it's the notes of all the things I could remember, so I could refer to those, and that looks good because, you know, they like to see sort of pieces of paper. Makes it seem so much more impressive and particularly telling the story of Jesus dying (we can't tell them what really happened) but that seems to work out really well.

It's a little bit of a mistruth but, I mean, we're trying to get the message out there about his kindness. That really works well because anybody who's a martyr goes down well, so we just let that story continue. We try to be as honest as with all those stories and the other things, it's just we have to be careful about the death part because if we said what would happen, that he didn't die, then obviously it's going to create problems with Jesus wherever he is because they're looking for him.

Reena: Do you know where he is?

Greg: No. So I just keep going from place to place in Italy and get quite a following … It's going really well. People are helping and working with me. The crowd is getting quite a few Romans, that's interesting getting the Romans in there.

The very first one that came was a soldier, a centurion, he came in camouflage so we couldn't see his soldier's clothes but we knew what he was. He just sat and listened and understood. It's nice to know that the message gets there, even to a soldier. He explained how he has to do as he's told, being a soldier. But … the thoughts he has, they can't control. They might be able to control his actions, and what he does, but they can't control the thoughts of what's inside him.

So he passed a message to a few others and there's a few other soldiers that come. It seems to spread like wildfire, more and more people are spreading the message. Been able to get some of the things that I've written down passed on to others as well, so they can read it. Yes, it seems to be quite a momentum going now.

One of the fascinating things about this account is that we get an insight into how Paul's fledging church officially began. Again, his behaviour is consistent with the enthusiasm that all he wanted to do was to spread the teachings of Jesus – and his way of effectively reaching people was to write down the teachings and also establish a formal way to meet to spread the teachings. Also, we see Paul starting to bend the truth to make his teachings that much more compelling and retainable. He starts introducing Jesus as being a deity, a god, or a martyr – which is the version of Jesus that we are most familiar with in current times.

This is consistent with Laurence Gardner's account that 'In his unbridled enthusiasm, (Paul) invented an inexplicable myth and uttered a string of self-styled prophecies that were never fulfilled … all social values professed and urged by Jesus were cast aside in the attempt to compete with a variety of pagan beliefs.'[1]

The next significant event sees Paul on his deathbed at the age of sixty-one. He is indoors on a bed and there are a few people, those who have been helping him with the work he was doing, in the room, feeling sad and crying. They know Paul is going to die, or they think he is going to die, as Paul's been ill for a short while. Paul, on the other hand, is ready to go.

Upon leaving his body, Paul reported feeling a little disappointment that there was a bit of a rigid structure in his teachings that was left behind. But he thought that it had to be done for it to become established. This session ended with Paul's soul receiving some healing.

4

EVANGELIST

Vices are sometimes only virtues carried to excess.
 – Charles Dickens

Greg's second session regressing into this life came as another surprise to us. He came to me a few months later for a therapeutic session, wracked with feelings of guilt and also a recurring thought of 'something went wrong and I am blaming myself'. So, using the verbal bridge of his recurring thought, we went straight into a series of body memories of a trauma.

When someone goes through trauma, the area of the limbic system in the brain that processes the narrative, the hippocampus, shuts down, while the amygdala, the area in the limbic system that processes emotion, fight or flight reactions and body sensations, becomes more active. In regression therapy, when the client drops into the traumatic event, often they consciously have no idea what is happening to them, because the hippocampus is shut down. However, the body consciousness holds these memories, and when we work with the body memories to clear the terror and emotions related to that trauma (called body therapy), we can then access the narrative and the understanding of what's happening. This is the process I employed with Greg at this point.

There was plenty of grimacing and gasping in pain, as Greg kept repeating that his arms and chest were held down and could not move, and his neck was burning, and he was coughing and spluttering. Once we had cleared all the body memories using body therapy, Greg finally started telling the story of how someone was trying to strangle him – being assassinated as a Christian in Rome. Keen to get the lead-up to the story, we went back to the first significant event.

He enters being a young man, around 23 or 24, with a black beard and wearing a whitish cloth over him. It's quite loose, just to let the air circulate. He finds himself on a donkey with his legs not free to move. He has got a leather bag with writings in it and taxes that he is collecting. There are some bags on the side of the donkey too. He is feeling fearful as he is carrying quite a bit of money and there is no one to protect him. Although he is confident that, as the local people know that he is doing the work for the Romans, they are all terrified. This is when Greg realises that he has popped back to the life of Paul.

Reena: How do you address the local people?
Greg: Hmm, well a lot of them are Jews, but I just address them by their individual names. I have a list before I come to each town of who the prominent people are and then I have to work out how much tax they need to pay and the time I've finished in that town, or part of the town, I go back with the money and go back again. It's like I am doing this all the time. I'm a bit young to do this sort of work, but I am good at doing it so that they've given me a free hand.
Reena: And what happens next as you are riding on this donkey?

Greg: Well, I'm coming to a commotion because there is a big group of people and I'm a bit concerned because I've got some of the money I've been collecting, not a lot but ... I'm a bit concerned that this is some sort of trap. Some of the people who do my sort of work have been robbed before and been left to bleed ...

Reena: And this big group of people – are they men and women?

Greg: Yes, but they don't seem threatening at all, they seem to be quite elated, they seem to be almost jostling to get into the centre of a crowd. It's almost like they are ignoring me so I feel really interested in what could be happening.

Reena: OK, so what could you tell me about the scene around you in terms of the weather and the ground?

Greg: On the ground, it's rocky, not much grass at all, just a few strands here and there, almost look like weeds rather than grass. There's dust and it's hot. The crowds, they are dressed in various clothes, most of them are in lightish colours, some have got little bits of colour like it's been dyed. So they've got a little bit like tea cloths that we have these days, you know this sort of marking on it, it's not a very thin cotton, it's a more coarse-type cotton, it's a real ... I think it's more of it keeps them warm at night-time as well but keeps the sun off the body during the day ... I really feel the excitement in the air.

Reena: So what happens next?

Greg: Well, before I am able to decide what to do, the group seems to be parting and there's this man coming towards me. He invites me to get down, to leave the donkey, the money and all of that behind and just embrace him.

Reena: Tell me more about this man?

Greg: He's dressed similar to the others but he's got very clear, piercing, loving eyes and he's got a black beard. Nothing's on his head, it's like the clothes are around the top half of the body and then draped down, he's got bare feet. He has the sort of clothes of someone who isn't very wealthy, [something] the poorer people, would wear. He's stood firm and bold. He's got a smile and it's almost inviting me to go up and let him put his arms around and hug me, and so I do that. And I just feel all this amazing energy flowing through my whole body.

Reena: Where is this energy coming from?

Greg: It must be coming from him. So I just, well, I just go with it, I mean it's so totally unexpected.

Reena: What does this energy do to your body?

Greg: It's almost like it's washing away things, it's like a lot of the worries and concerns and getting the job done and getting the taxes … I just don't care about that any more. I'm quite elated.

Reena: What happens next?

Greg: He finishes the embrace and he says, 'Come and join me.' And a few other people are saying, 'No, why do you say that, he's a tax collector?' And he's saying in the sea we're all … all the fish are the same, some are larger and some are smaller but they are all fish. And it's the same with people, all people are the same, they may just have different jobs and roles.

So I just walk off and leave all the things behind and it's as if, almost like, I just become one of the others. It's almost like the identity I had of collecting taxes was only when I had the donkey and the bags and all my written records of who I collected taxes from, and that was my role and I left that behind.

It's like I could become somebody new and they've all just accepted it now, and other things are coming up and we're starting to walk along and the crowd are following. It's almost like they're all wondering where they're going or what's going to happen and no one's really bothered, it's almost just like going for a fun walk except you don't know where you're going to.

Again, Greg's account of Paul meeting Jesus for the first time digresses wildly from the Bible and many other sources on the subject. Common knowledge holds that the tax collector that Jesus recruited into his team was Matthew, who was a disciple. However, neither the Gospels nor early sources name the tax collector as 'Matthew'. In fact, the only person that the Bible identifies as a tax collector that Jesus sympathises with is Zacchaeus. The Gospel of Luke claims that this causes outrage from the crowds that Jesus would rather be the guest of a sinner than of a more respectable or 'righteous' person – which fits into this account of Paul's.

In fact, there is not much in any source that provides accounts of Zacchaeus's later life, and what is available is contradictory. According to Clement of Alexandria, in his book *Stromata*, Zacchaeus was named Matthias by the Apostles, and took the place of Judas Iscariot after Jesus' ascension. On the other hand, Luke told us that Matthias was with Jesus since the baptism of John.[1] 'Matthias' is the Hellenistic version of the name 'Matthew'. Could Zacchaeus therefore be the 'Matthew' that Jesus recruited to be an apostle?

The later Apostolic Constitutions identify 'Zacchaeus the Publican' as the first Bishop of Caesarea (7.46).[2]

It is interesting to note that Caesarea was an important centre for Paul as well, who used it as a hub for his missionary journeys, and he was allegedly imprisoned here before being taken to Rome.[3]

Could Zacchaeus and Matthew in fact be the same person – as per Greg's account of Paul? The regression continues.

Reena: And what happens next after your walking? [very long pause] Do you only walk with this man?
Greg: Well, I'm just part of the crowd now, no different from the others, and that feels really good.
Reena: How many in the crowd do you think?
Greg: It was really solitary before but this just feels totally different. Hmm, about twelve, fifteen? It's hard to count the number. It's like there's enough people to be interesting but not too big to be overwhelming.
Reena: Who are the people of this crowd?
Greg: I dunno! But they all seem excited and chattering … There's two women and the rest are men. Similar sort of age, similar to me, young twenties. It almost feels like there's going to be something achieved. I don't quite know what it is and we've been given the choice of whether we become part of something, we just don't know anything at all, but it just seems exciting to be part of it. It's not like me at all to go off and leave all the taxes and the donkey behind, it's almost like I don't care any more now.
Reena: And what happens next?
Greg: We need some food, so we're stopping in a small house. I say house, it's a very cheaply built thing, like white smooth walls that have been made with some sort

of clay or something. It's just a doorway, I don't even think there's a window - it's very small. We're sat outside and the person inside has brought out a bit of food and is sharing it, so we all have a little bit of bread.

Reena: What else do you eat? Only bread?

Greg: No, there's some water and there's a bit of fruit, like dates. There's also something on the plate, I'm not quite sure what it is but it's like a dried fruit, some sort of plant or something. Something which he's perhaps collected wild. The bread's very lumpy and has grains in it. But it just seems so perfect.

The next scene saw Paul on the move with the same group of people, having left the house. The crowd is bigger now, people seemingly coming from different directions. They are following the person who hugged him.

Reena: How do you address this person who hugged you?

Greg: Well, I'm not sure, they kind of have slightly different names for him and he responds to all of the names, so it's a bit confusing. Some of them call him something with a 'Yeyal' ... not too sure what that is. It sounds strange but I just call him The One. It's almost like he feels [like] the special One. Yeah, I think we all have different names for him because it's almost like, I kind of feel like each of them have a different type of relationship with him and they kind of like to have a name that fits him. He responds to all of them, he ... But for me I call him The One. I like that.

Interesting how Greg refers to Jesus as 'The One' here, and 'Jesus' in his first regression. Normally, when people experience multiple regression sessions to the one life, they become more comfortable and sink into the memories more. Maybe as Greg became more comfortable and embraced the memory more deeply, he shifted from referring to Jesus as 'Jesus' to 'The One'.

Reena: Hmm … and they are all coming to see The One? These people?

Greg: Yeah.

Reena: And what's drawing all these people to The One?

Greg: Well, some people are talking about … perhaps he's going to be making some sort of plan, some of them are talking about him being the person to get rid of the Romans. Some of them say this word 'Messiah', but I don't think they … words like that … it feels like … not sure. They don't like anything that's overthrowing the Romans because they … I've seen what they've done with people before and they are all very frightened of them. It's almost like it doesn't matter when you're with The One. It feels almost like nothing can be defeated, you don't need swords or arms, just the group of us are able to almost do anything. It's almost like the Romans would wilt if we walked towards them, so I just go along with it and see what happens.

Reena: Are you a Roman or are you something else?

Greg: Well, I'm not a Jew, they call me a Gentile. I'm not really religious. I grew up in a village where there were Jews, it's just that we didn't do any of the things they do, so therefore they shunned us and that's why I was quite happy to do the job of collecting taxes from them, teach them a lesson.

This account once again contradicts the common knowledge that Paul was a Pharisee who held strongly to the Jewish traditions and rituals. It is the first time that Paul referred to himself as a Gentile. While I did not ask, this could imply that Greg's Paul held Roman citizenship due to his position as a Gentile, and his work as a tax collector, which is consistent with the accounts in the Book of Acts.[4] The regression continues.

Reena: Tell me more about the crowds that came to see The One.

Greg: The crowd? Hmm, well there's young and old, there's some women carrying babies, some children, not many, the children are with the parents and holding their hands, there's some older people having difficulty walking. There's some of them that have got wounds, there's one person who's like lost an arm, but they're all coming along.

Reena: What's drawing them to The One?

Greg: Well, there's going to be some kind of talk maybe, some of them are saying, plans to get rid of the Romans, but I don't think that is the case. But we'll just have to see what he's going to talk about.

Reena: And so just tell me what happens next.

Greg: The One is standing on a raised bit of land. I say land, it's all rocks but it just means his feet are at the same height as the nearest ones' heads but the hill is further down so people aren't all at the same height. And he's gesturing for everyone to sit. So we all sit and he's starting to talk.

He's just talking about how things can be done differently, how powerful love is. I don't quite understand what he means by that, but it's what he did to me and that's pretty powerful.

He's telling some stories, and he's telling the story of someone who had three sons, and the youngest son leaves home because he's not happy with how things are and feel that he's not getting a fair share. And how, when he comes back a little later, his father just gives him food and clothing. His other sons said, 'We stayed with you and we all did the things you asked for, yet you give all these presents to him and he did nothing, it's not fair.' And we all think to ourselves (well, *I* do), 'That's not fair, is it?' And he's explaining that with love you can forgive people and you can give them things that they need, it's not about giving everybody the same thing, you just give people what they need, when they need it; that's what love is.

So this is quite a different way of thinking about things. It's certainly got me thinking. A few people are chatting to each other about it, almost like it's an idea that no one's ever thought of before. It's almost like, 'Wow, yeah, we could do [that]'. It certainly got me thinking.

Reena: And what happens next?

Greg: Well, there's a woman with The One and she comes close to him and I guess I'm feeling a bit uncomfortable about why he's drawing women quite close to him, when this is men's work talking about these sort of things. It's not the sort of thing women do and yet he's drawing her up and he's saying how women are just as important as men. Well, this is a different idea altogether, women the same as men? They're supposed to stay at home and look after the babies and do the cooking.

Paul's way of thinking really is in line with both the Jewish and Roman's strong patriarchal cultures and systems at that time.

Reena: How does that make you feel?

Greg: Ah, a bit strange really. And he's talking about how it's not what job you do or who you are that's important, it's about how everybody can come through to the Kingdom of Heaven. It doesn't matter if they are young, old, male or female, they are all the same. And if all of them can come through to the Kingdom of Heaven, why are they treated differently when they are not in the process of going through to the Kingdom of Heaven? Hmm, that's got us all thinking about that one.

And then he says, what about someone who has a lot of money, can they take that through to the Kingdom of Heaven? They are saying, 'Well, no.' So then he says, well, if you can't take that with you, why do you need to collect it and hold it when you can help others? Oh my goodness … this is a bit of a new idea.

And he's walking forward and there's someone who's got some kind of disease, I don't know what it is. They're not well, they're like on a stretcher, I've never seen them before because of the crowd but they are always there. And he's moving his way forward and he's putting his hands on them and he's talking about bringing the Kingdom of Heaven down to them so that even the poor and the dying can feel it too. And he's saying how they can just go through to the Kingdom of Heaven in the same way as everybody else.

Well. He [the person with the disease] is certainly opening up his eyes and he's lifting his head up, others are helping to prop him up so he is partially sat, he's got such a smile on his face, it's almost like he's being touched, and there's a part of him that's about to change. I don't know, certainly quite an amazing effect he's having on everybody, including me ... some sort of buzz.

It's almost like ... thoughts of new ways of doing things, new ideas and more ... no one ever talks about ideas – well, come on, let's have more of them! Nobody ever talks about these sort of things. Everybody is always on about how to survive and keep out of the way of the Romans. We all have our little jobs to do and when we feel emotionally unhappy, we take it out on whoever's around and this is what everybody does ... and [this is] someone doing something completely different.

Reena: Tell me what more you are aware of?

Greg: Things are coming to an end now, walking away and the crowd dispersing. He's just called a few of us over.

Reena: Is that woman included as well?

Greg: Yeah. I think he's got a special relationship with her, I'm not sure. He seems to put his arm around her which ... it's not like a permanent thing, it's like when you meet someone you hug them, it's like that. It's brief and then it's finished, but he does it like it's a sign of affection. Everything's new so I just need to find ... he seems to be pulling a small group of us to one side, it was some of the ones who were together before the others joined us. He's calling us off and wants to talk to us as a group.

Reena: And roughly how many are in this group? [long pause]

Greg: About eight I think.

Reena: And what does he say to you?

Greg: He's saying something about we need to be fishermen for men or something. Do what he's doing, and, oh my goodness, how can we suddenly go through and do what he's doing? This is something entirely new …

We follow him and we find another house and get another bit of food given to us. One or two of them have brought some food with them and we're sharing it. It's not a lot, but it always seems to be just enough for what we need.

Reena: And what happens next?

Greg: Everyone's going to have to rest but we're all chattering and talking, the group are all quite excited. This is the first night, the first day, oh my goodness, if every day is like this … this is going to be exciting stuff.

The next event saw Paul in a group, at a table, eating with The One.

Greg: There's a group of us, the ones who are closest to him. I'm in this house with a big table and we're sat around eating our evening meal and he's saying this is going to be the last time we're all together and that he's going to die but it's for a reason. We're all a bit quiet about that. A few of them said no, we can't have that.

But we just learned to accept whatever happens happens, however unusual, because that is part of the journey that we seem to be on at the moment. Anyway, that's what I think, that's my view. The others may have different views. I don't talk much to the others about it. I'm more 'think about it'.

Reena: And it was a meal … what sort of meal were you having?

Greg: We had some water, there's some fish, it's like a dried fish that's cooked somehow. There's some bread – there's bread with everything – and there's some other things in with the fish and there's some vegetables of some sort, it's a bit like stew. Slapped onto a plate, it's very simple food but feels very filling.

This is slightly different to James' version where they were eating goat stew. However, both fish and goat were predominant foods that were eaten during those times. Fish was caught from the Sea of Galilee, and transported around the country. As with goat, fish was also served to honoured guests by rich patrons who could afford the delicacy.[5]

Reena: Are there men and women here at this meal?

Greg: Yes, there's Mary, who's sat next to Jesus – well, some people call him that … I call him The One. And then there's the other group of followers sat around him.

Reena: You are friendly with one another? What is your relationship like with the other followers … Mary and the others?

Greg: We all accept each other. It's almost like we treat each other how we've been taught to treat others. This seemed at first strange, treating people who were Jews or non-Jews, or women or men, all the same. But it's quite nice, I like it.

The next event sees Paul witnessing Jesus dragging a cross.

Greg: The One is dragging a cross ... he's got two hands to one of the pieces of wood and he's like pulling it behind him. And there are two or three Romans around him. One of them hits him occasionally. There's blood all over him, it's hard to recognise him like this. He's covered in blood, he's been beaten and whipped and his face has blood running all the way down it. There's blood coming from his head and shoulders. It's just that I know this is something the Romans have done to him and I'm just kind of stood there, I just don't know what to do. It was so obvious just following before but now something's happening to him, it's almost like I don't know what to do and the rest of the crowd are like that. And we're just kind of stood, almost like shocked, like paralysed with the fear and the shock. How could this happen? So I keep a bit of a distance away.

Reena: So just tell me a bit about the wooden cross?

Greg: It's not very big, it's like the wood is like circular, not very thick, maybe three inches thick and probably about the length of a person and a bit more. There's another piece that's been tied to it and there's like rope around the two pieces of wood in the centre. But as it's been dragged one of the pieces has been twisted so that it's not quite in line with the other piece but at a slight angle. The One is holding one of the pieces and dragging it behind.

Reena: Is it a dark wood or a light wood?

Greg: No, it's a light wood. It looks like some of the bark has been taken off it. I've got a feeling this has been used before for crucifixions.

Reena: Are both pieces of wood the same size or are they different?

Greg: Well one of them is slightly bigger than the other one and they are slightly, not entirely straight, a slight kink in them. But we all know what it's going to be used for.

Reena: And you're so confused, you don't know what to do ...

Greg: Just shock and horror. Just devastated how such an amazing person can end up like this.

Reena: What's your understanding of how The One ended up like this?

Greg: That he was tried and found guilty. Of course it was all stage-managed by the Pharisees and the Jews. Some of the Jews who don't like him want to get rid of him. I wasn't involved in that, but I am just following the procession. There's a few people on the side who've come to see this (all of them look equally shocked and devastated, frightened) and they are getting to a small clearing.

Reena: And what happens next?

Greg: Well, this clearing has got a small wall, very rough and ready, and the wood is on the floor and The One is being held. He's on top of the wood and they're taking nails and hitting the nail through each of his ... his wrists? Somewhere between the wrist and his palm, I think they're being careful not to cut open a vessel. They've been told to be careful where to put them, they do it to his other hand and feet. Almost like it's a cross but it's like an X instead of a cross. Then they pull this up to the wall and the cross is like leaned against the wall and he's just got his head drooped down.

Reena: In between the cross?

Greg: Yeah, his arms are in the air, his head's in the air and his feet aren't quite touching the ground because there's some wood slightly longer than his feet so his whole body is dragged on the wood. And there's blood coming out of where the nails have gone in.

Reena: What is his behaviour like? I mean, is he aware of the pain? Is he shouting?

Greg: No, he's not saying anything, he's just … it's like all the energy has gone out of him and the Romans stand around there. There's two others that have been treated in the same way so there's these three Xs where the three people are. All of them are hanging there. All of them have been nailed to the wood.

Sometimes I've seen these crucifixions where they've done them against the walls of Jerusalem and they're actually put on the big walls of Jerusalem, but for some reason they wanted to take him out of Jerusalem away from people so they found this little rocky outpost to do it. The Romans are just stood around, just keeping people at a distance.

In the interest of full disclosure, Greg, during the debrief, admitted to watching a documentary on television about ancient Roman crucifixion methods, and thought that this description of the position of the body may be more from conscious mind recollection of the documentary, rather than his own memory. However, according to Laurence Gardner, in the Dead Sea Scrolls the original holy sign of the cross was an X mark, which is now known as the St Andrew's cross. By way of later Roman influence the new cross sign was devised.[6] Maybe Greg's account was not far from the truth after all.

Reena: What else are the Romans doing apart from standing around and looking at the people?

Greg: Well, they're just Romans. They don't care about the people who've been crucified. They've been told what to do is to keep people away, so that's what they're doing. A few of them are taunting The One and taunting some of the others too.

Reena: How do they taunt The One?

Greg: They're saying that if you're special why can't you come off the cross and walk away? One of them is prodding with a spear.

Reena: Whereabouts?

Greg: In the body, but it's not like it's going in deep, it's just going in a little bit. It's almost like having fun, this is their way of having a bit of amusement. There's not many people around, I'm one of the few people there.

Reena: Who else do you recognise from the group who are there?

Greg: Well, there's Mary, that woman who is special to him, who he told me he was married to. There's a couple of the others who've been with him … men. And we troop away. I know he can't do anything; he'll have to die. So I suppose that's what I can do perhaps. That's the biggest way of thanking The One for everything I've gained and learned, is to go and do the same to others. Although my mind's not really on that at the moment.

The next scene sees Paul, in his early to mid-thirties, in Rome, after he had been to Cyprus and the outskirts of Rome, where he's got a group of people with him, who tried to establish the teaching of The One.

Greg: Well, I'm trying to get the teachings of The One established but it's proving a bit difficult … if we're caught by the Romans we get thrown into the arena. Or beaten. So we have to be very good and careful where we meet.

Reena: Where do you meet, then?

Greg: We meet in the cellars, or we meet in … once we met up in a barn on the outskirts of Rome, but then that's harder to get to. The cellars are easier because we can meet in smaller groups and it's harder for people to stumble in on us because we're out of sight. There's not many houses with these cellars but we have a few that open theirs. But the difficulty is that – and I tried to get some of these teachings established before on some of the islands – people started to go through and interpret them in lots of different ways and they started to lose their true meaning. At least now we're in a place where it's hard to keep this alive because of the Romans but trying to teach it in a way that is much stricter. It's more trying to keep what we've been taught but in a consistent way, because we can't meet in a more flowy way of the islands where it was up to us and people could come or not come. It was quite easy doing it there, but in Rome we have to be much more careful, so we have to teach it in a way, even if people are in small groups or they are going to a different small group, they'll get taught the same, otherwise they'll just get confused and we'll lose the message.

Reena: OK, so what happens next?

Greg: We were introducing some of the people that are working with me and helping me with this, coming up with ideas and suggestions of how we can do things.

Reena: Are there Romans?

Greg: No, no, they're followers . . that are helping do this teaching, but the subject comes up about women and I've been reminding them that their teaching about women was that all women were the same as men. And they are saying, 'Yes, but everybody in Rome doesn't like that way,' because in Rome there is an order of ... men, or the Romans and the non-Romans – the men and the women, and then the children.

We have to really keep to that sort of order in order to get some of these ideas in. It's not all of the ideas we were taught, but at least get some of them in. So I don't know, I don't feel too comfortable about this, but I think we'll experiment and try it.

So we introduce that idea into the teaching that men are separate and that men can be the ones that can teach others about doing this type of work and not women. It seems to work reasonably well because all other people who are working with me are men anyway, so ...

Reena: Who spearheaded that whole way of thinking ... about the men?

Greg: It's really come about because of where we're working in Rome and the difficulty of trying to get this message through in Rome where it's so ingrained of treating everybody in a certain order that to try to teach something too revolutionarily different just isn't getting through.

Reena: So it was a group consensus then?

Greg: Yeah, and it's basically about getting some message through that rings about the change; it may not be perfect, may not be exactly as we were taught, but at least it's getting something through. So I go along with this and everybody else agrees and of course the ones I am working with are males anyway, so we'll try to get the teachings out through males and this is what we agree. And we also agree that it's probably better that we don't get into relationships with women either.

The concern that we all have is that this is an important message and we have to go by ourselves to do this, and if we have women that are with us then we either would want to come back to look after them or they would come with us and they will be put into danger. So we are thinking that maybe it is better if we go by ourselves and people feel drawn to us to do the teaching, whether they are men or women then this is their choice, and then they can take that to others however they want, but it would be easier for us to work as and when and within the Roman culture.

So we do that and it's kind of not done as a forced thing but almost like an understanding and it seems to work quite well because we are getting the work out and each of the men are going to a different part of the city working with different groups. It means that they're fully focused on doing that, they are not caught up in having families or other things, so that's really helping things move forward, so I feel quite good that things are spreading within Rome quite well and it's got enough of the message for it to be powerful and to bring about a change.

Within the patriarchal Roman world in those days, it is conceivable that Paul had to adhere to some of the Roman ways for them to hear and receive his version of Jesus' message. Let's not forget that Greg's Paul was also shocked at Jesus' Nazarene teaching of equal treatment of women, earlier in the regression. Paul's patriarchal mentality comes through strongly in the Apostolic Constitutions. However, despite

Paul's appearance of supporting a male-dominated world, his letters made mention of his own female helpers: a servant of the church, Phebe (Romans 16:1–2), Julia (16:15) and Priscilla the martyr (16:3–4). He also mentioned in his epistle to Timothy (3:2–5) that a bishop should be the husband of one wife and that he should have children.[7]

This account that Greg gives of Paul is in line with Paul's struggle in reconciling Jesus' view with his own personal view of women, as well as the patriarchal Roman culture he was working in.

Reena: So how's the message being spread? Is it via word of mouth?

Greg: It's through small meetings and we have the meetings and people come who want to listen to it. We're very careful who we invite, because some of the members are getting caught and dragged away and beaten or put in the arena where they are brutally killed so we have to be very, very careful. But because there are so many people who are desperate for something new, there's no shortage of people coming.

It's almost like the more brutal the Romans are, the more people that come who want to know about what we're doing, particularly the ones who die holding the faith. Even some of the Romans are starting to come and secretly getting involved with what we're doing. Yes, it's a good job we kept males doing the work, it's a lot easier to draw the Romans in for that, they kind of understand.

Women come in and they listen to our teachings and they go off and work. And so, you know, we have people of both sexes, we even have some children that come and that's OK. So we have now about ten or eleven parts of Rome where we're working and now we're planning to take this to other parts of the Empire.

We'll keep this structure because it works really well and as people are trained they take this consistent message and we've got enough of the stories of The One and I'm going to take this to the other parts ... of the country and the Empire. People are going out with this and getting the message out there and it is spreading.

This is consistent with Paul evangelising and taking Christianity to Asia Minor and all of Europe – which was, at that time, predominantly under Roman rule.

In the next event Paul finds himself at the point close to his death.

Greg: I've had a feeling that it is my time. And it is not going to be very pleasant either. The followers of Christ are still being killed, persecuted and eaten alive by lions. So I am sat on a chair in my room and I am quite old with a bit of a cough. Hair is whitish and I feel quite content with everything I have achieved in my life. There is a knock on the door. I open the door and some soldiers come in and hold me. I can see by the door one of the followers skulking in the shadows but I can still know who it is.

Reena: Who is it?

Greg: He is somebody called Elema.

Reena: Tell me what happens next.

Greg: Rope is pulled around my neck, pulled tight and garrotted, coughing and spluttering. The worst part of it is that I can still see in the distance the person who betrayed me. I can't feel anger towards him, just disappointed. Then my life is over. And I feel myself coming out of the body and looking down and I can see one of the Romans lifts up a sword, takes off my head, and wraps it in sack material. And my body is just left there and my head is taken away. And I just go on my way.

It is interesting to point out that although there are no official records or accounts of how Paul died, tradition holds that he was beheaded by Romans under the rule of Emperor Nero in AD68, after his fifth missionary journey ended the year before.[8] Also, there is no account of what happened to Zaccheus in the later part of his life. Could the quiet garrotting by Nero's soldiers be the way that saw the end of the illustrious evangelist?

There is also a direct contradiction to Greg claiming Paul died by illness in the first regression, and garrotting in the second. Why? When someone goes through trauma, our brain and body go into the shock. In order to move in our lives (purely for survival reasons), our minds create coping strategies for us to continue on past the shock and trauma in a coherent manner, in the forms of denial, avoidance, shut downs, selective amnesia, or even fragmentation so as to not confront it – for confronting it means pain and fear. Breaking through coping mechanisms is key to obtaining the source of the trauma and retrieving the memory for transformative healing.

In Greg's case, the recollection of his death of being garrotted was clearly traumatic. So his psyche avoided it in the first regression. However, once the energy of the trauma was released through the use of Body Therapy at the start of the second regression, the suppressed memory was brought to the surface for him to confront and deal with.

Again, Paul dies with emotions of disappointment that the structure was too rigid and that they could not do more work with women, as The One had with Mary Magdalene. Paul also died with guilt: the message that The One had given was distorted when they got to Rome and Paul regretted changing the message and method to get it accepted. The more people that got involved, the harder Paul felt it was to change it, and it took on a life of its own.

When Paul met the spirit of The One in the Kingdom of Heaven, he apologized for letting The One down by distorting the message. The response he got was that there is no *one* message. People have to see the message behind the words; however it is expressed is fine. Everything he did was to carry the message into the very heart of where there was an absence of love, and Paul was embraced for that.

Frankly speaking, Paul's regressions provided me with the opportunity for the most learning. Paul is probably the most widely recorded biblical figure – with nearly half the New Testament accorded to him and his letters of Jesus' teachings. However, there is little record of his earlier days and death. On the other hand, there is minuscule mention of Zacchaeus, and yet it corroborates very nicely with Greg's earliest account of meeting Jesus.

Despite the inconsistencies with what little records are available, Greg's accounts during the regression are consistent with one another, and also provide a credible theory and insight into his fledgling Church, which has now grown immeasurably from his principles and teachings. His guilt and disappointment in himself is evident at the end of his life, knowing that his teachings deviated so much from the teachings of his idol that he was trying to emulate.

As The One said to Paul, each person will interpret the message differently, and there is no one message. At the end of the day, it is through Paul's efforts that Jesus is so widely known, and while the historical and ritual details differ, sometimes widely, the spiritual message has always been consistent – that of love, compassion and kindness.

Though maligned in many circles for corrupting the pure story of Jesus, the man and his family, Greg's Paul comes across as a person of great faith and devotion, who worked really hard, with earnest enthusiasm, in fulfilling his idol's request – to take the teachings to as many people as he could.

5

BESOTTED

I would not wish any companion in the world but you.
— William Shakespeare

Maya, a British woman of Asian ancestry, was the next person who emerged on this fascinating journey. She was a client of a student therapist of the Past Life Regression Academy, who spontaneously regressed back to the life of a biblical figure during one of the student's practice sessions. When the student heard that I was contemplating this book, she referred Maya to me. Not having much exposure to the New Testament at all, and having limited prior knowledge of key figures and events of the time, Maya was keen to explore this life more thoroughly, to assuage her own curiosity. Under the condition of anonymity, she agreed to share all the sessions exploring her memories as Mary Magdalene, including the ones she'd had with the student – where it all began.

Maya dropped into the life as a six-year-old girl, being aware of standing on beautiful spring-green grass with mountains in the distance, and little village houses dotted around. Her feet are bare and she is wearing a long white sheath, with a delicate silver-threaded loop belt around her waist. The dress around her chest is decorated with almost turquoise and thin gold embroidery. She wears bracelet cuffs around her wrists and a veil, which looks like a nurse's cap, around her head. She is on her own, communicating telepathically with animals and communing with nature, feeling peaceful, happy and still.

Maya: I'm not doing anything. It's like I just almost stand there. But even when I am walking this happens because I'm so open I think it just reaches out and touches other things. It's interesting. I can't explain it but it's as though ... It's like a spider web. And the spider web reaches out and touches all the other things and they touch me back. The spider web is almost like a telecommunications line back to me. So if one antenna (of the spider web) touches the squirrel it sends signals back and I kind of know what the squirrel is feeling almost. And then another tendril goes out to the mountains and I know what the mountains are. It's almost like a connection via the spider web. It's very beautiful. I am quite happy ... The other thing I am feeling is as though the Earth is singing. She's very happy. A slight vibration under my feet and she is really pleased and happy that there is life ... The Earth is singing and I can feel it.

The next significant event sees Mary running back home, because her mother was calling her back, with urgency in her voice.

Trainee: And how is she calling you?
Maya: 'Mary.' There's some excitement in her voice. And in the house is a boy and a girl. So I'm the youngest. They are my brother and sister ... so cute. They are looking at me with big eyes ... We're having a meal.
Trainee: And what's happening?

Maya: We are not sitting at a table. We're sitting on the floor, which is very interesting. My dad's there, as well. There is great excitement because they say someone is coming to meet us. Personally coming to meet me in particular.

Trainee: Have they told you who this person is?

Maya: They never say anything much. There's just this massive excitement but I feel really excited as well ... There's another family that's come to meet my mum and dad. The three of us are peeking through the door. Mum and Dad say they are important. I'm not sure why. They call us in to meet the visitors. I walk in. It's quite a big room. There's Mummy, Daddy, then there's another man and a woman. Oh, that woman is so beautiful. It's like she radiates peace. The funny thing is, I think she understands me.

Trainee: Do you know who this woman is, have you been told?

Maya: No. But there's an instant connection. She's a bit like me where she's so open and her energy reaches out and it touches me. She gives me this beautiful smile. I like her. I wonder if she can stay with us. Oh, there's a boy – and there's another boy. I think that they may be cousins or something.

Trainee: Tell me about the first boy.

Maya: He's very quiet. His cousin's a pain, very loud. Young thing. He's probably five. So I think I'm six [laughs]. This boy's a bit older. I find him interesting because he's very quiet but he's not shy, not retiring. He's very quiet and very still.

Trainee: And who is this boy? Is he related to the woman or the man?

Maya: He's related to the woman and the man. There's a stronger connection with the woman. The man is almost like the protector – like a warrior protector, but I know they're part of the family.

Trainee: And what happens next?

Maya: The woman smiles at me. It's a beautiful, radiant smile. I love the smile. The boy keeps looking at me, not the precocious one, the quiet one. He's a bit older than me. And it's funny because my mother has asked my brother and sister to take the cousin – but I am still to remain there.

Trainee: And what are they saying?

Maya: I don't understand the words that are being uttered – it's like I tune them out, but when I am speaking with the boy there is a connection and we are speaking through the connection. It's almost like no one else exists but me, the boy and the lady. It's funny because the boy's giving me this really intense look. It's almost like a feeling of ... again, no words are being uttered but it's almost like telepathic communication but not quite. It's not a Doing. It's a Being. It's almost like he is quietly pleased that we've connected. It's like a puzzle is in place almost.

Trainee: Do you know the purpose of this meeting?

Maya: I have no idea, but with the boy and I, we had to meet to connect. He has magnetism and I am drawn to him. But I don't want to play with him. I can understand what they are saying now, because just now when I was communing with the boy it's like everything else faded out. Then he said these things to me, telepathically, and then it's like the cone of silence fell. Now, I can hear the woman saying that the boy is going to go away for a while and then they will be back again when we are at a more appropriate age. I felt a bit of a sadness as I didn't want the connection with the boy to go. And I felt sad because I didn't want the connection with this lovely lady to go. I think she's his mum.

At the next significant event, Mary is at an event that sounded like her coming of age ceremony, when she was either twelve or thirteen. This is interesting because it is consistent with James' and Paul's regressions and many of the following regressions of the coming of age ceremonies that they seem to go through when they are approaching pubescence.

Maya: It's like I've been given my name. My name is Miriam now. It's a … I don't know what you call it. It's like a confirmation. I am a person now. It's something that everyone goes through. All the children go through. Trainee: Is it like a rite of passage? Maya: It's a naming ceremony. I feel like I've got my name, identity. In front of everybody, all the older people … I love my name. Miriam.

This revelation is quite significant. The Greek name 'Mary' is derived from the Egyptian 'Mery', and the equivalent to the Hebrew 'Miriam' all mean the same thing – Beloved. In the Greco-Egyptian culture, 'Mary' was not so much a name as a distinction, for those who were raised in a monastic environment until they were chosen to be betrothed.[1] So in being given this name, it is assumed that Mary's path was clearly marked for her. Unfortunately, this did not manifest as she'd expected.

Maya: My mum and dad are very kind, gentle people. There seems to be a little bit of an argument. They are arguing about something with some of the town elders … I get a feeling that they are not happy with the person that I am to marry. Once a girl has been named they either marry or they go into the temple to either serve God or be a priestess. Whereas for me it wasn't in my cards to be a priestess necessarily, and I think they are arguing about who I am partnered with and who I am meant to marry.

Trainee: Do you know who you are meant to marry?

Maya: I am very confused by this whole thing because all I wanted to do was to be with my animals and the plants. I am a little bit surprised because I thought my parents were going to send me to become a priestess, not marry. It felt overwhelming because I just got my name and my relatives are there and everyone's talking. I see my parents on the street with the elders arguing quite heatedly in the distance. My brother is there in the room. My brother is a man now … well, he's an adult, he is a lot older than me.

Trainee: What happens next?

Maya: The village elder storms out. And my mum is looking really upset, which upsets me. My dad is looking a bit tense. My brother is looking bothered by something.

Trainee: What happens next?

Maya: The celebration is over and everyone has gone home except for my immediate family. Again I see my mum and dad and brother sitting in a room having this deep, intense discussion. My sister is trying to distract me by brushing my hair. I've got beautiful hair. But I'm not distracted. I don't necessarily need to hear things to know things are not good. And I know it's got something to do with me. And I do not want to tune in or commune with them because I want to give them privacy.

Next, Mary regresses to a very personal, spiritual moment that she experienced. It is rare for these moments to occur in regression sessions. However, what is so compelling within this book is that, unbeknown to the regressees, another member of Mary Magdalene's family experiences something similar – which makes this experience extremely interesting.

Maya: I see a very deep blue, a cornflower blue, coming through. A colour. I don't know what that is. It says it's there to hold me … how can a colour hold me, I don't know … The colour is holding me, whatever that means.

Trainee: And what's happening?

Maya: I walk through the blue. I don't know if I'm imagining this or what, but it's like the blue suddenly turned into a butterfly and flew away and I am now in a garden. [laughs] It's like a rainforest garden. It's gorgeous. It's very pretty and very colourful and full of green. It's almost like an Adam and Eve garden. It's so weird! I don't know what one's got to do with the other. I don't know where I am.

Trainee: Just let it flow, let it happen. And what's happening?

Maya: It's really interesting. I can see all these little animals and butterflies and it's like I'm on a hill. And I look up and I see eyes in the sky and it's talking to me. [laughs]

Trainee: What's the sky saying?

Maya: It's very cute because the clouds make up a beard. It's giving me a warning. The sky's saying that the Earth is not going to be healthy any more. It's talking to me about the potential destruction of the Earth, of where I was standing as that six-year-old girl. The Earth's not going to sing any more. And he is talking to me about these changes that are coming through.

Trainee: Tell me about the changes.

Maya: He's showing me all this beautiful Garden of Eden almost ... melting slowly. Saying that she won't be able to sustain much longer. And he's talking about how the web of life – oh, now I get it – because so many strings of the web – it's going to be broken so there is a great danger that the web is going to collapse into itself. And it's something we can't let happen. Well, he's saying it's best for it not to happen but you know ... I don't understand because I'm twelve or thirteen.

The only thing I can feel is the devastation of the Earth and I ask how ... well, at first I ask why, because I don't understand why the Earth would choose to do such a thing. He says, 'Because the interconnectedness is broken – or beings on Earth do not see the interconnectedness so much, it's not sustainable for the Earth. It's all breaking'. So then I am saying, 'Why are you telling me? What can I do about this?' And he's saying that because I am so attuned to the web, it's almost like I can hold it. Just like how the blue is holding me, I can hold it.

Then he said there will be one who will come and work with me and be my partner and help me hold it. But it's almost like the grid and the web – it's like I'm holding it. It's only at that point that I realise that not everybody can do what I can do – like commune with the animals and the trees. I get now that my brother and sister and my mummy and daddy just can't do it. And I know inside me that the person who is going to come and help me is that boy. I know it because there was this connection between us. It's not just with nature, it's also with people. So everything as a whole.

The next significant event, Mary is back in the room where her mother, father and brother are talking.

Maya: But I'm not so nervous any more. I know how things are meant to be, so I'm OK. I know that their worries are not warranted because I know that everything has been put in place for the web.

Trainee: What happens next?

Maya: The village elder comes back – this is a few days later – and I think he's basically threatening my mum and dad. There is so much anger.

Trainee: Who's angry?

Maya: The village elder and my dad, there's just aggression between them. The village elder is trying to force my dad to do something he does not want to do.

Trainee: Do you know why he's trying to do this?

Maya: According to one of my siblings, my sister, I am betrothed to that boy but the village elder doesn't want me to be betrothed to him, as he does not like him now. He is about eighteen now. He [the elder] doesn't like it and my family apparently is quite a high-status family in the town, in the village. So marrying me off to that boy would automatically give him a high status and they don't want him to have the high status.

But I don't understand why because to me all I'm seeing is this web and he is going to help hold the web. I'm not understanding why they don't want the web to be held. Don't they understand the Earth can't sing?

[laughs] But no one understands my language. My brother and sister do, but I think there is also a deep understanding within them; there is a good, deep connection between us.

Trainee: Is there anything else we need to know here?

Maya: My mother comes to me. She's beautiful. She has got long, dark-brown hair, ringlets. She wears a veil. Very soft, gentle face. She tells me I have a choice.

Trainee: And what's the choice?

Maya: She tells me that I am betrothed to that boy that I saw. It's not like he's poor, it's not like he's got no stature. Status isn't the thing. I don't know why that town elder doesn't like him. Or [I can marry] someone else of a slightly higher standing, equal to our standing – like a rich merchant's son. I look at her and I say, even though I know she won't understand, that my destiny is with this boy. So no matter what happens, whether the town elder, whether I, whether my parents – it doesn't matter who wills it, what will happen is I will be with this boy. So she takes the message back to the village elder and my father and the village elder is so angry.

Within the Christian tradition, Mary Magdalene is held to be a prostitute, with little, if any standing, within the community. The four Gospels included in the New Testament have little to say about Mary Magdalene until the crucifixion, apart from claiming that Jesus cast out seven demons from her (Luke 8:2 and Mark 16:9).

However, Jacapo di Voragine, a thirteenth-century Archbishop of Genoa, wrote *La Legende de Sainte Marie Madeline* from church records. In it, he stated and gave evidence that Mary Magdalene had indeed a high standing in society, through the lineage of both her parents. Her father was called Syro the Jairus, and he was the Chief Priest, subordinate to the Jerusalem High Priest, a Pharisee. Syro was a Syrian nobleman, whose wife Eucharia was of royal kindred – descended from the priestly Hasmonaean House of the Maccabees, who reigned in Jerusalem from 166BC until Roman occupation from 63BC.[2]

This is consistent with Maya's account in her regression of the high stature that they hold within the community. Also, it is interesting that their family had a quarrel with an irate elder, who did not want her to marry the 'boy' due to him being of lower stature. It seems that this elder could be the Jerusalem High Priest, to whom her father is subordinate to, which accounts for his threats.

Trainee: So what happens next?
Maya: Three days later there's a big contingent of people coming to the door. It's the merchant and his wife. They have come with presents and gifts. They ask my mum and dad if I would be betrothed to their son. My mum and dad call me in. I don't quite like the look of the son. He is very hard-faced.
Trainee: Has he got a name?
Maya: I think it's a D-A-E – there's a W somewhere. I think it's D-a-e-w-u-d-e. Something like that. [laughs] But let's call him David.
Trainee: And what happens?
Maya: Oh, yes. Hard-face. Don't quite like him. But for some reason, to maintain the fabric of my thought processes – this role has to take place. I feel a part of me has tried but I know I have to do it.
Trainee: And what happens?
Maya: The next year or six months, there is this grand party and we get betrothed. We do not consummate the

marriage. When he came to the marriage bed, people outside were cheering and doing all sorts of things but he was so drunk he just collapsed on the bed.

Trainee: How do you feel?

Maya: Relieved! [laughs]

Trainee: And what happens next?

Maya: He's quite a bit older than me. He's twenty or twenty-one but I am just thirteen. I am not that old. I am of a marriageable age but …

Trainee: And what happens next?

Maya: I go and sit outside. I am feeling quite distraught because … I'm confused because I know that to keep the fabric I had to be betrothed to this person but I am not happy. I don't want to be with him and I'm yearning to be with the other boy – whose name I still don't know. I don't quite like what is happening. Later on we do end up consummating the marriage and it's been quite unpleasant. But now I have a boy, a little son. About a year or a year and a half.

Trainee: And what's his name?

Maya: He's got the same name as his dad. Daewude. So let's call him David junior.

Trainee: What's happening now? How old are you now?

Maya: Probably about fifteen. David senior beats me. He doesn't understand the fabric and the web. All he lives for is for profit and for going to other women. I don't mind when he goes to other women. It makes me feel quite relieved really. I'm happier when he is not here at home. His son has got a jumpier disposition but he adores his dad. I teach my son about the grass and the trees and the animals and sometimes he listens to me, a bit enraptured, and at other times he goes off and plays with his toys. I can't blame him really – he's one [year old]. [laughs] But I don't feel that connection with my son that I felt with 'the boy'.

Trainee: Is there anything else of significance here or can we move forward?

Maya: I think this abuse, the beatings, make me feel quite despondent as well. The other thing is, because I'm in the city, I can't feel the Earth. What I would like to do is move to the country but my husband would have none of that.

[The next significant event sees Mary when she is about sixteen, and her son is two.]

Maya: I am getting really annoyed with my husband and all his beatings. I'm not in the expanded, bliss feeling. I feel small and crushed and ... So I told him six months ago I wanted to leave him and he beat me ... I got really hurt. But even if I left him, where would I go? The only thing that keeps me going is that he travels a lot for work. He's a merchant, he goes and he trades. So one day [when he went away], it was the day after one of the days he beat me, I picked up my son and I went to my brother's place.

Trainee: What happened?

Maya: My brother looked at me and was quite surprised because he didn't realise that I was going through all this. I told him to hide me. He was really gentle and sweet, to keep me there ... me and my son, for a little while, while my husband trades.

In that community it's disgraceful for a wife to leave her husband, so I know eventually I have to go back to him. And it sickens me. It really does. But my son plays with my brother's children. I see the connection that my brother and his wife have. I'm not envious of it, but I wish I had it because it's a lovely connection, because my husband and I have a very hard connection.

Trainee: And what happens next?

Maya: I go and stay at my brother's for a couple of months and there is this great excitement because this man is coming to our part of town, the country, where my brother lives. This man's name is Yeshua. My brother says that it might be a good idea for me to go and see him and hear him talk. I look at my brother like he's a madman because I don't understand why he wants me to go. But he says, 'Just do it. Everyone else is doing it.'

My sister lives near my brother so she takes me by the hand and says, 'Let's go.' My sister-in-law can take care of the boys, the children. So I went off to see this great man talking called Yeshua. I see this crowd and this man sitting on a rock talking. Again, that very quiet, intense, still way of being. There's something about his eyes that grabs me but when I'm in the crowd he looks at me and then our eyes meet and then I feel it – that connection.

It's only then that I recognise him as being that boy – the other one, the other half who has got to hold the web. He's far from being a boy now … His voice has got a beautiful magnetism. A charismatic thing. When he talks he looks at you individually … it's as though he talks directly at you. But when his eyes met mine there was a spark, like a spark of recognition. Like a [she makes a gasping sound].

At this point it becomes clear what the political reasons are for the elder, the Pharisee, to denounce Mary's marriage to 'the boy', whom we now know is Yeshua or Jesus. At this

106

point, Yeshua had adopted the Essene way of Being, and was considered to be a Nazarene – the spiritual leadership of Essenes. He was openly and publicly opposing the rituals and practices adopted by the Pharisees. To the Pharisee, Yeshua was a rebel, and thus could not be seen to have a raised stature via marriage to the daughter of yet another Pharisee.[3]

Trainee: And what was the message that Jesus was saying?

Maya: He was talking about peace and balance in the sense that balance is the gateway towards peace. Almost like if there is a balance of power there is peace. If there is a balance of … these are not his words, just the way I'm interpreting it … there's a balance of yin and yang and there's peace, right?

So it's all about that if there is a balance in the environment, there is peace; and imbalance causes chaos. So even within your body, if there is an imbalance of something there is chaos – or disease or illness, which is chaos. So he is just talking about peace and how peace is the perfect balance of everything and this is what we should strive for.

And the way towards the peace and the balance is love, but not love as in romantic love or whatever but love and respect of everything. So knowing that there is a place for your neighbour and there is a place for power and there's a place for trees and there's a place for birds and plants and what not, because once you start loving all these things you leave them be, you respect them. Then there is a balance. You don't overpower. And it's not about adulation, it's not about worshipping, but it's not about oppressing and treading on; it's about peace.

It's about respect and balance; and also the thing is when you worship something or someone you put them on a pedestal so they are not in balance with you. So this way, if you just respect them and love them, then there's a balance and then there is that peace.

His words touched me deeply, because of what I had just left behind. I can feel within my relationship with my husband and moving on from my son there is a massive imbalance there. And I can see that it resonates with a lot of people there, but I think they are also feeling: 'It's all very well to say but how do you do it?' Because a lot of them are poor and they are being trodden upon and suppressed. And that's when he says, 'It starts with you. If you sit and feel 'I'm being oppressed', well, you are. But if you pull yourself out of that and if you just align yourself and balance yourself energetically, then your whole being will shift and the balance will come to you by just being'.

Trainee: So what happens next?

Maya: He looks at me and it's like he can't tear his eyes off me. So the whole time he spoke, he was speaking looking at me. [laughs] But nobody else noticed because he is incredibly charismatic and maybe everybody else in the audience felt like that. Although just after he finished, his eyes caught my eyes again and everyone left. But I was still sitting there. He had told me in that telepathic way to stay – it's not telepathic, it's through the connection, it's through the energy. He grabs me by the shoulder and he picks me up. He helps me stand. Again, no words, but I know he is really happy to see me again and I was really happy to see him. And he gives me this hug and I feel the most intense love connection. It's so amazing. It's like all parts of us are connected.

And I notice my sister weeping and I pull away from him and I ask her, 'Why are you weeping?' and she says, 'It's because you are weeping.' I didn't realise I was crying but it was because I was so happy. My sister knows all that has happened with my husband.

Trainee: And what happens next?

Maya: We can't talk much or anything but he has asked if he can see me again. I say as long as I am in my brother's house, yes.

Trainee: And then what happens?

Maya: And then I go off almost floating because I'm so happy. The next day Yeshua comes to my brother's house and we go for a walk. But the first place we went to was a little hut. I call it a hut because it's not as big as our house. And his mother is there and I feel that connection again. She comes and all she does is she gives me an embrace. She just looks at me and that's all I need. No words need to be uttered because I know she's part of the fabric as well.

She gives me bread. We are hungry so she feeds us. Then she suggests to Yeshua to take me out somewhere. We just go outside. It's funny because we can't ... it's like we need to touch. Even when we are eating, we need to touch. Even when we walked up a hill, we were holding hands and he was telling me what he had been through and I was telling him a little bit about what my life was like. Not going into the great detail about my husband. But he's quite sharp so he actually asked about him and I told him what was happening. And the thing is we had to do this very quietly, because most of town knows I am married because my husband's family is of a high standing. We've got a high status and to the outside world it's the most glamorous marriage.

So Yeshua and I have to be really careful with our affections in public because, like I said, it's a travesty and it's punishable by death for me to consort with another man while being married. But I can't help it.

So anyway, in the privacy of our natural world, he asked me what was happening and, when I tried to gloss over it, he wouldn't accept it. And then I had to tell him. And he was very tender about the whole thing. And then I tell him words that could have got me killed if someone else had heard it. I asked him if we could be together. And he said … he too knew it was our destiny. He knew but I also told him about the vision that I had had and I said, 'I don't understand how it can be our destiny because I'm already with this guy and I'm not understanding how we can be together.'

And in amongst conversations like these we were talking about the web of life, we were talking about the Great Mother Earth, we were talking about animals, interconnectedness, everything being whole – all these lovely bits of conversation that I love having. So just being with Yeshua … he is my other half. There is a deep understanding there. But then the time comes when my husband is scheduled to be back home and I have to leave the comfort of my brother's house to go back home, with my son, back to all that beating.

Trainee: And what happens?

Maya: [long pause] … This gets worse and I feel it more because I had a week or two of bliss … It's like heaven and hell. And it's almost like the very essence of duality.

Because I had so much love [with Yeshua] and there is so much anger and hatred or fear here.

Trainee: And what happens?

Maya: I try and get my brother to go and have a chat with my parents to get them to intervene on my behalf. My brother is a merchant as well, you see, and is quite well regarded in the community. My husband likes my brother but my brother loathes my husband. My parents, although they feel quite sorry for me, they can't do much. So my brother decides to step in and ask. My brother doesn't say anything about Yeshua – he just says to my husband, 'You have been hurting my sister and it might be an idea for both of you to go your separate ways and find happiness.'

My husband goes absolutely livid at my brother and says it's none of his business. Then he hits me more because I had complained to my brother. And he forbids me to go and see my family so I feel even more trapped and really low. I really feel like I'm in hell.

[The next significant event sees Mary, still around sixteen years old, in a white sheath dress, drenched in blood, lying on her side in the road, bleeding from her womb. She is in pain and, while there are people around, she is not aware of them. Emotionally she is numb.]

Maya: I think I'm being lifted and put on some form of … some vehicle of some sort to be taken somewhere. The vehicle is being pulled by some person, almost like a cart … it's long.

Next, Mary is aware of being on her bed. She had passed out for a while. Awareness dawned on her as she realised she had lost a child through miscarriage.

Trainee: Do you know who the father was?

Maya: It was that person I married. The one I was forced into a marriage [with].

Trainee: And do you have any other children?

Maya: I get a sense there's a boy called David but I'm not sure if that's the one I miscarried or if it's the surviving son. It's all very confused, mixed up. I think they gave me a drug to keep the pain at bay. But what I do feel is that this man that I married is even more angry with me. Because one of the reasons he married me was for me to breed and miscarrying really isn't an option. It's almost like a failure.

Trainee: And how are you feeling?

Maya: Physically it still hurts. I'm feeling very numb now but sad ... sad. I think she might have been a girl that I miscarried.

Trainee: Is there anything else here that we need to know?

Maya: My son David – I think he is still living. He comes to see me once in a while. But I'm not in the right place to play with him or be with him. He's feeling very, very sad.

Trainee: Is there anything you'd like to do or say to him at this point?

Maya: No. I know it's selfish, but I just want to be alone for a while. I feel anger.

Trainee: What's the anger about?

Maya: Because I lost ... Well firstly I'm in a marriage I don't really want to be in. It's made me really angry because the only thing I have for my children ... he gets more violent, not physically violent now, because I'm in bed and you know there are people actually looking after me.

Trainee: Do you know why you miscarried?

Maya: I know I miscarried very late. I think my second trimester or something. I felt massive pain and then there was just blood and I know I went walking to the market or the shops or somewhere.

In the next significant event, Mary is out of the bed.

Maya: He (husband) has taken to beating me. And David, my son, he sees this and he is not too sure whether to ... I think he is starting to get a slightly cruel streak in him. Like this is OK because he really looks up to his dad. His father adores him. He's the heir ... and I think that hurts the most. That David's going to get this ... I'm afraid he's going to be like his father: cruel and a bit cold. He doesn't get the lighter essence. I've tried teaching him but, he thinks whatever I say is worthless and useless.

At the next significant event, Mary, eighteen or nineteen, is gathering some of her few belongings because she is going to run. She feels relieved and sad. She was torn as to whether to take David Jr, but because he is so much like his father, she decided not to. While her husband and son went on a trading trip, she runs to her brother's house with her sister.

Trainee: What happens next?

Maya: [pause; hesitantly] I think my son hates me.

Trainee: How old is your son?

Maya: Four-and-a-half maybe.

Trainee: And what's happening?

Maya: I left my husband and my son hated me for that.
But I go and stay with my brother. He gives me a place
to live. And the town folks don't like what I've done.
They say all these awful things to me. Because of my
brother's standing in the town and also that of my mum
and dad, they don't kill me. My brother and parents
could almost bribe the people, the officials, so they
don't kill me. But I am a pariah. So is my son. I am an
absolute pariah. I have completely lost all my standing. I
have nothing – no reputation, just nothing.

For more than two thousand years, Mary Magdalene has had a
slanderous reputation. And it seems it started from here – the
decision she made to break free from an incredibly abusive
marriage. Judea, in her time, was a patriarchal society that did
not take kindly to women leaving their betrothed husbands –
especially when theirs was a high-standing marriage, blessed
by the high-standing Pharisees. While she was not killed, her
reputation was severely blackened by her merchant husband
who was trying to save face and not lose his status or
reputation.

Trainee: And what happens?
Maya: But in losing all of that … It devastated me.
There was nothing for me to hold on to about my son –
who hated me. That's when it happened. That's when I
started to walk with him. Yeshua asked me to be with
him and to go with him and I said yes. He didn't listen
to the lies that were being told about me because he
knew the story, the whole story, and it didn't matter. He
loved me for who I am. So that's how I started to walk
with him and that's how we got together.

The regression went on to briefly explore the crucifixion and touched Mary's death slightly. As this is redundant to what I explored in greater detail in later sessions, I have not included the excerpts of that part of the session.

This account could explain why Mary's reputation was so sullied during that time and also within the Christian tradition. There is nothing in the Gospels that mentions that she was a prostitute. In fact, she was portrayed as more as being the Apostle of Apostles. However, on 14 September AD591, Pope Gregory I labelled her as a prostitute. By doing so, Pope Gregory essentially removed her from the leadership position, and removed her intimate relationship with Jesus, something that we see a glimmer of in this regression.[4] This is further substantiated by Laurence Gardner in his book *The Magdalene Legacy*. In it, he writes about Pope Gregory I delivering a sermon, where he confirms Mary the Sinner and Mary of Bethany to be one and the same, equating the seven demons that she seemingly carried with the seven deadly vices.[5] However, in 1969, Pope Paul VI released a revision of official church doctrine, saying that Mary Magdalene was no longer deemed a prostitute by the church.[6]

Maya's first regression into the life of Mary Magdalene has been truly eye-opening. She shed light on a Mary that is complex and multifaceted – an incredibly intuitive and spiritual soul, and the daughter of a high-standing Pharisee and Sadducee, who due to power and political reasons was married off to someone she did not want. From a tender age, she'd endured years of domestic violence and abuse at the hands of her husband.

Due to very patriarchal cultural rules, punishing women who leave their wedded husbands by death, she found it tough to leave him. However, she proved to be incredibly strong by making the difficult decision to break free of her husband, despite cultural perceptions, enduring her reputation of being spuriously sullied and the hatred of her son, to start pursuing her true path.

What more will be revealed of this enigmatic soul?

6

BETROTHED

The greatest happiness of life is the conviction that we
are loved; loved for ourselves, or rather,
loved in spite of ourselves.
– Victor Hugo

Nearly a year later, Maya came to me to participate in this
book. Over two sessions, we explored the rest of Mary's life
through regression. While we did briefly review Mary's life
when she was younger, it was not done in the depth that the
student had recorded. So, to avoid redundancy, this chapter
will focus on the part of her life just before she leaves her first
husband to the end of the crucifixion.

We start the session by going back to a time when Mary
was seventeen or eighteen. She was up on the balcony of her
house when she heard Yeshua was back. She went to listen to
him again. At this point, she is aware of and gives a rundown
on Yeshua's family members. She calls Yeshua's mother Ma,
who was very nurturing and was like her own mother. She
called his father Pa. His name is Yosef. Yeshua had two
brothers – the second brother she addressed as Mattius and
the younger one Yamez, who was her friend. Yeshua had a
younger sister whom she addressed as 'Baby'.

Upon glancing at Yeshua's face, she described him as being
quite handsome in her eyes. His face was quite angular with
high cheek bones. His nose had a little ridge that was a bit

sharp. His eyes were very deep hazelly-brown – in some light it was hazel, in some light it was dark brown. He also had longish hair, which made him look quite roguish. He was very thin, unlike her then husband, who was big built.

Maya: I've done something I'm not meant to do. [pause] Yeshua … he went off the second time and he came back. We had very little contact but he was starting to speak up against – in small groups – he was starting to speak against people like my father and also against … not exactly like my husband and his father but that sort of class. And I got some word about this so I snuck into one of the little groups he was talking to. But he wasn't speaking against them. He spoke for what they were not doing. So he was talking more about everything being equal and … He was talking about 'there's no greater power than love' and things like that. He was saying he disagreed with some of what the leaders were saying.

I sort of disguised myself – there was a shawl around me – and I snuck into one [meeting]. And then I started to sneak into a few more. Oh, and he was also talking about women and having an equal place in the house – things like that … that our society and our community don't really practise. His words gave me hope, because I didn't have it in my own house. Anyway, my husband heard that I had snuck out one day and he hit me and told me to not do it again. I got a bit defiant and I then kept going more. He found out and threw me out.

This account further confirms that what Jesus was preaching was against the normal customs and beliefs of the very hierarchical and patriarchal Judean society.

118

Curious to get a little more information about this part of her life, of whether she left her husband, as she claimed in the previous chapter, or was thrown out, as she mentions here, I persisted to explore it more. I started to work with her, taking her through the trauma slowly and carefully, until the energy of the trauma cleared and more detailed information came out.

Moaning that she hurts, Mary stammered that she is alone, wearing a luxurious dress of blue and green, with a gold belt and embroidery. She is outside, in the market square, surrounded by buildings. It is busy, hot and dusty, and she chokes out that she is thirsty.

Maya: I'm stumbling. I'm thirsty. Beaten. Beaten by my husband. I cannot do it any more … On my left face. My left hand. Stiff left hand from the shoulder down. Left eye bruised, left face … just bad. He hit my face because I'm pretty. He always hits my face.

Reena: OK. Just tell me what happens next.

Maya: I faint. But just before I faint I hear a commotion. I think there are some people at the market place that have taken notice of me. And they all … I don't know.

Reena: And what's the next thing you become aware of?

Maya: His face …. It's my heaven! [giggles] It's that cool respite… gentle eyes; angular face; a beard and a moustache; longish, roguish hair; beautiful, gentle eyes. A little smile.

Reena: Just tell me what happens next.

Maya: I close my eyes and I feel like I'm lifted. Someone's lifting me and I faint again. I'm quite badly injured. The face I saw is Yeshua and in his presence I feel safe, that nothing bad can happen to me.

Reena: OK. Just tell me what happens next.

Maya: I'm in a cool house, I think. I hear a big commotion outside. But inside it's so peaceful. I feel the presence of a woman. She's gently stroking my forehead. And I think she's wiping away some sweat or something, I don't know. It's very gentle, dabbing like that. And I feel Yeshua's presence in the room.

Reena: Are you aware of who this woman is that's stroking your head?

Maya: It's a mother figure of some sort, but I'm not sure if it's Yeshua's mother or mine. I think it's more Yeshua's mother. But there is a very maternal feel. I'm not terribly conscious. I'm sort of conscious in and out. Far away but here. I think I've been badly beaten this time. I don't feel any rage inside the house, but outside there's so much rage. I hear it and I don't like it. I feel it. But inside it's cool and calm. It's bathed with peace and love.

Reena: Do you know what happens next?

Maya: I feel some energy on my face. It just feels really nice. [long pause] It's a bit tingly as well. It's cold on my shoulder and then it stops. I think my hand is broken at the shoulder. Not at the shoulder but just below, just somewhere here [indicates a point on her left upper arm].

Reena: And what's happening to your arm at the moment?

Maya: It might be that the flow of energy is trying to go through smoothly but it stops. I feel really heavy and I cannot open my eyes. I can't see anything. It takes a while but then [it] moves and the energy is flowing quite nicely down the hand. But it hurts. And my neck hurts too.

Reena: Let's move on and tell me what happens next.
Maya: I have a fever. That's why the maternal figure dabs my forehead with cool water. I understand now. I was slightly delirious before. She is trying to cool my physical body down. My hand feels a lot better. But I still need to rest it.
Reena: What happens next?
Maya: Headache. But the energy can move now … It's almost like life force. My hand was broken and it stopped. I don't know how it couldn't flow nicely. It was like a jagged flow. But I can feel it flowing now. Like a river. [Maya's arm jerks suddenly; she sighs] Ah! I feel a lot better. But I still have the fever.

During the debrief, Maya mentioned that her arm was bent and broken. When the life force flowed in a straight line, the bones straightened and aligned. The regression continued.

Maya: My head is a lot better now. My arm is still healing but it's a lot better. I think I'm at Yeshua's house. That was Yeshua's mother.
Reena: And just reflecting on your time in the house when you were recovering from your beating, what exactly was done to you to help you in the healing?
Maya: Oh, I don't know. I was in and out. All I know is Marta was sitting there dabbing my head with cool water. I was semi-conscious. I don't know. It was the feeling that the energy was jagged and then it started to flow. The energy stopped at the hand and then it started to flow.
[In subsequent regressions, Marta emerges to be Mary's sister.]
Reena: Does it feel that it's healed or …?

Maya: The bone still has to fuse a little bit more but ...
[long pause] How it happened, I do not know. I was in
and out of consciousness.

Reena: OK. If there is a time when you are cleansed of
seven demons by Yeshua, I'd like you to go to that
point now and describe what's happening.

Maya: This is that point. [pause] This is that point.
[pause] This is that point. There were no demons. The
fighting. My husband was ... my husband ... How do I
explain this? During this time the wife was the property
of the husband. But when I refused to go back to my
husband after he beat me, he couldn't handle the shame,
so he made up a story of how I was having an affair.
How I had so many affairs. He made up stories to hurt
me. He didn't want me to tell stories of how he had hurt
me and I left him because he hurt me. He turned my
son against me. But he hit me so many times, I couldn't
bear it any more. It was going back to hell.

Reena: And is this the demon that Yeshua protected
you against?

Maya: There was no demon. It was a story that was told
about me. It was a role for ... it was a role that people
... I think, I don't know ... but it's a way that they
could reconcile the stories that were told by my
husband, to the sort of person I was when I was just
helping people after I became better from the beatings.
The people outside, when there was so much anger ...
they were the people who were coming to get me to
take me back to my husband. And Yeshua – and his
mother, the whole family – they stopped them by saying
that I was hurt and I needed to be healed.

[At the next significant event, Mary got coy and very
embarrassed.]

Maya: Yeshua and I talk quite a lot. He shares with me his dreams and his vision and it was one that I believed in, one that I shared. Our society was very structured, very hierarchical. There were definite ways of doing things and it was quite controlled. He talked about ways where that wasn't important – it was all about love, unity and equality. He talked about an age, if you wish, where there were not such strict rituals, or maybe an age where there was more freedom. He told me about where he went when he was sixteen, seventeen. He went to schools in Egypt, he says. In the Egyptian areas anyway. Within his school he saw how it was run, where men and women … It wasn't so ritualised, strict, so controlled. It was more free-flowing. He also talked about the community, where it's driven not by power but through mutual respect and acceptance of each other. He talked about some of the learnings he'd been through, some of the arts. All this knowledge he had learned, so there was a deeper knowing within him. He talked about being part of this … This was very difficult for me to comprehend. He's part of a priesthood, but it's a free-flowing priesthood. It's not linked to one temple or one place. It's like a priesthood that walks. That's how I understand it. When he was talking to me about this, it was all very new, all very revolutionary. But even as it took me a while to understand it, it is something in principal that I shared with him, a belief that I shared with him. I guess he saw that. One of those times was under the twinkling skies. We were sitting in his garden and chatting and he said to me that he had feelings for me.

Reena: What does he say?

Maya: Oh! [laughs loudly] It is very private! [laughs loudly] It is private! [laughs again] Well ... He said to me before he had seen strength and beauty within me and something about he sees it again ... But he's had feelings for me for a while. When he said this to me, my heart fluttered even more wildly. But I was a little bit ... I held myself back because I had been with another man and had another child. I felt dirty and slightly unworthy of him because in our society it's all about pristine, virginal girls.

Reena: And what did he say about that to you?

Maya: He said he really didn't care. He said it's about the essence. This is something he will keep repeating to me through my life because it's something I've felt a bit guilty of. But he keeps saying that that was a choice that wasn't mine, I was forced to go into that. And it was part of the culture. But he said that he doesn't care about the culture. It's all about the energy inside, the essence within. And he still saw me as being pristine. I wasn't dirty or used.

Reena: What happens next?

Maya: Although my heart is fluttering wildly, because I thought so highly of him and quite lowly of myself, I take a while to ... commit, if that's the word. He is very patient, gentle and coaxing. Until one day my fluttering heart fluttered too much for me to ignore. [laughs] That's the only way I can describe it. And then I said to him, if he would have me, I would commit my life, my soul to him. So we had a very simple, basic, very quiet, secret ... ceremony.

Reena: Did it follow the traditions of Jewish weddings or did it follow some other ideas?

Maya: It followed the traditions of his priesthood. His priesthood.

Reena: And what did it entail?

Maya: It was a bit different 'cause my pa didn't know – or didn't want to know. My ma was not allowed to be there. Marta and Yazarus took the roles of my ma and my pa. Yazarus my brother.

Her brother, Yazurus, could be a reference to the Biblical Lazarus, who was raised from the dead by Jesus, according to the Gospel of John. The Biblical Lazurus was said to have two sisters, Martha and Mary, which is in line with what Maya claims too about Yazarus. Could they be the same person? The regression continues.

Maya: [after a pause] Oh. [sounding surprised] I'm feeling rather hot and expansive. I'm feeling like I'm going to expand. I feel quite floaty. Like the sun had entered me, the sun! [pause] This part of the ritual was quite secret. It was just done by the head priest of his order.

Reena: Does this order have a name?

Maya: I've no idea what it is. [pause] Zadok. Zadek. Something like that. But it's not ... it's a union ... Oh, I know! It's a union of spirit, it's not a physical union. It's a ... Oh, this is so different from my old one with the other guy. The one with the other guy was more material and physical but this is more spirit. I think when I was floating and that feeling was ... I felt the union, like it's the union of two souls, and it was very expansive and very hot and very floaty.

Later on, Maya reveals that what it felt like, was that for a split-second their spirits leave their bodies, unify and then go back into their bodies united. So they have each other's essence in the body. It felt like total bliss because they were totally aligned and their spirits and energies were in the same vibrations, in resonance. 'It's a Sacred Union. And we will forever be connected,' she says with a smile.

I ask if Yeshua has any of these spiritual unions with any of the other disciples and am told emphatically: 'No, this is only done with me.'

The revelations of her union of spirit are incredibly fascinating and revealing. Firstly, her naming the order Zadok/Zadek is key. Through long prevailing custom, the Davidic kings (the lineage of Jesus) were allied to the jointly dynastic Zadokite (Zadok) priests. Described in the Old Testament book of Kings as the son of King David, King Solomon was installed by the High Priest Zadok in the tenth century BC, thus starting the reigning line of the Royal House of Judah that prevailed for 300 years. While the Hebrew Pharisees and Sadducees refused to accept Jesus as the legitimate royal heir, the Nazarenes and Ebionites did, therefore making his claim legitimate under the laws of Essenes.[1] According to this tradition, only the head of the Zadok priest, given the distinction Michael, can cement wedlock of the heir of the Davidic Line.[2] Maya's revelation that the head of the Zadok priesthood conducted the ceremony cements the fact that they were proclaimed the rightful dynasts of the Davidic bloodline and shows their standing within the Essene community.

An interesting fact here is that the prevailing Zadok priest at that time was the son of Zacharias, John the Baptist.[3]

Mary goes through the list of the few people who are there at the ceremony – Marta and Yazarus, her sister and brother,

Yeshua's mother and father, and several priests and priestesses were there but Yamez, Yeshua's brother, was not. He had gone away. She described the venue of the spiritual union to be outdoors. The head priest was either in a cave or a hollow in a tree, and she and Yeshua were outside watching him. His priests and priestesses stood behind him, in a crescent formation, chanting and murmuring as Yeshua and Mary were told to hold hands, look into each other's eyes, open to one another, to flow and merge spiritually. The ritual of the union of spirit was known to a few but not to the masses. There were some elements of Judaism but not so much. To Mary, as someone who lived within the Judaic culture, it was foreign yet familiar.

The Sacred Marriage, referred to as the Hieros Gamos, is an ancient bridal ceremony that is conveyed by the Song of Solomon.[4] The mysteries of this intimate, powerful, Sacred Union of spirit, while it is not known to all, could be only known to those who have been initiated into the traditions of the Davidic and Zadokite succession lines, which could explain the need for secrecy.

The sacred act of Hieros Gamos reputedly also includes the act of anointing with ointment. Curious about this act, I asked about it. Maya revealed that there were many events where she anointed Yeshua's forehead. Yeshua believed that he and Mary were equal. They were so connected through spirit, that whenever he left without her or when he addressed a big group, the anointing was like a little ceremony between them; not only was she giving him her blessing, she was giving him access to the energy within her, to help him to further spread the message or do what he needed to do.

She also reveals that he anointed her too, but she did it more as he was the one who did most of the work. He anointed her before the birth of their children and when she talked to the group of women. It was a way in which they connected with each other and for them to channel more energy throughout their union.

She also confirmed that they never anointed the feet, unless a death was involved. She chuckled and said mischievously that kissing of the feet occurred occasionally – more out of affection than anything else.

The next significant event saw Yeshua telling his brotherhood about his union with Mary.

Maya says, laughing, 'The term "wife", "partner", doesn't sit well. We use a deeper term that describes that we are unified in spirit not just in the physical plane. A few of his brothers were a bit shocked and appalled because they've heard of my reputation. They do not know the full story. Or some choose not to believe. And that term, which I cannot get now, also is an indication that I am Yeshua's equal, which some of the brothers, because of their upbringing and the culture, it just cannot sit with them. So they are very uncomfortable – whereas the females were thrilled.'

Mary goes on to say that Yeshua's sister was there. Mary is also aware of two groups of people. The first group stays and walks with Yeshua. The other group of people is a bridge. They work in the material world but are connected to them. They include Marta, Yazurus and Yamez, who was ecstatic when he'd heard about the union.

Maya: He [Yamez] had taken over the family business (merchant) and he'd grown it. He's doing well.
Reena: What things did he merchant?
Maya: Anything that would make money, I suppose. Eventually he went on to metals but beforehand … silks and agriculture. Just a merchant. It's interesting how he and Yeshua were working in line but he was doing it in

the physical world and Yeshua was doing it in the more spiritual sense.

[Mary goes on to say that Jesus' other brother, Mattius, is not prominent in her life. He came and went, came and went. She got a sense that he did not like her and he did not approve of Yeshua and her having a union. In fact, he was very angry.]

Reena: What is he saying?

Maya: It's not saying but a feel[ing]. He may have said to Yeshua but Yeshua's kept it to himself. Mind you, it didn't change Yeshua's way of being towards me. I also get a sense from Mattius that he is not a patient fellow. And I get a sense that he ... Yeshua's getting prominence because he's a priest and he's doing what he's doing, he's talking a lot and because of his bearing, and what he is saying, people listen to him and they respect him. Yamez has then taken on the role of being the family merchant. He has taken on the family business, which should have gone to Mattius as the second brother but it didn't. I don't understand why it didn't. I'm just glad my friend is happy. But Mattius ... it feels like he has missed out, that something is owed to him. There's anger ...

[The next significant event, Mary revealed a rather dramatic event.]

Maya: Marta came. She panicked. She's panicking. She'd seen Yazarus lying on the bed and he wasn't breathing ... or was breathing very slowly. And his hands were clammy.

Reena: What are you doing at this moment?

Maya: I was in the garden. Marta had been running with ... She was panicking. So some of the other people came running behind her, wondering what was happening. Marta was in a state. I was clearing something in the garden. I stopped and I was holding her. And she was babbling. Raving on like ... because she was panicked. So the first thing I did was try and calm her down. She described how Yazarus was and how he'd been like that for a couple of days. She said he was like a dead man. He hadn't eaten, didn't wake up, just nothing. She wanted Yeshua to come and heal him. Of course, he is my brother, so I had to go. I panicked. Then I took my husband, Yeshua, and he ran home – to Yazarus's home. To my family home. And I saw him and my heart almost stopped beating. Yeshua told me to stay outside and he walked in. He's a tall man, is Yeshua, so he had to bend down to go in.

Reena: What happened next?

Maya: He put a hand over Yazarus. He put his hand down like that. [gestures hands scanning an area about ten centimetres above the surface of body] And when he got somewhere around here [indicates the upper chest area] he knocked three times. [she knocks]

Reena: In the chest area?

Maya: Just under the throat. Somewhere here. [she knocks again] Three times. Yazarus coughed and jerked. And Yeshua did it again. And he asked Marta to get some water. And he put his hand over the water. Yazarus took a sip – well, he put it on Yazarus's mouth, so I'm assuming Yazarus took a sip. He waited a few minutes and put some more water [sic]. He did this a few times for about an hour – with the water. And then eventually Yazarus opened his eyes. He had eaten too much of a particular plant or herb. And what it did was, it caused him to ... it caused everything to just slow down. It caused the heartbeat to slow, it caused the breathing to slow.

Reena: And what did the knocking on the throat area do?

Maya: It's not the throat, it's just there, somewhere here. [gestures] Just under the throat, above the chest.

Reena: And what effect did that have?

Maya: What all this was, because when everything slows down, people could die because they don't fulfil the physical needs of the body so they don't eat, they don't drink. It's not that the herb kills the person, it slows everything down and it's the dehydration that kills. So this just shocked the system back. And then the water just started to bring the person back. Just starting to put fluids into the person. Yazarus took a while to get the body back into a functioning state.

Reena: How long did it take him?

Maya: I don't know. Three weeks? But what Yeshua was doing was scanning the life force, the energy life force of the body. And he found out where it was depleted and he knocked it back almost. And Yeshua also gave energy to the water, so when Yazarus took the sips of the water it became slightly more potent than just giving him water ... I am in awe of my husband because he has the ability to work co-operatively with energy. I try to learn but I do not have the amount of skill that he has. Although what he did with Yazarus, I could have done as well because I understand.

The area that Mary indicated that Jesus worked on is the location of where the thymus, a pinkish-grey two-lobed gland, is located in the chest. For a long time, the function of this organ was not understood. Now, however, modern medicine recognises this gland is closely related to the immune system, stress and general well-being. It has the role of master controller that directs life-giving and healing energies of the body and is strongly influenced by an individual's physical environment, social relationships, food and posture.[5]

The healing knowledge that Jesus and Mary Magdalene had was, and still is, renowned. Josephus, in his book *Wars of the Jews*, explained that the Essenes were very knowledgeable and practised in the art of healing, having received their know-how from the ancients.[6] So it makes sense that Jesus applied all his knowledge to help his brother-in-law.

Reena: What happens next?

Maya: The people around the village are surprised to see Yazarus alive and well, the strong, healthy man he is. They too think a miracle has occurred. Yeshua is very skilled at what he does.

Reena: Has he ever told you how he learned these energy skills?

Maya: Mm. He learned it when he went to school all those years ago. He learned it from different – he calls them 'masters'. But [to] what he has learned he has added his own knowledge and skills too.

Reena: Did he tell you what schools he went to to learn these energy skills?

Maya: He went quite far. He went to the ancient land of kings just across the sea. He went by boat ... It's what we refer to as the Land of the Desert with the big ... the big structures. They are in the shape of the pyramids. He went there but he went further [afield] as well.

Reena: And what other places did he go to?

Maya: He went to the ancient islands of Greece. He said they all added to his learning and teachings. He also went, he tells me, to a place with very, very big mountains. It is not far from where we live — he says there are big, tall mountains. Sometimes he talks to me about his travels. He did a lot of travelling when I was married to that other man.

[The next significant event finds Mary in the events just before the crucifixion.]

Maya: I'm holding my daughter's hand and I'm pregnant. This is the daughter I share with Yeshua ... Emotionally it's like I'm split. I'm distraught but I'm not. I think in that time I've grown and I've developed a different sort of presence. I'm a lot calmer, more centred, older. I feel I need to be strong for Tamar and my unborn son.

Historians speculate that Jesus was crucified between AD30–37. It is also said that Mary Magdalene was three months pregnant when he was crucified. This is consistent with this regression. Historical annals also hypothesise that in September AD33, a daughter was born to Mary Magdalene. She was named Tamar (meaning 'palm tree'). There are also many references claiming that the daughter's name is Sara — however Sara is a distinction. In Hebrew, Sara means princess, and so she was called Tamar the Sara. Tamar was the original matriarch of the Royal House of Judah, and the name of King David's sister.[7] Our regression states that while Mary Magdalene was indeed pregnant during the crucifixion, she was pregnant with their first son, having already borne her daughter. As you will find, subsequent regressions will reflect and account for these memories of Mary's that Tamar (Sara) was indeed a toddler, consistent with the time that Jesus was crucified around AD37.

The regression continues. When asked about what was happening with Yeshua, Mary says that he is very hurt.

Maya: I think they've physically beaten him. Ah, now I understand why I'm half-distraught and half-not. Because we were joined in spirit, the part that's distraught feels sad for him because physically he's hurt, but his spirit is very much alive. And I can feel that. I know it will be well … I ask one of the lady follower sisters to take Tamar away. Not too far away from me but just slightly away. And I take Ma and another one of the sisters and we decide we were going to be with him when they put him on the cross. It's not just a torture element. It's yet another form of humiliation because they punish the lowest of the lows on the cross. So it's another form of disgrace and we wanted to show solidarity, so we go. And we want him to see us and we can give strength. And I think for me it's because my spirit's connected to his, it just feels that I need to be near him so he can get more strength from my spirit. So he comes bearing it … the cross. I see Yamez lurking around. I'm not quite understanding what he's up to, but my focus is not on him. And Ma is crying because Yeshua's body is so broken, it's so scarred.
Reena: Just describe what you can see.
Maya: The broken, scarred body? And the nailing … They are doing it on the peak of the hill. We are somewhere down here, where the crowds are, but we are slightly in front. We can hear the sound of that. [she makes hand gestures] The nailing. We were not allowed … I didn't see the whipping or the … It's quite quiet.

There are a few gasps of pain but it's quite quiet. The other two are moaning. Again, I'm ... It's a weird feeling. It's like I'm half-distraught but half-I-know-it-will-be-OK. And then they raise him. Ma almost faints with anguish. The other sister's rather inconsolable.

Reena: Are there any other physical marks on him where he's been hurt?

Maya: Yeah. [she uses her arms to demonstrate the crucifixion position] So his hands are like that. The nails go in there ... the wrists. So the hands are like that. [she demonstrates] His head is kind of droopy. His beautiful hair is all matted and bloody.

Reena: Is there anything on his head?

Maya: No. Nothing on the head. Just bloody. Mind you, everything is blood and brown so I can't see anything on the head.

Reena: And what about his feet?

Maya: His feet are like that. [she crosses her ankles] And there's one nail through this part. [gesturing to where the ankle joins the foot]... It must have been excruciating but he's relatively quiet.

Reena: Is there anything else said or done?

Maya: There is this horrible man, one of the soldiers. I don't understand why but he takes a big stick and smashes it into the shin. Aren't these men in enough pain already?

[She then went on to talk about the reaction of the many people who were watching.]

Maya: Oh, they were openly weeping. Some were jeering, some were weeping. It's like a mixed ... It must have been weird because Ma is inconsolable, almost on the verge of collapsing. The sister is inconsolable but I'm just staring at him. I'm really at peace and calm and

… [pause] distraught and yet I knew everything was going to be OK … Because of that union, I knew his spirit was OK so I knew it wasn't him.

Reena: Does this person look like him? The person on the cross?

Maya: Totally. You see, it's not a physical knowing that it wasn't him, it's an energetic knowing.

Reena: Do you think anybody else knows?

Maya: I don't know. Ma and the sister certainly didn't. They were inconsolable … It was one of those 'being in denial' things and probably hoping and praying it wasn't him. But at that point when I was kneeling under the cross and looking up, I knew it wasn't him because the spirit was the same – the spirit was healthy, the spirit was fine. Even though my eyes were telling me differently.

Reena: What happens next?

Maya: The crowd goes. The three of us, we're still kneeling under the cross. We were still there kneeling. I think Ma might have spat on the horrendous man who hit the shin with the big stick, which was very unlike Ma. She was distraught. She would never do that otherwise. Anyway, Yamez comes and takes us. Yamez asks for the body to come down. That body is not dead. That body looks barely alive.

Reena: And who does he ask?

Maya: Oh, the guards. For some reason they do it.

Reena: OK. And what happens?

Maya: Yamez … Ma wants to rush up and have a look at the body but Yamez stops her. He gets the guards to get the person ready for taking him to the burial ground – the family burial ground.

Reena: Do the guards think he's dead?

Maya: The guards just do what Yamez says. I'm not sure why.

Reena: How do they get the nails out of the wood?

Maya: I don't know.

[Could it be that at this point Yamez keeps the family away from the body because it is the body of the Substitute, and not of Jesus?]

Reena: What happens next?

Maya: Yamez takes us to the burial ground ... It's quite hilly. Maybe white ... white ... it's not hard rock, it's white hills where chambers have been dug out. Like a little hole in a little chamber. And each narrow tunnel, each chamber, had rooms for the family members.

Reena: And how do you actually get into this place?

Maya: I think it's just ... We just walk in. There's a hole in the hill. Like a little thing and you walk in. Little rooms. And we go into one of the rooms where the female members were meant to anoint and prepare the body for dead. And there he is. Lying down. Alive ... But he doesn't have ... Do you know where the man whacked the shin with a stick? That wasn't there any more. He had blood up here [she demonstrates, by the head], he had blood on the back, his face was really bruised and scarred, matted brown hair with blood, beard matted, scars all over his chest. Very thin. He was thin before but he's a lot thinner. He's just bones.

Reena: What about his hands and ankles?

Maya: His ankles had rope marks where it was tied. His hands had rope burns.

Reena: Are there any marks where the nails went in?

Maya: No. [pause] He had a broken hand though.

Reena: And the person that was on the cross before, had they been nailed or had they been roped on the cross?

Maya: There were nails. It was nails and rope.

Reena: It was nails and rope on the cross. And now you can see the rope marks. Can you see where the nails have been in?

Maya: No … At that time, I had so much relief. Not relief but just joy of seeing … When I saw him he was breathing but very shallowly. So it was … It didn't compute in my head that they were two different people physically. My essence, the spirit, said that's not him on the cross. But it said it is him on this slab. But the mind just wasn't making sense of it all. It was a very emotional time. I just didn't get what was happening. I was just happy to be able to see him and to feel him. But as I was cleaning the wounds, I realised that they were not there and I was a bit quizzical. But it never entered in my conscious mind that someone else went through it. It was a spirit thing.

Mary then revealed that Ma, Yamez and her daughter Tamar were in the hole in the hill with them. She said that Tamar was possibly three years old. According to her, Yeshua was unconscious and barely breathing. When Mary began to clean the body, Ma stood away with her daughter, inconsolable. At this point she revealed that Yeshua's sister's name sounded like Salome.

In the New Testament Gospels, there is mention of Jesus' sisters at the cross and at the tomb. Some Gnostic Gospels also state that Jesus had sisters. The Vatican's *Apostolic Constitutions*, as compiled in the fourth century mentions 'The Lord and his sister.'[8] This is consistent with Maya's recollection of Jesus' sister. Although the references are made for Jesus having more than one sister, as opposed to these regressions, where there is only reference to one. There are also historical references that refer to Jesus' sister as Sarah-Salome, which makes this consistent with James' identification of his sister. Again, 'Sarah' is considered a titular distinction and Salome the name. The regression continues.

Maya: I feel sorrow for this poor body is so beaten ... like I did before when I saw him. But I know our spirit is strong. His spirit is strong. So it's very confusing. Ma is almost inconsolable. [long pause] I try to explain to her quietly that the spirit is strong, but I don't think she can hear it.
Reena: What's she doing at the moment?
Maya: She's just crying on Salome's shoulder.
Reena: OK. What happens next?
Maya: Yamez comes with ... ointment and also with the priest – and he passes them to me for me to bathe and dress the wounds. He's so badly beaten. I'm surprised he survived. It's interesting how his body is broken but his spirit is strong ... The priest puts his hand on Ma and is comforting her. I think the priest knows that Yeshua's spirit is strong too. But anyway, I just tend to the body and I speak to him. I speak about our daughter and our son. I speak to him and I say I know his spirit is there. I wet his lips with water. It's a bit parched. And that is all I do. I bathe the wound and I sit with him. I dress the wounds and I sit with him. More often in silence. Until his eyes open.
Reena: And how long has it been before his [Jesus'] eyes open?

Maya: We wait a few nights until Yeshua came to. It was quite scary because we thought he wasn't going to make it. I think by this point Yamez went to get the priest of the sect, and he was there as well. I think he was doing some chanting. But I knew Yeshua's spirit was fine … It took three days or something, three nights, two or three days and nights. And it was a relief when his eyes opened.

Reena: And what happens when he opens his eyes?

Maya: It doesn't surprise me because I know his spirit is strong but I feel … [chuckles] joy. It's a funny feeling within me. I grasp his hands and I lift his hands to my lips and I kiss his hands and he closes his eyes. I know it's probably a good thing to tell the others but I do not want to leave his side. And I'm the only one there so I just stay there, just holding his hand, waiting for him to open his eyes again.

Reena: What happens next?

Maya: Ma comes with Salome and Yamez and I tell them quietly what's happened. Ma is so overwhelmed. So they sit with me and they bring food. They normally bring the food so they sit there with me and wait until Yeshua's eyes open … His eyes open again. The look of relief on the family's faces is palpable. Ma rushes to him and holds his hand and weeps, but quietly. She feeds him just a touch of water. He doesn't speak. He just has a very weak smile and he goes back to sleep. This happens a few times until he starts getting a little better and then we feed him – mush initially and then water. It's like the physical body has to become as strong as his spirit. It's like that.

It took him a few hours to really come to and regain consciousness. He looked rather surprised that he wasn't dead because he had fully expected to die. He looked relieved. He gave me a hug. He held his little daughter. He held his sister and his mum and his brother. He hugged his priest. The priest left and then Yamez was talking about how he had spoken to the Governor and bribed the guards to bring him down before he had completely died.

[Interesting to note here that whilst James did arrange for the Substitute to come down before he had died, in Mia's own regression of James, the account was that things went wrong and the Substitute did die either on the cross or just after been taken down. This plan clearly went awry, which accounts for James being so distressed.]

Reena: And how did he convince the Governor to do that?

Maya: Because he was a powerful merchant he had connections. And there was bribery as well. Money and bribery ... [long pause] This is something Yeshua told me afterwards, after he and Yamez had had a little chat. He had asked someone else to bear the burden of the cross in order to save Yeshua. So what had happened was Yamez had access to Yeshua during the time of the torture and the beatings. I didn't, Ma didn't, no one else did in the family. And he knew that Yeshua was so weak he wouldn't survive even carrying the cross to the hill, much less bear being on the cross. Besides the beatings, Yeshua was also not given food or water for several days and nights. So he managed to get someone to take the place of Yeshua and it was quite easy because Yeshua's face was unrecognisable because of all the tortures and the beatings. So it was just [a case of] getting someone else in the prisons ... and then to just bear the cross.

Reena: And how did they convince that person?

Maya: Because of his love for Yeshua. He didn't want Yeshua to die. He was one of the followers who was caught.

Reena: Oh, and the rope marks from his arms and legs, this had come from prison rather than the cross?

Maya: Yes ... If this got out, that Yeshua was still alive, he'd be hunted and killed again. So it had to be kept very, very quiet. We had to leave. The little group had to disband and leave. So the brothers and the other sisters were told that ... I hate saying this, but there's a little inner, trusted group and then all the other followers. So the inner, trusted group were told that he was healed. He didn't die on the cross but he was very nearly dying and he had to leave to escape and to recuperate. Which was true as well but they thought he was the one on the cross. A few – the bigger group – were told that he'd died and the whole story about how he came [back] to life ...

Reena: Can you tell us exactly what that is?

Maya: That he had died but his very strong spirit had come and given some messages to the inner group and almost they were following his word. They were not told of a physical resurrection but more like a spiritual one.

Capturing the crucifixion through the eyes of Mary Magdalene was fascinating, especially given how consistent her account is to James' account given through Mia. Both James and Mary Magdalene were in the first tier and understood the depth of the entire story, compared to some of the others, and this came through in both regressions.

Besides the crucifixion, her account of the Sacred Union and what she'd experienced with Yeshua was so deep and profound. Their relationship flowed a lot deeper than being husband and wife, sharing a life and children ... they shared a soul. She truly was the closest companion he had, which is befitting of her strength, compassion and the love that she had for him.

7

BELOVED

All, everything that I understand,
I understand only because I love.
     – Leo Tolstoy

This next part investigates, in some detail, Mary Magdalene's life after the crucifixion.

Maya: I see us all getting on a boat. There's Tamar and Marta. I'm a bit sad because Yazarus, he's not coming with us. He has to stay.

Reena: Have you been involved in these discussions about where you're going?

Maya: Me? I think so, yeah. Yazarus has to stay because he's taken on my pa's role within the community. But it's good in a way because he also follows The Way – the way of Yeshua. So he's like a bridge into the community. He's like a mouthpiece. But he has to stay, which saddens me. Yeshua is getting into the boat. He's still a bit frail and weak but at least he's standing.

Reena: Who else is getting in the boat?

Maya: Yesoos [their newborn son]. I'm carrying him. There is a different boat for Ma and Salome. Yamez is in our boat.

Reena: Are you all going to the same place or to different places?

Maya: The different boat's going somewhere else.
Reena: Has anybody told you where this boat's going to, that you're getting into?
Maya: Yes, we are going … We have to go away because otherwise Yeshua would be … Our family's not safe here. And nobody can know Yeshua is alive. So we are going further away. We are going to … France, I think.

During this regression, and others, the regressees use modern terms and names to express themselves or describe their experiences. For example, during that time, the area that Maya refers to as 'France', in which they docked, largely made up the region known to the Romans as Gaul.[1] However, Maya refers to it as France because though the memories are accessed through her subconscious mind, they filter through the conscious mind in the current life and use the preconditioned neural linguistic pathways to communicate it to me – the therapist. It helps put it into context for her as she goes through her experiences. The regression continues.

Reena: OK. Just describe the boat you are getting into.
Maya: It's quite a basic boat, with sails, but quite big. Yamez uses it for his trading so it's easy for us to be smuggled on board almost. But the quarters are quite nice, quite comfortable. Yamez gave us his quarters. He is lovely to us. It was a long trip. Rather uneventful but it made me a bit ill. I haven't been on water like this for a long time before. A few storms here and there but …
[Mary reveals that they were blown off course due to unexpected winds. They bypassed France and ended up off the coast of Spain. Her travel companions were not worried as James had contacts in all these places. He traded as they just waited near the ship, for winds to

settle and blow in the right direction, for them to resume course to France.]

Reena: Do you have a name for the place where you've landed?

Maya: It's spoken in a foreign language – I don't understand. But Jerusalem was very dark and ... not dark, but rigid, whereas this place is very bright and upbeat. Tamar really liked it there. We didn't stay for too long. The wind has righted itself and Yamez did his business and has resupplied stocks and [we] got on the boat and ended up in France.

Reena: OK, whereabouts in France do you end up?

Maya: It's a quiet coast. When we were in Spain, Yamez kept our identities relatively quiet. He didn't mention our identities. But in France his friends knew of us and it all had to be kept on the 'down low' [sic]. We had to walk through the forests.

Reena: Are you still calling yourselves by your original names or have you changed your names in some way?

Maya: We keep our names.

Reena: OK. Just tell me what happens now.

Maya: We walk through the forests and hills to get to a village. I don't know how Yamez made all these preparations. Sometimes he's amazing, that man.

Reena: Does this village have a name that you find yourself in?

Maya: Aq ... Aqui ... Aqui ... Aqui ... Aquitaine? Something like that anyway. It's kind of a foreign tongue.

In Gaul, Roman writers noted the presence of three main ethno-linguistic groups in the area: the Gauls, the Aquitani, and the Belgae. Maya was referring to the second group, the

Aquitani. These were a people living in what the Romans called Gallia Aquitania, what is now southern Aquitaine and south-western Midi-Pyrénées, France, in the region between the Pyrenees, the Atlantic Ocean and the Garonne, present-day south-western France. They spoke the Aquitanian language, related to Old Basque.[2] After the sessions, when Maya was asked if she'd had prior knowledge of this, she seemed surprised and emphatically denied it. The regression continues.

Reena: What else is happening?

Maya: Nothing. We just set up ... like there's a little cottage, hut, for us. It's a very simple life. And Yeshua is still not strong so we just need to be there for him to recuperate and to survive. It's nice because we can have almost a relatively normal family life, which we didn't have the opportunity to have before. But Yeshua gets very impatient and he says that he needs to walk again and there are messages he needs to spread. I'm frightened ... I'm frightened he'd be found out. The Romans have got far-reaching arms. And it's almost like we're under their nose. We get stories of how other followers are being killed and persecuted by both the Romans and the Jews. And that they have to communicate with each other via secrecy and symbolism. And I don't understand why Yeshua wants to continue on this mad quest whilst I am pregnant with our third son. But he's quite insistent. So he and Yamez devise a plan where he is to go off to the islands in Greece. He's been there before, Greece. So he can go underground and be part of that priesthood as well. He wants to be in touch with that priesthood. To teach, to spread the word, to do what he wants to do, to do what he needs to do. I don't like it so I say I will remain here. I like this place. So far it's safe for our children. They're having fun. Tamar's going to school. She's having a good time.

Reena: Whereabouts do you get your money from to buy food and whatever?

Maya: Yamez. We have our own little garden but Yamez provides for us.

Mary then talks about their interaction with the local people. She and Yeshua talk to them, and teach them. She revels in the fact that they are so open to their teaching, due to their beliefs about spirits and different deities. This is a nice change to what they had faced in Jerusalem. She learns and communicates to them in their language, which is a dialect of French. She revealed whilst her mother tongue is Hebrew, her father made sure that she learned French and Greek when she was younger as it was important for her family. Though she knew and understood French, she found the accent of this place very different, so it sounded really foreign from what she was used to.

The next significant event sees Yeshua boarding the boat to go to Greece.

Maya: I have to put my heavy heart aside and say bye-bye but he knows I'm not very happy. [chuckles] He says he can see the wrath of all of hell in my eyes and he can feel it in my spirit and he says it's a good thing he's leaving. And I say to him it wouldn't be there if he had chosen to stay … He says bye-bye to the children.

[Then Maya talks about her three children.]

Maya: Yosef (the youngest) is a mere babe – he's about three or four months. Tamar is about seven – six, seven.

Yesoos is about three or four but he's an imp. He is so mischievous. He is just really curious and mischievous. Tamar is very gentle and sweet but she has been through a lot. The deep memory of the pain has made her wise beyond her years. But she's still sweet and gentle. Sometimes I wonder about David ... His father has turned him against me and I haven't been there to defend myself. He turned everyone – most people – against me. But that is a time long in the past. It hurts but there is so much else going on.

There are traditions and rites in annals that set the scene for two possible nephews of Joseph of Arimathea – the elder named Jesus and the younger named Josephes. The inference is that they are sons of Jesus Christ and Mary Magdalene.[3] According to Laurence Gardner, historical records show that Mary Magdalene's second son was born in AD44,[4] which would make Tamar eleven years old, as oppose to Maya's claim of her being seven. As we've seen in the previous chapter, the historical records do not tally with Maya's and others' regressions on Tamar's birth either.

The next significant event saw Mary walking with Marta, when she saw a man in the stocks. Feeling sorry for him, she placed her hands on his cheeks, and his face brightens at the show of kindness. She felt good doing it but she feels a deep sense of weariness.

Maya: Marta and I were going to our little hideout in the forest where I'm with the children, Tamar and Yesoos and Yosef. Those are my kids. [wistfully] I haven't seen Yeshua in so long. He's gone off to another part – Greece – to do whatever he needs to do. I needed to stay away and hidden for the sake of the children. But in

my own way I'm quite respected and revered by quite a
few of these people in France, in the villages around, so
they come and hear me speak. And Marta is there and
Yamez comes once in a while to visit. And sometimes
he transports Yeshua back and forth for visits as well.
Reena: So what else happens?
Maya: I continue teaching. In fact, there are more and
more people coming to hear me. Well, they want me to
speak to them. I'm a bit frightened because ultimately
I'm here to take care of my children – to make sure
they're safe from people from Rome or from Jerusalem.
But my heart is in the message and the teachings, so I
teach. And there are demands for me to go to other
villages. Initially I was a bit reluctant and a bit hesitant.
But they're very persuasive ... I talk to them about
being kind to each other; about [how] love and
compassion is the biggest message; about equality; about
the soul. I teach them about different aspects of life. I
do not teach them about the one God. I teach them
about there being an existence of supreme love from
which we can draw strength. I teach them about the
Way.
Reena: Why do you not particularly talk about God?
Maya: No, I do not talk about the *one God* because they
have their beliefs.
Reena: Ah, it's a way of avoiding their beliefs.
Maya: No, it's a way of incorporating their beliefs,
because whether there is the one God or the many gods,
it doesn't matter. It's the fact that there is a supreme
connection of love. That is the most important message.
And the Way is the way to live in that love and be in
that love. There is no point in fighting like our leaders in
Jerusalem used to – about pernickety points, about

different rituals, about different details, because in the fight, they lose the way to love, they lose the way to Be, and I didn't want to do that with spreading a belief of one god versus many. It was irrelevant to the way that Yeshua teaches. Sometimes it is hard but I get a feeling that when they listen to what I'm teaching, they think of Utopia, because these are villagers, these are peasants that I'm talking to. Simple people. And there has been some suppression by their lords. When I teach it gives them hope. It gives them lots of hope ... When she was [old] enough, Tamar came with me as well.

Reena: And what about those who are in control and in power?

Maya: I also teach them about using energies, different types of energy. I also teach them about the energy of plants and using that to heal. One of the lord's babies was very ill. The mistress heard from one of the workers about me, so she brought the baby to me to be healed, which I did. And she then kept coming. The mistress kept coming ... I don't ask for payment. I do it out of love.

[She then went on to describing the baby's symptoms.]

Maya: There was always high fever. He got very hot. Because of that he cried a lot. And he had big pains in the head. And there was something with the heart, which no one picked up, but when I put my hands on his body I could feel his heart wasn't so healthy. It was not as robust as my babies were, the heart. Yes ... [long pause]

[She then described the ways she healed him. She used a herb that the locals thought was a weed, so they did not think it would work. And she also put her hand on his forehead and drew it away. She had specialised in working with herbs when she was a child, working with the Earth.]

Maya: I used to go to the fields. It's almost like they speak to me but not quite. I just knew what to do. That's how I knew what to ask Yamez to bring to me to bathe and dress Yeshua's wounds. I knew what to give him internally and externally.

The next significant event saw Mary's reputation growing. She was called 'Madonna' and they embraced her teachings of the Way, and what she had to say.

This is consistent with the historical trail. Whilst Jesus' mother Mary was referred to as the White Madonna, Mary Magdalene was dubbed the Black Madonna. The Black Madonna started to be venerated in AD44 in the Languedoc regions of Provence, where nearly 200 of these ornamental representations had been discovered in France by the sixteenth century. The Black Madonna is deemed to be wise, and the representation of the Holy Spirit on Earth.[5] The other reason for her being dubbed Black Madonna is because in many paintings she is dignified with the black robe of a Nazarene priestess, of the Essene order.[6] This term then confirms her as practising and teaching the Essene way within France. The regression continues.

Maya: This mistress told her friends about me and about my abilities so I was working with quite a lot of children who were not so well. Until the grand princess of Aquitaine – she's not like the 'Queen' queen [sic] but she's the head family of that region – she came. She needed some help ... I'm not fighting for power. So if there's an opposition, to me it doesn't matter, because I've got enough people who want to hear about the

Way. I'm not saying that their way is wrong, I'm just teaching about the Way, my way. And in fact when the mistress of the bigger Aquitaine – let's just call her princess, shall we? – and her husband ... They are very open. They are very open to the Way, to what I was saying. They are open to me healing with herbs, they were open to all that. They were very supportive. They understood that I was of no threat. It took me a while before I told them who I was and exactly where we've come from and who Yeshua was, because I was just scared of their connections. So I didn't tell them about that until very much later on, but again it was irrelevant to what I was teaching.

[In the next significant event, Yeshua comes back and stays for a month, before heading back to Greece, where he stays with a priesthood and spreads the Word. In a separate session, Mary reveals that Yeshua also spends his time in the northern part of Egypt, where he learned his spiritual truths or beliefs. So he kept going back there once in a while to keep in touch with his brotherhood.]

Maya: He is looking very ... His body is not so strong. He is quite frail. He never fully recovered from that ... His body never fully recovered. Yamez is telling me that [he] has heard some news from Mattius. He had shared it with Yeshua and it made him a bit more upset. I think Mattius had gone off to teach the message but he was caught and killed. Yeshua is a bit devastated that Mattius has died in a violent way I think ... All the followers have gone underground.

Timeline-wise, Mary reveals that Yosef is now about three or four, cheeky Yesoos is about six or seven, and Tamar is about eleven – approaching puberty. She chuckles and says that Yesoos is very curious and loves Yamez's life. He thinks it is very exciting, as instead of staying in the village, he wants to explore the world. Yamez has promised Yesoos that when he is old enough, thirteen, he will be able to join him, with his parents' blessing.

In the next significant event, Yeshua is ill.

Maya: His body is on the verge of giving up but his spirit isn't ready to move on. I joke with him and I keep saying to him [that] his spirit is stronger than his body.

Reena: Where is his body at the moment?

Maya: He's in our little hut, cottage, in France. The children are there and his head is on my lap. Yamez is there, Marta. Again I'm torn. I'm split because I'm devastated that Yeshua's body is giving up, but at the same time I know it will be OK. Spirit-wise it will be fine. It's very wearying, living like this.

Reena: OK. Let's just go through it slowly, the things that happen.

Maya: Oh. Yeshua knows he's ready to go. He's feeling a bit sad because he knows ... He says that things will be hard for those who choose to follow the Way. He's sad that very little can be done about that by him at the moment. He feels that sense of responsibility. He gives his blessings to the children and tells them how proud he is of them and how much he loves them. Tamar, in her very quiet wisdom, is sad but she understands what's happening. Yesoos (in his mid teens) and little Yosef are very sad. Little Yosef is like the baby of the family so he is very tender. He didn't go through the hardships Tamar did and he doesn't have that curiosity and that robustness of life that Yesoos has. Yeshua asks

Yamez one last favour of taking care of his children. Yamez says: 'I'll take care of them as if they are my own.' Then Yeshua slips away very quietly. His head was on my lap the whole time. He went away peacefully but the only worry was for the people who are following the Way – for their safety.

Reena: What happens next?

Maya: The priest does the final rites. [long pause] And I let my husband go. And again I can still feel his spirit so one part of me is fine, but the other part of me is just [sighs heavily] … I will miss him. For as long as I live I will miss him. We had a funny relationship because we were apart for most of the time and yet we were still connected with that spirit. We were so connected. But I always knew … one part of me always knew, his body was there, which gave me comfort. This time that knowledge that his body is not there, it saddens me, but our spirit is still joined.

Reena: Tell me what happens next and particularly to the body.

Maya: We cover the body in white linen and we take it outside the hut. Yamez, Yesoos – they are carrying the body. The priest is in front in the lead, then the body and then the four of us follow behind. Myself, the two children and Marta come behind. And then we burn the body and we let the ashes go with the wind. It's almost like a ceremony to set the spirit free from the body. Yamez and the priest stay with us for a few days. The people in France, they were not privy to this. The village where I'm staying [is] on the outskirts, but they still send me little things like food, just to help me. And when Yamez goes, he takes Yesoos with him with the promise he'll take Yosef when Yosef hits puberty.

The regression turned towards Yamez's family, specifically his wife.

Maya: I do not meet her. He speaks of family but not much. He is too involved in our dramas. [laughs] He gives everything – he gives his time, he gives his energy, he gives his love, he gives his money. He gives us everything ... He's been more than a friend. We couldn't have done this without him. Yeshua wouldn't have had the extra life without him. But he was especially close to Yeshua ever since they were children. Yamez is a special soul.

In the next significant event, Mary is aware that both Yesoos and Yosef travel with Yamez.

Maya: It's good for my boys really to be with him, although I miss them. So Tamar [twenty-one] and I decide we're going to walk and teach. Marta's not with us now ... She's left ... At this point I have no idea [where]. She left a few years ago ... All this while I have been teaching Tamar about the Earth and the energies of the Earth. Teaching her the Way. Teaching her about using herbs, healing. So we decided we're going to just walk and teach. And we're going to work with the Earth's energies as well. So we go. We just walk and teach. For days and days, sometimes. Because I had done a bit of this walking and a few mistresses know about me and the Grand Mistress knows about me, I have free rein to walk ... We don't mention about crucifixion. It is not the core message of the Way. We just say that my husband started to teach and he was a very brave man because he started to speak out against leaders because his belief was so strong and for that he was punished. But his spirit never died, I said. It's not exactly a lie. It's what he did that's the most important thing.

The next significant event saw Mary, old, in a cave.

Maya: There are some people and my daughter. I hold her hand and I ask her to continue this work, to continue working, to continue spreading the message, to continue working with the Earth … We work with the Earth's plants but we also work with the Earth's energies to help people, help ourselves. We need to work with the Earth to enable, for example, crops to grow at their best with the most nutrition. We need to work with the Earth and the energies so that we get the most from just living, just life. And just developing that understanding of the Earth and working with it instead of using the Earth was quite important in the work I was doing – which I shared with Tamar.

The regression moved on to her children. Mary was aware that Tamar was married and had a child. Whilst her sons occasionally come and go, she does not keep in touch because she constantly walks and moves from one place to another. She is connected to them via their spirit, which is strong and happy, so she does not need to see them. At this point, Yosef is still a young man finding his way. Because Tamar walks with her, she knows more about her.

Later, during the debrief, Maya revealed that whilst she did not know where they were, deep inside she felt that Yesoos had got married within the family. This is consistent with James' regression that Yesoos – Jesus Jr – had joined the early

Christian community in Britain and married his cousin, James' daughter.

In Britain, within the beautiful and colossal ruins of Glastonbury Abbey, is the Lady Chapel. Outside the south wall of the chapel is a stone inscribed with the words 'Jesus Maria': could this be related to the consecration of the chapel by Jesus Jr in memory of his mother? The Corpus Christi College in Cambridge holds the seven-volume *Chronica Majora*, which holds a collection of ancient records from the Benedictine Abbey of St Albans in AD793. In it, there is a record that the chapel was built in AD63 Glastonbury – the same year that Mary Magdalene died in France. Whilst there is no indication that Jesus Christ ever came to Britain, there are a number of instances when the younger Jesus travelled to Britain, with his uncle, Joseph of Arimathea, who is also James, Jesus' brother.[7] These historical accounts correspond to these memories revealed by Mary Magdalene.

Maya also revealed that, whilst it was Tamar's role to keep the teachings sacred and safe in France, it was a tougher role as she'd had to draw souls to her, without knowing whether it was the right soul or the wrong soul, or whether it was a dangerous soul or a good soul. Yesoos' role, however, was to move around and spread the Word. It was easier as he did not stay in one place for too long and so sought people out, so he was drawn to people who he could trust to teach.

This is a significant insight because tradition holds that Catharism is a tradition that is based on the teachings of Mary Magdalene and carried on by Tamar. In the departments of Ariège and Aude, where the Cathars lived in the Middle Ages, the earliest traces of Christian religion can be dated to the fifth or sixth century, that is, the period between AD414 and 507. This is timed with the arrival of the Visigoths to the region. The Visigoths were Arian Christians, and did not believe Jesus was the Son of God, nor did they believe in the Trinity. Neither did the Cathars. Also, of all the branches of Christian belief, only the Cathars ever accepted that Jesus and Mary Magdalene were married. This was probably because their ancestors living there in the first century had met Mary and Jesus as a couple and, undisturbed for centuries, these beliefs were then passed down from father to son or from mother to daughter for hundreds of years.[8]

Apart from oral tradition and painfully few written texts, we will never know much about the enigmatic Cathars. Due to the perceived threat they offered to the Catholic doctrine, Pope Innocent III attempted to eradicate Catharism, first peacefully, then forcefully through a series of crusades and inquisitions over thirty years when the Cathars refused to surrender their beliefs and were killed by the Church as heretics.[9]

The regression continues as Mary went to her own death point. She is about sixty-ish, and finds herself in a cave in France.

Maya: There's a candle in the cave and it's time for my spirit to leave my body.

Reena: And this cave you're in: is there a name for it?

Maya: No, it's just a cave ... It's quite high up and I can see – well, not now because I'm in the cave – but from the mouth of the cave I can see the lands.

Reena: And this cave that's high up, how do you get access to it?

Maya: I walked up. This was before I was this ill. It was also a safe place.

Reena: OK. Just go through slowly what happens. Just go through the death, when your heart stops beating, and then just tell me what happens.

Maya: I slip away. Tamar is next to me. She doesn't realise I've slipped away. We are very close, she and I. We've been through a lot together. But I am glad she has her own family and I know she will keep the teaching alive in her own way. There are some people but they are all either asleep or meditating or something. Their eyes are all closed but it's OK. I just slip away ... Tamar and I did lots of walking to spread the message, spread the Way. There are some people in the cave but I am happy to go and be reunited. [sighs heavily] The body is weary so it's time to go and I pass the work on to my daughter. She can continue with this Way. My sons are not with me but that is OK, it doesn't matter. They have their own lives. Word will get to them. It's fine.

I feel very warm. I get a sense I've done this many times before so I'm quite practised at it. [laughs] It's like my spirit lights up the cave for a while. I feel that. It takes me a while to leave the cave and then I float off ... I was quite happy with that life. Quite satisfied. Because I felt I had passed everything on to the right person, who would do the right things with it.

In the twelfth-century *Chronica Majora* of Matthew Paris, it was confirmed that Mary Magdalene died at La Sainte-Baume in AD63,[10] in the Provence-Alpes-Côte d'Azur region of south-eastern France. It lies 40km (25mi) east of Aix-en-Provence. The Grotto of Mary Magdalene is a Christian pilgrimage site to this day, and her relics, including her skull, found in 1279, are held within her tomb in Saint Maximin la Sainte Baume – declared as Christianity's third most important tomb by the Vatican.[11]

So, why did the Church denounce Mary Magdalene, even going as far as calling her a prostitute? Laurence Gardner's hypothesis is that the succession via Apostolic Constitution is the reason why the Church began to denounce any women who were closely involved in the ministry of Jesus. They wanted to denounce any form of family hereditary claims to the succession of the Church, thereby strengthening the Apostolic Succession through followers dating back to Peter and Paul.[12]

This was taken further by the third century, when a process of segregation had commenced in churches led by the Romans, where men performed the rite and women worshipped in silence. In 1977, Pope Paul VI, the same Pope who in 1969 had released the revised Church doctrine stating that Mary Magdalene was no longer considered a prostitute, reaffirmed that a woman could not become a priest.[13] In doing so, the Church acted contrary to how women were treated within the Nazarene community, and within Jesus' ministry.

The good news is that, in 2016, under the leadership of Pope Francis, Mary Magdalene was officially declared an Apostle and Pope Francis elevated the day long set aside for a memorial to Mary Magdalene into a feast day, thereby lifting her to the level of the Apostles. In an article for the Vatican newspaper, Archbishop Arthur Roche wrote that St Mary Magdalene's new feast day, 22 July, was a call for all Christians to 'reflect more deeply on the dignity of women, the new evangelisation and the greatness of the mystery of divine mercy'.[14]

Later on in the year, on 2 August, Pope Francis also announced the establishment a 'Commission of Study on the Diaconate of Women' and named twelve members to it, six of them women, including one American – Professor Phyllis Zagano, who teaches at Hofstra University, Hempstead, NY.

These are positive signs that the Roman Catholic Church is opening their arms to the involvement of women to take more active leadership roles within their church[15] – mimicking more accurately how Jesus actually led his ministry, and perhaps contemplating opening the doors to slowly acknowledging Jesus' bloodline.

Maya's portrayal of Mary Magdalene's role in Jesus' life was of a tender, deeply loved and constant companion. This is consistent with Laurence Gardner's historical research of their relationship: 'From the outset of Jesus' mission, Mary Magdalene is seen as a constant in his life.' Not only did she travel with him, she confided in him, shared energy with him, was a companion to his mother and sister, and gave birth to and cared for his children. She has been documented as Jesus' consort and the Apostle of Apostles – she was whom Jesus kissed and called his blessed one. She was closer to Jesus than anyone else.[16]

She was indeed his soul mate.

8

DEVOUT

A friend is one that knows you as you are; understands where you have been; accepts what you have become; and still gently allows you to grow.
– Elbert Hubbard

During her first regression as Mary Magdalene, Maya was asked if anyone in that life was familiar to her in the current life. It is common for people experiencing past-life regression to recognise characters from that life as families, friends, acquaintances and even perpetrators in their present incarnation. It is customary to determine this during a therapy session to gain insights on soul contracts and life lessons. This knowledge gives clients a deeper understanding into their relationships and current life lessons.

Maya identified that Mary Magdalene's sister, Marta, reminded her of Sally, a colleague and acquaintance of hers. Sally is Irish, currently residing in Britain. In contrast to Maya, Sally is thoroughly knowledgeable about the New Testament and went to church and was brought up with the teachings. However, when she was about eleven or twelve, she started to question everything that she was being taught. When her teachers, priests and parents could not answer her questions, she expanded her search and read up on Judaism and Islam, which eventually led her to the more esoteric study of spirituality – Gnosticism, Sufism and the Kabbalah.

When Maya informed her friend of this, the revelation not only surprised Sally, but she struggled to accept it. However, she did agree to explore more and participate in this book. As with the other participants, I gave her a wide berth when entering the life, as opposed to specifically asking her to go back to Marta – again, making sure that no leading suggestions were planted into Sally's subconscious.

Sally entered into a past life where she found herself in a grove of olive trees with a well. She was a 32-year-old female, wearing simple leather sandals, a long, simple, hessian or linen dress, with a hessian or linen cover over her hair. It was light, and there were children, animals and other women there with her. They were fetching water and collecting olives from the trees.

Sally: [long pause and heavy sigh] There are some buildings and there's a courtyard in the middle – open, with some trees for shelter. There's a big table. The table is shaped like a big U. It goes around. And there's a meal being prepared, like a feast.

Reena: Who's preparing the meal?

Sally: There's many people. There's a lot of activity, there's a lot of people running around.

Reena: Could you tell me a bit about the activity, please?

Sally: Preparing food, preparing the table. It's like we're expecting someone. It's some sort of celebration. There's a lot of excitement about people coming, as though they've waited a long time.

Reena: Who are the people preparing for the celebration, in relation to you?

Sally: Some of them are family. Some of them are friends. Some of them are … it feels like a community.

It feels like we're connected ... everyone feels like family.

Reena: Is there anyone from your immediate family there?

Sally: An aunt. I think the people that are coming are my family ... The guests have arrived. There are eight-altogether ... one woman and seven men. We are very happy to see each other.

Reena: Who are these men and woman to you?

Sally: It's my sister.

Reena: The woman is your sister? What's her name?

Sally: Mary.

Reena: Is that how you normally address her?

Sally: I think I call her Maya.

At this point it is interesting to note that Maya's choice of pseudonym might have been more than just a passing fancy. Maya and I had both avoided giving Sally details about the preceding regressions, including the choice of pseudonym. This raised the possibility that Mary Magdalene really was known as 'Maya' to her close family. After the session, the fully conscious Sally said it 'felt like that was my name for her, not everybody else's name. It was something that the family called her.' The regression continued.

Reena: OK. And who are the seven men?

Sally: One is her beloved.

Reena: How do you address her beloved?

Sally: [long pause, sighs] Joshua.

[It soon became evident that Sally was referring to Jesus, which gave us yet another variation on his name. While Mia and Greg had referred to him as Jesus, Maya had called him by his original Aramaic name of Yeshua and

Sally was now using another westernised version of that, Joshua.]

Reena: OK. And who else is there? The other six men?

Sally: Peter. Simon. James. Andrew. [long pause]

Reena: Who else is there?

Sally: [long pause] I can't see him. He's at the back.

Reena: OK. That's fine. And what is this celebration for?

Sally: It's a return. They've been away for a long time.

Reena: Away from where?

Sally: From home … Home is where the community is.

Reena: OK. And how are you feeling now that they have returned home?

Sally: I am very pleased to see them. But there's mixed emotions because there are stories of troubles that follow them so …

Reena: What are some of these stories?

Sally: That there are many enemies and that there are many that they are not pleased with, particularly from the elders – the Pharisees. We are watchful of … [hesitates] … spies. When there are large groups that come together, it's difficult to know who everyone is. When there are faces we do not know, we don't know what information will go and so there is less ability to trust and therefore their safety [sic].

Reena: Who would send the spies?

Sally: Those of the Pharisees, the leaders that are jealous of the following and the message. The message of individual right and power. The message of love and connection to God. Those that wish us to be enslaved, they would rather this message was not delivered.

Whilst Sally and Mia have not met or spoken to one another about their regression, it was interesting to note that both of them conveyed the same message that Jesus was speaking of, and the Pharisees were unhappy with.

Reena: How do you feel about these messages?
Sally: Frustrated that it's not a truth that's known to all.
Reena: Just tell us what happens next.
Sally: There is a feast. Many people. It's a joyful celebration. But all the while I have a sense, a feeling, that it won't be long-lived, and that it would be foolish to let [our] guards down.
Reena: How do people address you in this community?
Sally: As Marta.
Reena: And are you Maya's older or younger sister?
Sally: I feel very protective of her. In some ways she seems so much younger but in other ways she seems so much older ... there's a wisdom and knowledge in her.
Reena: In what way does she seem younger?
Sally: She can be very playful and light, and sometimes I envy that lightness she has because I think I worry for her and the community, and sometimes that worry wears me down.
Reena: What role do you play in the community?
Sally: Often an advisory role. There are several who are keeping things in order, although everyone contributes. And even though I'm a woman, my impact is valued.
Reena: How is this community addressed? Does it have a name?
Sally: We try to avoid being too public. We prefer to remain out of public view, out of sight, as much as possible ... Sometimes there is conflict in the community because the intention is for peace and

sometimes it's difficult to see how there can be peace without first fighting for that peace, and this creates a lot of disruption, because there are those that want to go and fight for the truths, for what they believe in. And yet this goes against everything that we are trying to create.

Reena: What are your views on this?

Sally: It's difficult to find the balance. Because when there is fear there is weakness. And when there is weakness there is danger. And sometimes it's wiser to hold one's thoughts and to keep those truths only for those who have the ability to recognise and to understand – the eyes to see and the ears to hear. More selection is required in who this message is portrayed to.

Reena: Is there anything else of significance about the celebration?

Sally: [sighs heavily] There's a lot of wine consumed. And lots of singing and dancing.

Reena: And what happens next?

Sally: Some very heated discussions between some members of the community and some of the visitors … About what's going on outside of the community and what needs to be done. The people are being lied to, downtrodden and becoming more and more powerless as people come in, and it seems that they take more and more.

Reena: What's the general consensus of what is to be done?

Sally: Some want to fight. There is talk of a rebellion. An uprising.

Reena: What is the view of Joshua and Maya?

Sally: They don't involve themselves in these debates … It's like they are just observing, absorbing everything that's being said. Others are arguing for a peaceful way, to remain focused on remaining in the place of sanctity, physically, mentally, emotionally. Honouring the divinity in all things and therefore loving and accepting all things and all beings and all peoples regardless of what they do or say. That by remaining in a place of love we can conquer anything. But others are too impatient and they want freedom now. They want to liberate the people and they say we must stand up to them, that we must have our own truth, our own leaders, our own voice.

Next, Sally was navigated to the most significant part of the celebration.

Sally: Before the feast starts, there's a moment when everyone in the space joins hands and then there's a blessing over the food, over the gathering, over everything that has been provided, and in that blessing there's a huge amount of energy being generated and I can see it radiating out of everybody over the whole space. It's almost like everything lights up.

Marta then reveals that though Joshua and Maya lead the blessing, everyone is involved and contributes – including the smallest and youngest.

Reena: What happens to the food and the drinks that have been blessed?
Sally: It's optimised. It provides us with everything that we need. The vibration of the food and the liquid that's to be consumed has been elevated and therefore we need less of it to be sustained.

Reena: OK. In terms of the liquid, you did mention that there was wine. Is there also water?

Sally: Yeah.

Reena: OK. How was the water obtained?

Sally: The water came from the well.

Reena: How about the wine?

Sally: [long pause] There is like a storehouse. There are skins and there are jugs – large vases – that hold some of the wines. But something is changed in the quality after the blessing.

Reena: What is the celebration for?

Sally: The celebration of Sacred Union. Coming together. Unity. Love. Reconnection. Oneness.

Reena: Is this celebration of Sacred Union for the entire community or is it between specific people within that community?

Sally: We're all one. What is celebrated for one is celebrated for the whole.

Reena: OK. How often are these celebrations conducted?

Sally: There are many celebrations. This one is quite unique.

Reena: In what way is it unique?

Sally: Because there is a unique intensity in the energies that are currently around the table.

Reena: And what has brought about this unique intensity of energies?

Sally: There is a particular freq— like a frequency of Maya, Joshua and the others that is amplifying what usually happens to a lesser degree. And those that travel with them all spread out amongst the others so when the energy starts to flow and it reaches those, it's as though it creates a grid that amplifies and boosts everyone else as it goes around the space. It's like an electrical circuit and it's pushed on by the next to the next. And then at points it's heightened and then it continues on around until it comes back to the beginning and then it continues.

Reena: You mentioned this intensity is particularly unique at this time.

Sally: Yes.

Reena: Are you aware of what happened with Maya and Joshua for them to have had this intensity?

Sally: They have both been in training for many, many years.

Reena: Is that all that's significant with the celebration?

Sally: Yeah.

Though Sally did not know anything about Maya's regression, Sally gave a wider participant's perspective to Maya's more personal perspective to the Sacred Union shared between her and Jesus. It is interesting to note that the perspectives of both memories of this ceremony are complementary. Could this account of the Sacred Union be the Feast of Cana that is written in the New Testament?

Also, Sally's account gives a plausible explanation to the 'Turning water into wine' miracle that Jesus performs at Cana. Whilst the energy did not change the water's molecular structure to wine, it certainly added a special quality to the food and drink, making it that much more satisfying to consume.

The next significant event took us to a large cave that many people were living in.

Sally: It's not just one cave. I feel like I'm moving from cave to cave, reassuring people ... Members of the community. There's a lot of quite worried faces. The children don't seem to mind. The children are playing with sticks and rocks.

Reena: What are the people of the community worried about?

Sally: There's been some persecution and there's been some attacks on some members of the community. It was no longer safe to stay where we were. There are those who would keep us silent so it was safer to move.

Reena: Where are Maya and Joshua at this point?

Sally: Out somewhere teaching, we are not entirely sure where.

Reena: And how about Peter and Simon and James and Andrew and the person who was at the back. Where are they?

Sally: As far as I know they're together.

Reena: OK. And just tell us more about the worries.

Sally: Concerns about how to survive, being discovered, finding a place of safety to put or store the teachings.

Reena: How are your teachings communicated?

Sally: Mainly verbally but some has [sic] been written down.

Reena: What's the material that these teachings have been written down on?

Sally: I haven't seen them. They haven't been shown to me. It's very frustrating for me but as a woman there are some things I am not allowed to experience.

Reena: I understand. Is there a specific person that's in charge of the teachings that have been written down?

Sally: Much of the teaching is from tradition. It's been handed down orally ... for many generations.

Reena: And how did those oral teachings get written?

Sally: It was decided that it was important that a written record be created so that future generations would be able to understand the message as it was portrayed at the time, not in a form that could be distorted as the story changed. Even the words of the most recent teachings are being altered to suit the purposes of those who are in power – a distortion of the truth.

Reena: Is there anything else significant about now?

Sally: It's just that so much has been distorted and there have been so many lies.

Reena: Is there anything else of significance with these people, and community in the caves?

Sally: This is a place of sanctuary.

These caves sound very similar to the series of caves found at Qumran, within which historians suggest the Essene community used to live. Qumran is also the area in which the Dead Sea Scrolls were found. The Dead Sea Scrolls, estimated to be created between 400BC and AD300 are said to be the library of the Essenes and their teachings. In 1991, the Huntington Library in California received pictures of the 900 scrolls and passed them to scholars for study. They found the scrolls had very similar linguistic style to that attributed to Jesus in the New Testament. For example, the language that Jesus used in the Sermon of the Mount (Matthew, chapter 5 5) is similar to the Blessing of the Wise from the Dead Sea Scrolls.[1]

This would indicate that Jesus, Mary Magdalene and Marta were integral members of the Essene community and that Marta's account is a fascinating insider's look into their lives and way of Being.

The next event took us to a meeting between Joshua, Maya, Marta and a few other men. Marta reported being very, very frustrated and irritated.

Reena: What has frustrated and irritated you?
Sally: Because there is a naivety and almost an arrogance. It feels as though all of them are completely blind to what is really happening and what is going on. And I know that Maya and Joshua know exactly what the next phase is going to be. And because I can see exactly what's coming, it's as though the men have been completely blinkered to the truth and they still think that they are going to succeed and that somehow they are going to be able to overcome the status quo, the powers that are currently enforced [sic]. And it's almost as if they've been … It's like a delusion that it's all going to work out perfectly.
Reena: What do *you* think is going to happen?
Sally: I *know* what's going to happen.
Reena: What do you know?
Sally: We've already seen it.
Reena: Who are the 'we'?
Sally: Maya, Joshua. That in moving forward he must be presented as the 'sacrificial lamb'.
Reena: And how did you see this?
Sally: Waking dreams. And there is communication between my sister and I that is more like telepathy. And when I look into their eyes, both of them, I can see it. And I know that they know. But to the unseen, the smiling faces that they present show a very different story … Because they don't want to scare everyone. And because it must unfold in the way that has been destined, and if others knew then it would not proceed

as it must. And the others can't be trusted to hold the energy.

Reena: So who are trusted to hold the energy?

Sally: Very few. Only those that can see ... Myself. Judas. There are other women. There is a group of women.

Reena: How many in that group?

Sally: Twelve. There are twelve men in one circle. There are twelve women in the other circle.

Reena: Can the twelve men see?

Sally: No. If the twelve men got out of their heads and out of their arrogance they would see.

Reena: Is Judas part of the twelve men?

Sally: Yes. But he spends more time in his heart.

It was then established that Marta, Mary Magdalene and Mary, Jesus' mother, were all part of the group of twelve women, and that Joshua was part of the group of twelve men.

Sally: The group are sat around in one of the caves, in a circle. I'm permitted because I am serving. And there is an irony because I can see so much more than they can see.

Reena: So there's only the twelve men in this room, not the twelve women?

Sally: And Maya. Some of them are not happy that she is part of their circle, that she is admitted into the circle and that I am admitted into the circle.

Reena: And you are serving. What are you serving?

Sally: Wine. There is also bread and olives. It's a sustenance ... throughout the meal, it suffices. The bread and olives have been blessed. It's sufficient.

Reena: OK. So what's the end result of this meeting?

Sally: Each has been given instructions according to his role in the proceedings … irrespective of what happens, they must go forward and continue to teach and to pass on the message truthfully.

Reena: What stops Joshua from informing the other group of twelve about his role of being the 'sacrificial lamb'?

Sally: Because if they knew, they would try and prevent it. They still believe that he is going to be able to conquer and to become a leader of the people.

Reena: OK. Is there anything else of significance here?

Sally: It's just incredible that in arguing amongst themselves and bickering amongst themselves and vying for position and for status within the space, within the circle, that they are missing all the important information that's being given to them. If they did open their hearts and if they did pay attention, they would know what was being told to them and they missed it. They weren't listening. They were caught up in petty squabbles and they were not listening. And they treated me with disdain for being just a woman. And yet I took the time to see what was really happening, as they could have. And it feels like they wasted the most precious moments that they were ever going to be given.

Marta's account of the Last Supper is not terribly dissimilar to that of James'. Whilst she did not mention the goat stew, she did mention the olives, wine and bread, as did James. Also, James did say that there were fifteen in the room, and by Marta's count there were fourteen. This is in line with Laurence Gardner when he wrote that the Apostolic Church Order claims that both Mary and Marta had been present at the last supper.[2]

It was interesting to note in Marta's account that the community they were living in was extremely patriarchal – and very similar to the Jewish and Roman society that existed during the time of Jesus. This is illustrated in a few Judaic books – including Deuteronomy 22:23–27 which states that 'A virgin who is raped in a city should be sentenced to death because she could easily have cried out for help.' He also mentions that the Palestinian Talmud states that 'The words of the Torah will be destroyed in fire sooner than be taught to women.'[3] So Marta's frustrations can very easily be understood under this oppressive regime.

It is also interesting to note the parallel of society's perception of women whose importance was almost completely wiped out from the Bible, and disregarded within the wider Jewish community, as well as that of the Essenes during the time of Jesus. Greg's account of Paul also highlighted this imbalance between the male/female roles and explains his continued pursuit of dismissing female teachers from his ministry. However, as we are now living in the time for the Divine Feminine to rise and to balance with the Sacred Masculine, it is interesting to note that we are getting accounts from some key women during the biblical period.

The next event sees Marta packing as much as she can.

Sally: Because we have to leave. And it's urgent.

Reena: Just tell us about the urgency of the leaving.

Sally: The separation, the disconnection. The illusion of separation has been achieved. And therefore we must go forward alone.

Reena: How has that illusion been achieved?

Sally: Joshua is no longer with us.

Reena: Were you there when he became no longer with us?

Sally: [after long pause] Yes, all of the women were present. In one way or another.

[In navigating Marta back to that scene when Joshua was no longer with us, she became restless. There was lots of movement, but silence. It took a fair bit of coaxing and cajoling for her to verbalise what she was experiencing. Finally ...]

Reena: Can you tell us about the emotion you're feeling?

Sally: Frustration.

Reena: Go on.

Sally: It's frustration that it has to be this way; that people are just unable to see or recognise the truth.

Reena: And what is happening around you?

Sally: Crowds of people and soldiers.

Reena: What are people crowding up for?

Again, she was reticent to answer the question, and she became quite restless. After another long pause, Sally expressed her need for a toilet break. It was evident that she was unable or unwilling to talk directly about this event – which was the crucifixion. This is the normal occurrence of participating in or witnessing a trauma of a close loved one.

When someone goes through trauma, our brain and body go into shock – the deeper the shock, the deeper the trauma. In order to move in our lives (purely for survival reasons), our minds create coping strategies for us to continue on past the shock and trauma in a coherent manner. If the trauma is too intense for the individual to cope with, the psyche disguises it in the forms of denial, avoidance, shut-downs, selective amnesia or even fragmentation, so as to not confront it – for confronting it means pain and fear. However, people will display different symptoms of the trauma – e.g. PTSD, phobia, phantom pain, psychosomatic disorders, anxiety or addictions – due to the suppressed memory of the trauma that still exists.

In a therapeutic setting ensuring that the psyche feels safe and breaking through coping mechanisms is key to obtaining the source of the trauma and transforming it. In Sally's case, witnessing Joshua's crucifixion was clearly incredibly traumatic for her and so she was resistant to revisit it. Only once the emotion of the trauma is released, through gentle coaxing, and the suppressed memory is brought to the surface and dealt with, can the memory be released or integrated healthily into the complete psyche of the person. In a therapeutic sense, this is how regression therapy can bring about deep healing for people.

The next sequence of events demonstrates how techniques in regression therapy are used to release the strong pent-up emotions and bring about relief and an understanding of the traumatic events Marta witnessed/experienced.

When the regression resumed, I invited Sally to go back to the event where there were crowds of people and soldiers and allow the memories to come through.

At this point Sally began sobbing uncontrollably for several minutes as I repeatedly urged her to let out all the emotion. Allowing her to take her time, when the emotion finally subsided, I invited Sally to describe the emotion she was feeling.

Sally: A combination. Of rage and sorrow.
Reena: And what made you feel all this rage and sorrow?
Sally: The level of suffering that humankind was capable of inflicting on one another. And the stupidity.
Reena: And what specifically happened to make you feel so?

Sally: Because Joshua had volunteered for a very particular role. But there was no need for the level of suffering that they inflicted. And the pain that he experienced. He was beaten and whipped. Humiliated. Such cruelty.

Reena: Were you there to witness the beatings and the whipping?

Sally: Some of it was public.

Reena: Were you there to witness the public ones?

Sally: Some of it. We were trying to send energy to keep him strong. But it was so intense and the physical body can only maintain so much. And in our sorrow our energy was weakened because we weren't able to maintain our state and therefore we were unable to help him as well as we might have done. And for that I feel great shame and great sorrow.

Reena: What else did they do to him that you witnessed?

Sally, still releasing her personal anguish of witnessing the hurt inflicted on Joshua, started to weep again. Once again I repeatedly urged her to let out the emotion. When Sally regained her composure, she relayed what she had witnessed.

Sally: It was bad enough that he was beaten and had nails driven through his flesh on to the cross.

Reena: At which points on his body were the nails driven?

Sally: His feet. And through his wrists.

Reena: Where was Maya when all this was happening?

Sally: We were together. And Mary.

Reena: Where exactly are you witnessing this from? Were you amongst the crowds or somewhere else?

Sally: Just in front of the crowds. But on top of all of that, it was the goading, it was the jeering, it was the negative energy of the soldiers and the crowds that was the most painful of all. Because none of them could see that the whole point of it was to set them free.

Reena: At the time of the nails going through the flesh, was Joshua conscious or unconscious?

Sally: He was in a trance state.

Reena: Was that to minimise the physical feelings of what he went through?

Sally: Yeah.

Reena: OK. And what happens next?

Sally: I think we're there for quite a long time. Many of the crowd leave. Bored. The negative energy lessens and we're able to regroup. Many of the other women are still there.

Reena: Are the men there?

Sally: Some of the men. But there's almost an energetic grid that's been set up so even the women that aren't nearby we can connect to, we can tune in to … We're sending healing energy too.

Reena: And then what happens?

Sally: The soldiers are checking to see if all of the men on the crosses are dead.

Reena: How many men are you aware of there, that you can see?

Sally: Three.

Reena: And the soldiers are checking to see if they are dead. And then what happens?

Sally: [after another long pause and much restless, tormented movement] One of the soldiers has a spear.

Reena: What is the significance of the spear?

Sally: Because at first he jabs his feet to see if there is any movement. Which there isn't.

Reena: And what happens next?

Sally: Then he's prodding the body with the end of the spear to see if there is any movement. And then he puts the spear into his side.

Reena: And what happens next?

Sally: Very little comes out. Because the blood flow has been slowed down.

Reena: What's slowed the blood flow down?

Sally: Being in very deep trance ... The soldier is a bit perturbed by this. And when he looks at us we just smile at him. That makes him even more perturbed. He doesn't like us. He can feel something. Especially now the crowds have gone and it's starting to get dark.

Reena: What happens next?

Sally: We're chanting, quietly ... Some men arrive ... They speak to the soldiers and tell them they've done their job. They give them some money and then they take the body down ... We leave.

Reena: Who leaves?

Sally: All of us.

Reena: What happens to the men and the body? Do they go with you?

Sally: Yeah. We follow them. We give the appearance that we're lamenting. And wailing. Some try to follow us but we say no. This moment must be private. We use our intention for that energy to keep them away.

Reena: What happens then?

Sally: I'm making sure that people stay away from the body.

Reena: Where do you take the body?

Sally: To a small cave.

Reena: What happens to the body there?
Sally: We circle the body and we send healing.
Reena: All the women?
Sally: Yeah.
Reena: Any men?
Sally: I think I can see one or two men. It's not all of the women – just those that can be there. The rest are tuning in from elsewhere. It's not safe for everyone to be seen together.
Reena: How many women are there?
Sally: Three or four.
Reena: Who are the women? Yourself?
Sally: Mm. Maya. Mary.
Reena: Anyone else?
Sally: There's one more. I'm not sure of her name.

Later, Sally said that although the name Sarah came to mind, she did not want to say it, thinking it was conscious mind interference. Could it be Sarah, Jesus' sister?

Reena: And what happens to the body as you're sending healing?
Sally: He's brought out of the trance. But he's very weak. The body has sustained a lot of damage. So the body is wrapped.
Reena: Can you tell us how the body is wrapped? Is the face wrapped as well or just the body?
Sally: The whole is completely covered while healing is sent. Put back into deep sleep; deep, deep trance. He needs to sleep. The body needs to sleep. It needs rest for the repair to happen.

At this point, it is interesting to note that Marta was clearly not one of people who was let in on the secret of the Substitute. However, it is also not clear whether she was working on the Substitute or on Joshua himself, as the entire body is wrapped, including the face.

The next event took us back to her packing to leave because the country and environment she was in was not safe.

Sally: There's a lot of anger, there's a lot of disappointment. Many people feel let down. They feel that in some way, Joshua let them down. He wasn't the saviour that they thought he was going to be, because they feel like he didn't save himself so how could he save them? And this is the message that's been broadcast, spread.

Reena: So what about that makes it unsafe for you?

Sally: Because there are some who are still teaching the true message and in order to ensure that message doesn't reach the ears of the people, those in power want to destroy any who are still speaking that truth – they want it wiped out completely.

Reena: So who are you leaving with?

Sally: There's a small group of women and children. One or two men. We have belongings loaded on to some animals and we're travelling. The intention is to get out of the country, to go as far as possible.

Reena: What means of transport do you use?

Sally: Walking, yeah. Sometimes we take turns on the animals. But mainly walking.

Reena: Who are the men the women go with?

Sally: James, Joshua's brother.

Reena: Who are the women?

Sally: Maya. And Marianne.

Reena: How many children are there?

Sally: Four.

Reena: Whose children are they?

Sally: They belong to the women that are coming with us.

Reena: Does Maya have any children?

Sally: No, but she's pregnant.

Reena: Do you have any children?

Sally: [pause] Yes.

Reena: How many children do you have?

Sally: Well, there is a child with me. I don't know if it's my child. There is a child holding on to me quite closely. I feel very close to this child. I don't know if it's mine.

Reena: Who is this child?

Sally: It's a girl. I think it's a girl. The child's got long hair.

Reena: How old is the girl?

Sally: About six. Five or six, I think. It's difficult to tell.

This is very interesting in the sense that in the subsequent part, Marta realizes that the girl is actually Mary Magdalene's child, and not her own. So, it is consistent with Mary Magdalene's regression that Mary was pregnant with her second child, whilst her eldest child, her daughter, was a young girl during this time.

What I also found interesting is that a year later, I conducted the regression of Tamar, Mary Magdalene's and Joshua's daughter. You will see that this account was nearly word for word the same between Rose (Tamar) and Sally – although they live oceans apart and have never spoken to each other or communicated about their individual regression sessions with me. This is also substantiated by Laurence Gardner, who writes, 'Sara/Tamar, is independently listed as one of the women who was on the original voyage as Marta's companion.'[4]

It is details of similar accounts such as these that make me believe that these lives are not made up, but are true memories of the past. During the debrief, after the session, Sally also mentioned that she felt like she really wanted this girl to be her child as they'd had a close relationship. The closeness of their relationship is also reflected in Rose's regression.

The next event took them to their destination, where Marta is aware of big cliffs in where she thinks is France.

Sally: [after a very long pause] We go by boat to … From a big boat to a smaller boat to a beach. There are people waiting.

Reena: And do you still have the two men and several women with you and children?

Sally: I think so. There seems to be quite a few people in the boat.

Reena: Where is Joshua, do you know?

Sally: At this point we don't know. He went the other way.

Reena: When you left the other place, did he leave with you?

Sally: [after a very long pause] Not that I'm aware of. I don't think it was safe for us to travel together.

[By this time, it had been around three hours and I thought it would be prudent to start bringing the session to a close. So I 'navigated' her to her death point.]

Sally: I feel ancient but I don't know if I'm that old.

Reena: And whereabouts are you?

Sally: It feels like I'm inside. A small stone building. It's quite small. And there's matting on the floor. A fireplace. It's like a hearth, so there's a fire. And there are some people there.

Reena: Who are the significant people you can recognise around you?

Sally: It's hard to tell. My eyes are quite blurry.

Reena: And how are you feeling?

Sally: Tired. I feel a little bit sad as things didn't work out as we wanted them to.

Reena: Which country are you in?

Sally: [long pause] I'm not sure – it might be Britain. We might be Druids. But I don't know if that's a dream.

Reena: And at the point of death, did you have a beloved of your own?

Sally: No. And I don't think I did have the child.

Reena: Whose child was it?

Sally: My sister's.

Whilst there is no historical mention that Marta passed away in Britain, there is however tradition that she died in Tarascon, in the south of France. In fact, there is a church that has been built there in her memory, Église collégiale Ste Marthe, with a third-century crypt that houses her remains.[5] It is interesting that Marta did not quite know where she was as she approached death, as it was a haze to her, so she may not have the memories of where she actually was at the point her heart stopped beating.

Nevertheless, as Marta mentioned that she was in Britain, I navigated her back to the point when she actually travelled to Britain.

Sally: We have visitors from the community and people who've travelled and they are going to Britain next and I want to go with them.

Reena: Was Maya with you when you made this decision? And if she was, what did she say?

Sally: Feel like I'm putting my foot down and just saying I want to go.

Reena: So she obviously wasn't happy about it, was she?

Sally: I don't think so.

Reena: OK. Did anyone else from the place [where] you were with Maya go with you?

Sally: There were quite a few people in the party that went.

[Marta then gave an account of wanting to see Britain because of stories that she had heard of places of great energy and teachers who had wisdom.]

Sally: I wanted to do something for *me*.

Reena: Was James in the party when you left?

Sally: Yeah, I think so, yeah.

Reena: Did any one of Maya's children go with you?

Sally: Yeah, I think so, yeah.

Reena: Which one went with you?

Sally: Boy. I think. I'm not sure. I can't say.

This was again consistent with James' account that Jesus' son, Jesus Jr went with him to Britain.

Wanting to know about the most significant event(s) for Marta in Britain, I 'navigated' her there.

Sally: [after another long pause] An energy centre with high priests. A big stone circle ... There's a ritual, a ceremony ... Connecting to Source and generating energy. Energy that's used to heal the land ... There's

190

great power here in this circle. The energy of the land. It's like a portal.

She then described the stones as being huge, and that there's an altar and there are upright stones and there are stones that lie across them. Later in the debrief, Sally said that it was StoneHenge but that name did not come to mind whilst she was regressed. She recounted that there were thirty people involved in the ceremony, while Marta and Maya's son (unnamed as yet by Marta) were part of the inner circle.

Marta's impression of Britain was that it was primitive, barren, green, cold and sparsely populated. The people seemed primitive to her but she liked them. Her impression was very similar to that of James – who said they were loud and unrefined. She recalled there being fights between and within the tribes but there was an element of peace, and no signs of troubles with the Romans.

The great similarity and connection between the ancient Hebrew culture and religious belief and the Druidic population of Britain has been pointed out by many eminent scholars, including Sir Norman Lockyer, Edward Davies and W.M. Stukeley in their respective books.[6] These historical accounts are consistent with both Marta's and James' memories of having a close connection and integrating with the people of Britain and their beliefs.

After this event, Sally had been under trance for nearly four hours. So I navigated her soul to a place of healing for rejuvenation, and brought her out.

Besides the honour of sharing her perceptions of the story, I could not help but conclude that Marta was entirely devoted to the cause. Dismissed by virtue of her gender, she was nevertheless a key player in this story, by being a female backbone of support for her sister's family, at the expense of her own life. Her accounts of being part of the Druids in Britain just add to the evidence of ancient Israelite relationships and ties to British traditions.

9

DOUBTER

To thine own self be true, and it must follow, as the night the day,
thou canst not then be false to any man
– William Shakespeare

Mina is an American lady, currently residing in northern Europe. She got in touch with me to experience a between-lives session a couple of years before this book was conceived, when she spontaneously went back to this life in biblical times. Before this session, Mina had little to no prior knowledge of figures in the New Testament, apart from Jesus. A few years later, when this book was being planned, I reached out to Mina and asked if she would like to explore this life even more. She agreed.

So we explored the memories of the life of Thomas, a gentleman whose inquisitive mind led him to naturally doubt Jesus' work, but also led him to follow his heart in pursuing answers to his questions, which ultimately led him to great faith.

Mina entered the life in a middle-aged male body, with brown sandals on big feet. His legs are big and bare, and skin is brown. His torso is also big, covered with brown cloth. His hands are large, and he has longish brown hair, as well as a brown beard that covered his upper lip too. He entered the memory standing on dry land, being aware of people walking around – no one that he recognised. What was significant in this was that there was a building in front of him that he wanted to enter. At the debrief, after the regression, Mina mentioned that this building felt like a specific place. It was more decorated than a residence would be, and the floor was patterned, though the size could not be worked out.

Upon entering the building, he finds that he is sitting with some others, and feels colder.

Mina: We just feel the connection. I can feel it very strong [sic]. There are other people there and we become like – one connection. It's different from outside.

Reena: Tell me more about the difference. What happens outside?

Mina: There's lots of scattered energy outside. But when we go inside, we unify our energy together ... There's a harmony that happens between us.

Reena: And what is the significance of that harmony?

Mina: It's like connecting a universal rhythm. It's like being in this ... It's like a wave, a wave of energy together, and it's not as fragmented as on the outside.

Reena: Can you tell me more about the others? How many others are there?

Mina: I don't know exactly but there's one on my left, and on my right, and we're ... I think we're in a circle. The one on the right is smaller than I am.

Reena: Are you the biggest man there, just in terms of size?

Mina: I don't know. I can't see that far.

Reena: OK. The one on your right is smaller than you. Is it a man as well?

Mina: I don't know. It's more feminine. But the one on the left is definitely a man.

Reena: Do you know them well?

Mina: I believe so.

[At this point, he could not remember how he addressed them.]

Reena: Could you describe the whole process of unifying energy from the start to the end – what you're doing?

[Mina's body suddenly stiffens and tenses up.]

Mina: Mm. I can see the arms and hands.

Reena: Do you link arms and hands?

Mina: Yes. It comes from the ground and from the sky as well. There's a strong track from the ground right now. And there's the cross, the cross is the body, the ground and the sky, through the arms … It's getting stronger.

Reena: And what does your body feel like with all this energy going through you?

Mina: It feels very strong and very alive.

I felt very excited when he started talking about the movement of energy through the body, using the symbolism of the cross as the connection of the body to the Earth and sky and arms with one another. Whilst I know that the traditional symbolism of the cross as a crucifix has deep meaning within mainstream Christianity of the blood sacrifice of Jesus to atone for the sins of the masses, I personally have always found it uncomfortable that a Roman instrument of torture and execution is used to spread a deep spiritual message. This alternate viewpoint about the cross that this regression provides (and the meaning behind it, about connection and Oneness with all) resonates a lot better with me. It also is consistent with the way of Being that some of the other regressees share, in subsequent chapters.

The regression continues, and after he enjoys some pleasurable minutes of connecting with the energy, we go to the end. Mina's body makes a jerking movement.

Reena: That was a big jerk. What happened there?
Mina: [softly] It was like there was almost no body ... There was like a free space. It's like I'm above it all. There's an anchor in the body.
Reena: This anchor pulls you back into the body?
Mina: Yes.
Reena: What do you do in this free space?
Mina: [softly, in wonderment] I can see far away ... I can see other people that are far, far away ... that I should go and speak with. We are going to exchange understanding ... They have another way to understand the connection – the connection between the human form and the spirit form. I like to go and hear what they know and tell them what I know.
Reena: And are these people, are they in the same land that you are in now or is it a different land?
Mina: It's a different land.
[During the debrief, Mina mentioned that this was a memory of him consciously having an out-of-body experience to gather information. When part of Thomas floated up high, he could look far distant and see there was another group of people who had this connection. He knew that he had to go there to speak with these people to learn more. It was so interesting to feel like one could rise above all the noise and just know very clearly, even at a long distance geographically, where there would be a similar vibration to connect to and exchange with.]
Reena: Describe these people for me.

Mina: They are more Asian … I think they are Tibetan.

Reena: And how do you come to the decision of talking to them? Do you come to it yourself or are you assigned it?

Mina: My spirit knows.

Moving to the next significant event, Mina's body moves quite a bit and turns. Back in his body, Thomas finds that he's walked for a long time, and he is getting colder. At the end of the walk, he sees a building with a wooden door.

Mina: I'm going inside. It smells different.

Reena: What does it smell like?

Mina: [deep breath] I don't know – just different.

Reena: And tell me about the building you are in now.

Mina: It has very high ceilings and it's very long and there are doors off of each side of it.

Reena: What's it made of?

Mina: Mm … Wood and stone. There are paintings.

Reena: Tell me about the paintings.

Mina: [pause] I can't see it entirely. There are all these colours and there are figures. A lot of them.

Reena: And what's the most striking colour there?

Mina: It's blue … There is a young man and he's an Asian man … He doesn't have any hair. He's wearing a robe. He's leading me somewhere.

Reena: Where is he leading you to?

Mina: It's like a number of people and they're sitting and I'm going to sit with them. I think there's a man there who seems important and he's talking. They are showing me pictures.

Reena: What do these pictures represent?

Mina: [pause] It's of the body, the human body.

Reena: What's the significance of these pictures?

Mina: There's a seed, it's like a seed that's in all of us. We are talking about that ... It's a seed that's planted. It's the thing that ... He says it's the same in all of us.

Reena: Tell me more about the seed and the relationship with spirit and body.

Mina: The seed is the deepest thing there is ... and I think it's ours. But it is and it isn't.

Reena: And tell me about the importance of the seed to the Asian men and you.

Mina: We are discussing whether it is or it isn't. [laughs] It's funny because it either is or isn't and it doesn't make any sense inside the brain. But it's like an opening hole to an understanding ... that the form ... it's like the form is just a function. There's so much we don't know and don't understand.

Reena: And is this the main message that you've come to this place to spread?

Mina: I think it's actually them telling me this. I came to learn something.

Reena: I see. What is the most significant learning?

Mina: I Am That. I Am That ... I and That are the same. The form is a function of That and to connect to the seed we know. And there's an illumination ... There's a ... We are making ourselves so busy. It's always there.

Reena: And what do you do with this information, with this teaching?

Mina: I'm integrating it into my understanding. Then I'm going to go home.

Again, one of the main messages that permeates through all the regressions is that we are One – with Source or God. We are all a seed of divine, and there is no separation between ourselves, others and God. Our divinity is all the same. 'I AM' that 'I AM'. Mina's regression just consolidates this message.

The regression continues with Thomas being at his home.

Mina: [breathes deeply] There's a window and I'm lying down.
Reena: Where is home?
Mina: Near Saudi Arabia.
Reena: How many days did that journey take?
Mina: Hundreds (mostly walking).
Reena: And tell me more about your home.
Mina: It's made of clay, it's small … I think I'm alone. I don't see anybody else … I feel foreign. It's my home, but it's not my home.

As Thomas had entered this life whilst he was middle-aged, I wanted to know more about his life that led up to this point. So we went back to the first significant event that he was aware of. He accessed a memory of him being a little boy.

Mina: I have a brother.
Reena: How do you feel about your brother?
[Mina's face lights up as she chuckles happily. Later, she mentions that she could feel the bond and sweetness and the playfulness that they shared.]
Reena: Is he an older brother or younger brother?
Mina: I think we're the same.
Reena: How do you address your brother?
Mina: I want to call him Christian. I don't know why.
Reena: And how does he address you?
Mina: He calls me Thomas.

Later, in the debrief, Mina mentions that Thomas had a special childhood nickname for his brother, which would not leave her throat. For some reason, 'Christian' was the name that spontaneously popped out. Also, when asked if Christian's build was as big as Thomas, Mina responded that he's a little smaller, and softer and finer in general.

> Reena: And tell me more about your brother and your relationship with him.
> Mina: We're like the same. [long pause]
> Reena: Were you born to the same mother?
> Mina: Yes … Ma.
> Reena: Same father?
> Mina: Yes … Papa? Abba?
> Reena: And are there just the two of you with Mum and Dad or are there more in your family?
> Mina: I think there's more.

This is an interesting part of the regression because Thomas reveals both his name and the fact that he and Christian are blood twins. The name Thomas is derived from the Aramaic or Syriac 'Toma', equivalently from the Hebrew 'Teom', meaning 'twin'. The equivalent term for twin in Greek is 'Didymus'. The Nag Hammadi copy of the Gospel of Thomas begins: 'These are the secret sayings that the living Jesus spoke and Didymos Judas Thomas recorded.'[1] This is where we had the first clue that Mina's Thomas really could be the Apostle Thomas.

In the next significant event, Thomas goes to a point where he and his brother have grown into teenagers. He is aware that they have two more siblings – a brother and a sister. During this time, Thomas felt quite alone, and started to experience what seemed to be a shamanic event.

Mina: I don't know where I am and I feel like there's a ... predator, there's some kind of animal near me ... a not-so-nice animal.

Reena: What are you meant to do with this animal?

Mina: I just have to be very careful.

[In navigating Thomas to the most significant part of the encounter with the animal, Mina's body jerks.]

Reena: What's happened to your body?

Mina: [sighs; long pause] Um. It's like ... [sighs] It feels like the animal and I have joined ... energetically ... because I feel a lot stronger.

Reena: What sort of animal is it?

Mina: Some form of ... of ... cat. Big cat. I think I'm now a man ... I feel grown-up now. I just feel really strong. I'm not afraid any more.

What we can gather from Greg's account of Paul, Mia's account of James, Maya's account of Mary Magdalene, and now Mina's account of Thomas, is that children within this community seem to go through a coming-of-age ceremony to mark the change from boyhood to manhood. Whilst Paul's account was more in line with the Jewish tradition, Paul clearly was not comfortable with it. Whereas with Thomas, a shamanistic approach was used by way of a power animal, which he totally embraced. The following excerpt from the Crystalinks website made sense of it:

'In the shamanic world, everything is alive and connected, bearing an inherent virtue, power and wisdom. Power animals represent a person's interconnection to all life, their qualities of character and their power, their inner self. Humans find a symbiotic relationship with power animals especially as it relates to experiences in higher Consciousness. Power animals most often appear to humans in dreams, meditations, initiations and visualisations. In shamanism they could physically manifest briefly as if seeing a spirit.[2]

Thomas' spiritual journey did stress the connectedness and Oneness with all – and the connection to his power animal could very well be a step in his learning more about the Oneness and interconnectedness with all. At the end of the regression, when asked about the significance of the cat, Mina mentioned that cats are alone and strong ... and merging with the characteristics of the cat, his power animal, gave Thomas what he needed in his life moving forward.

Next, Thomas was navigated to the point that was the most significant between Christian and himself.

Mina: [in awe] It's so beautiful ... It's like our hearts are one.
Reena: Yours and Christian's?
Mina: [nods] We have the same understanding.
Reena: Did Christian also experience the cat?
Mina: I'm checking. [pause] I think there's something else for him. He's lighter than I am.
Reena: Does he share with you what he has to experience?
Mina: Yes. He sees through the veil.

At this point, we'd had a break and a debrief, due to the intensity of the session on Mina. The next day, as we were starting, Mina started to feel cold, and went back to being in the room where Thomas had first felt the connection with the Earth and sky and everyone around him.

Reena: Who are there?
Mina: Christian and James are there.
Reena: Who is James?

Mina: The other brother.

Reena: And your sister?

Mina: I think she's on the right?

When asked, Thomas could not remember how he had addressed her.

The identity of the name of Thomas' brother as James is fascinating. Some have seen in the Acts of Thomas (written in east Syria in the early third century, or perhaps as early as the first half of the second century) an identification of St Thomas with the Apostle Judas, brother of James.[3] The regression continues.

Reena: Do you know the person on your left?

Mina: I think it's Mark.

Reena: And who is Mark?

Mina: He's not a brother but he's one of the brothers.

Reena: So not a brother born by your mother. Is that what you're trying to say? [Mina nods] So how many other brothers are there that are not born of Mum?

Mina: [long pause] Eight. And from this, I think there's two or three women as well.

Reena: Can you tell me more about the women?

Mina: I know them all. [pause] I don't know their names.

Reena: That's fine. Just tell me what you feel about the relationship. Are they close to you?

Mina: All of us are close.

Reena: So there are eight other brothers, then the three of you, the blood brothers. So that's eleven, plus three women. Fourteen in all. [Mina affirms] And this room that you're in ... What's the significance of this room?

Mina: It's a place where we meet and we make it sacred together.
Reena: Have you been to this place often?
Mina: Yes.

This place being of significance to Thomas, I thought it would be good to find out a little more ... so I navigated him back to when he first was aware of being in this room.

Mina: I'm a little nervous.
Reena: Just roughly how old are you?
Mina: I think I'm a teenager.
Reena: And what happens next?
Mina: I'm being told something significant. I'm being told about the connections.
Reena: Who tells you?
Mina: It's Christian ... Jesus .... and he's telling about the connections. And I think that he reminds me of the connection that we had when we were children with one another. And I think that it's a special thing that we have with one another. But I can see that he is right.
[This was a key point when Thomas first refers to his twin brother as Jesus.]
Reena: And you're referring to him now as Jesus as opposed to Christian. Did the name change or what is the significance of this difference?
Mina: Yeah. He ends up having a different ... Hmm ... How do you call it? It's like he becomes more knowing, more wise.
Reena: And does this happen as part of *his* initiation? [Mina affirms] What was his initiation like?
Mina: I don't know exactly because I wasn't there.

Few texts identify Thomas' twin. In the Book of Thomas the Contender, part of the Nag Hammadi, it is said to be Jesus himself: 'Now, since it has been said that you are my twin and true companion, examine yourself ...'[4] Within this regression, the identification of James being Thomas' brother, and there being a sister, is consistent with accounts of Jesus' family structure given by the other regressees. Could Thomas the twin be this enigmatic brother, who's been given so many names by the others?

The reason why Mina could have spontaneously called Jesus 'Christian' could be illuminated by Flavius Josephus in his first-century *Antiquities of the Jews*. He made two claims that Jesus was called Christ (or Christos), and that 'Christian' referred to the followers of Christ.[5] Maybe Mina was making reference to Jesus being called Christ as she was tapping into the energetic connection of her brother, before he became 'wiser'. The regression continues.

Reena: And when you're there for the first time with him and he explains the connection, is anyone else there with you?

Mina: I'm pretty sure that James is there. Or somebody. I think it's James. I think there's other people that are there too. I don't know them.

Reena: Are you aware of how they got to that building?

Mina: [perplexed] No. I don't know ... I'm just feeling confused.

Reena: Tell me more about 'confused'?

Mina: It just feels like he (Jesus) is beyond my brother now.

Reena: And how does that make you feel?

Mina: I feel sad. [sighs heavily] It's not sad, it's ... it's a little empty, a little ...

Reena: Do you still feel that connection with him like you did when you were young?

Mina: Yes. But it's bigger than that. I can see at once he's different. He's changed. Perhaps I'm a bit jealous.

Reena: What are you jealous of?

Mina: Sharing.

Reena: Sharing him?

Mina: [affirms] But at the same time I can see that there's something beyond him there. It's just maybe a little unusual. [softly] It makes me question myself.

Reena: And what is it about yourself that you're questioning?

Mina: Just … just … this … whether to be this or that. There's a physical world to be part of.

At this point, we find that Thomas begins to query and doubt things. Tradition states that Thomas is best known for disbelieving Jesus' resurrection when first told of it, and demanding to feel his wounds before being convinced, thus earning his the title 'Doubting Thomas'.[6] However, from this regression, it is clear to see that his doubts started before because of this big change in connection he felt with his twin brother, Jesus, and balancing between the physical realities that he is used to, and the spiritual world that his brother is leading. What made this even more interesting is that before being regressed to Thomas, Mina said that in her current life existence she had no idea that he was known as Doubting Thomas before this regression.

The regression continues to when we went to the point when Thomas made his decision.

Mina: I'm outside.

Reena: Are you a little older? [Mina affirms] And tell me more about outside.

Mina: It feels like the sky is opening up ... My heart feels more open ... Now I know it's true, the fact that everything is the same.

Reena: And what do you decide then?

Mina: [resolutely] I have to share the message.

Reena: Are you alone?

Mina: Yes. I went to find out for myself how I felt about it.

Reena: And now that you know that you have to share the message, how does that make you feel?

Mina: I feel good, I feel full.

In the next significant event, Thomas watches Jesus healing people with the energy through his hands, where he allows the energy to flow freely through him. Thomas is amazed and confused with what he is witnessing.

Mina: There's a part of me that thinks it's not possible. [pause] But I can *see* it is possible. And he's just ... he was just normal before.

Reena: Do you share your confusion and your thoughts with Jesus?

Mina: Not all of it but some of it.

Reena: And how does he respond?

Mina: He says, 'Trust me, brother.' [laughs] And he knows that my heart has had a hard time. But he is very compassionate. And I feel softer then.

At the next significant event, Thomas is at the birth of Jesus' child.

Reena: Who's giving birth?

Mina: I think it is. [pause] It's so beautiful.

Reena: And did she give birth to a boy or a girl?

Mina: It's definitely a boy.

Reena: And how do you address the woman?

Mina: I call her Mary.

Reena: And is it their first child? [Mina affirms] And what is the most significant part of this event?

Mina: I have a connection with this boy. I will care for him. I will have to care for him at some point. And that's just ... We are connected ...

Reena: It's nice to have such a close connection. This connection you feel for the boy: is it something similar you share with Christian? [Mina affirms] Do you share this connection with anyone else?

Mina: No.

This account is an inconsistency with the other regressions, where Jesus' and Mary's first child is a daughter. However, according to Laurence Gardner, if Jesus was the royal successor of the Davidic Lineage, the dynastic succession would terminate unless he had a son.[7] So whilst the daughter was their first biological child, the birth of Jesus' son was very significant as he was the first child that would continue the dynastic line. This could account for why Thomas meant that their first child is male.

The next significant event sees Thomas travelling, but he does not know why and where. Jesus is not there. Thomas thinks that Jesus was killed through his body being tortured.

Reena: What happened to his spirit, even though his body's been tortured?

Mina: It's still there. I know he's fine.

Reena: Do you connect with his spirit through the process of torture?
Mina: As I always have been ... We can merge.
Reena: And can you merge at this moment?
Mina: [affirms] I can see it really clearly that the body is just one form. You can go beyond it. I have mixed emotions about it. I understand but I am still sad about it.

At the debrief after the regression, Mina said, 'I don't feel like he was *on* the cross. I mean, I know just from knowing Christianity that they say he was on the cross, but the only thing that came out of my mouth was that he was tortured. It was just that he was tortured, not that it was that image of him hanging on the cross dying. I didn't have an image of him hanging there.'

This is consistent with the other regressions that Jesus was not hung on the cross. Mia's James and Maya's Mary Magdalene mentioned that he was tortured to the point of near-death, but substituted on the cross, a turn of events orchestrated by James – and after which Jesus was healed through the ministrations of Mary Magdalene and Mother Mary.

Thomas' knowing of Jesus' spirit and Consciousness being fine, whilst his body was in pain, is also very similar to Mary Magdalene's sense of being split and confused when she was witnessing the crucifixion – where half of her grieved for the death of her husband and the other half felt he was fine. These similar experiences are consistent with James secretly orchestrating the substitution and only informing the family afterwards.

This is probably why there is nothing in the Gospels of Thomas to indicate the notion that Jesus died for people's sins and then rose again.[8] The regression continues.

> Reena: And does he have a message for you in this spirit form? [Mina affirms] And what is the message for you?
> Mina: He just says serve with those who want to know and share with those who want to know.

In the next significant event, Thomas is in a place he calls 'Arab', with a lot of people who have diseases. Arab is not the land that he grew up in, but where his current home is. This is eerily consistent with Mia's account when James mentioned that his second brother went south after the crucifixion, never to be heard from again.

> Reena: So what is it about this land that drew you there?
> Mina: I don't know. My body just knew to come. My soul knew to come.
> Reena: OK, that's fine. Tell me more about the disease. Is it a disease of the skin, the organs, the mind?
> Mina: It's everything. It's all connected. You mostly see it on the outside of the body ... [wrinkling her nose] It smells.

The disease that Thomas is referring to could quite probably be leprosy, as symptoms include loss of skin pigment, odour, and an apparent outbreak of papules. The Mesopotamians became familiar with leprosy during the third millennium BC. It was already becoming globally distributed in the seventh century BC, and was unquestionably present in Palestine by the fourth century BC.[9] What is fascinating about Thomas' take on the disease is that whilst the symptoms were physiological, he took a holistic view on the cause of it.

The regression continues.

> Reena: And what drew you here to this place?
> Mina: Just the direction. And there's spirit here. There's a strong one. It's almost like the land has spirit here …
> And there's close connection between people. And the land as well.
> Reena: How did they receive you?
> Mina: I find the right people … For sharing the …
> [pause]
> Reena: … the message of the connection? [Mina affirms] And they are receptive? [Mina affirms] OK.

Afterwards, at the debrief, I asked Mina to identify the country that Thomas had gone to. She said it was Syria. Timeline-wise, during the regression she confirmed he was in Syria after he had been to Tibet, and both before and after the death of Jesus. He had been to Tibet before the death of Jesus.

The timeline of Thomas' travels is especially significant. He is known as the only Apostle who went outside the Roman Empire to preach the Gospel, in Syria, ancient Persia and as far as India. Logistically, the route between the Roman world and India, which was Rome's source for large quantities of fine muslins, pearls and spices, was well established. So it is feasible that Thomas did go to Tibet, as Mina recalls. However, there does seem to be some controversy as to when Thomas went to south Asia, and where in India he stopped.

According to tradition, it was from the ancient city of Antioch in Syria that St Thomas the Apostle was commissioned to take the Gospel eastward. On a trading vessel plying between Alexandria and the Malabar Coast, St Thomas the Apostle reportedly arrived in Kodungallur in AD52. It is also commonly believed that St Thomas established seven churches in south India before being martyred in Mylapore (near Madras) in AD72.[10]

However, on 27 September 2006, Pope Benedict XVI gave a speech in the Vatican in which he recalled an ancient tradition claiming that Thomas first evangelised Syria and Persia, then went on to western India, from where Christianity also reached southern India, inferring that Thomas did not go to south India. Since this statement was perceived to be a direct violation of the religious beliefs of many St Thomas Christians in India, they condemned it.[11]

Our regression takes this controversy one step further. According to Mina, Thomas travelled to Tibet before the crucifixion, and lived in Syria before and after the crucifixion. Whilst this is in line with Mia's regression as James, where he was not aware of his second brother being there during the crucifixion, whether Thomas made another trip to south Asia after the crucifixion is unknown. However, given the number of days that it had taken for him to go to Tibet in the first place, it would seem unlikely that he would make the long arduous trip twice. The regression continues.

At this point, Thomas was navigated to the point just before his heart stopped beating. He finds himself outdoors, still in Arab (later identified as Syria) – and there is water not too far away.

Mina: There's people coming after me. I think they might have something … It's like they're military but I don't think they're military.
Reena: Who do you think they are?

Mina: [sighs heavily; long pause] I don't really know … I don't know these people.

Reena: And are you aware of why they're after you?

Mina: They're not connected.

Reena: To the energies? [Mina affirms] What is the significance of that to them coming after you?

Mina: They think I'm lying.

Reena: Does it threaten them in any way?

Mina: Yes … It's not their understanding. I've been shot by something. I'm very old.

Reena: Where in your body have you been shot?

Mina: Chest.

Reena: And what do they shoot you with?

Mina: It's like a form of arrow … spear-like.

Reena: And what happens next?

Mina: They're standing right above me. They're watching me die. It's OK.

Tradition holds that Thomas was indeed killed by four soldiers armed with spears, a fact not known by Mina before the regression. However, again, Mina's recollection is that Thomas was martyred in Syria, and not south India – as tradition would have it.[12] What is also interesting is that Mia's James accounted that Thomas was killed by Roman soldiers – which is consistent with historical accounts that during those times, what we now know as Syria was occupied by the Romans.

Once Thomas' heart stopped beating, I checked to see if his spirit had left the body, or if it was still holding on to the body.

Mina: It's still holding the body.

Reena: Where in your body is the spirit still being held on to?

Mina: Right behind the sternum … They're picking me up – those men.

As the sternum was still holding on to the trauma of the piercing, I then used body therapy, a therapeutic aspect of regression, to help shift the energy. I simulated the spear using my hands, and directed Mina's hands to hold on to mine and pull – as though she was pulling out the spear. When she pulled it out, Mina groaned and coughed – an indication that her body was expelling the trapped energy of being speared.

Finally, Thomas' spirit was released from the body and he travels to the Spirit Realms where he met and merged with the soul of Jesus.

Thomas' existence is pertinent for us because even when he felt unsure, jealous and doubting, he searched within himself to find what he resonated with. Only when he was sure, did he live out the principles of Jesus' teachings. Nobody forced him to choose a path, not even Jesus. Thomas was also physically quite alone throughout his whole journey. However, he is inspiring because he never felt alone because he was energetically connected to Jesus, the Earth, the sky and everyone and everything around him.

This connection and self-resolution enabled him to take the teachings of Jesus further than anyone else who was close to Jesus at that point.

Through Mina, Jesus also advises us not to fear those who do not know The Way because we will make waves though our actions – 'The Way' is to illuminate, for even the smallest waves of illumination can enable them to Be with and in Light.

10

FORGOTTEN

It's never too late to be what you might have been
– George Eliot

Rose resides in Singapore, and I got to know her fairly well while I was living there. When I moved, we kept in regular touch. During one of those conversations, Rose told me that she had gone to see a psychic who told her that she had experienced a life during biblical times. I told her that when I visited Singapore, I would regress her to that life, so we could explore it.

The opportunity presented itself four years later. I was visiting Singapore, and I dropped Rose a note to see if she would be willing to explore this life, and share the regression in the book. As with all the other participants, she agreed on the condition of anonymity.

What unfolded was yet another unexpected twist in this journey – she went back to the life of Sara (Tamar), the daughter of Jesus and Mary Magdalene.

She entered the life in a female body of a child of five, who was aware of her little feet being bare. Her very thin body was wrapped in some cloth that was rougher than a blanket. Her long, browny/red hair was wet after bathing. She noticed that she was on a beach, where she'd been bathing, and there were lots of happy people, who were bathing too. It seemed to her that it was like a gathering, a festival.

Reena: Is there a significance to the bathing? Or was it more for fun?

Rose: I don't really understand by the … it was fun but I don't think it was *for* fun.

[She was also aware that whilst she knew everybody at this gathering, her family members were also present.]

Reena: Who is the most significant person you are aware of at the moment that you can see?

Rose: I think it is my aunt … Mara. She put the blanket around me, so she's standing with me.

Reena: Did she bathe with you?

Rose: Hmm … No.

Reena: Who else are you aware of around you?

Rose: Now I see my dad. [giggles delightedly] I love my dad so much. Everybody loves my dad.

Reena: How do you address your dad?

Rose: Ya'Ya.

Reena: Ya'Ya, OK … and how does Ya'Ya address you?

Rose: Lamb, 'my lamb'.

Reena: That's very sweet. How does that make you feel?

Rose: Special.

Reena: Who else are you aware of now? Mara, Ya'Ya …

Rose: There's so much love here. So much love. I'm just really happy … I don't think my mother's here.

Reena: How does that make you feel?

Rose: OK.

Reena: How do you normally address your mother?

Rose: Mama.

Reena: Is there anything else of significance?

Rose: Hmm… [pause] The sun is really, really beautiful but … I just know this is a special moment. The Light is very beautiful … I can feel that. Everybody feels it.

Reena: Tell me more about this Light ... and what you can feel and what it is doing to you ...

Rose: I look at my Ya'Ya and he's in the middle of everybody, and everybody is feeling the Light. It's more of a feeling than a ... I just know it's important.

Reena: What is Ya'Ya doing in the middle?

Rose: It looks like he's praying ... Everyone else is praying now.

Reena: Are you praying as well?

Rose: No, I'm just watching them.

Reena: How about Mara?

Rose: No, she's just standing by me.

Reena: What are they praying about?

Rose: I don't know.

Reena: What's happening with the Light as everybody prays?

Rose: Well, there's a lot of Light. It's very golden, it's very light, it's yellow. Everybody is just very still.

Reena: How does this Light affect you?

Rose: We will all carry this Light.

Reena: What's the significance of this Light that you are carrying?

Rose: I will always remember.

At the end, Rose reveals that what Sara had experienced with the Light was the Oneness. It's almost like she could see the Light connecting everybody. Whilst in her past-life body of the five-year-old child, she could not explain it very well. She could feel it so strongly, and could see the connection between all of the people. 'It was almost like a hazy light over the whole scene. It was just so beautiful,' Rose said.

In the next significant event, she is in her room, in her bed, on the floor. It's dark and she is awake. Her Aunt Mara is there with her, sleeping on the floor. She also shares the room with whom she first identifies as Mara's three-year-old boy whom she refers to as her cousin. This identification changes a little later. He is very cute, and is always asleep. She is still five. She described the room as a place where others sleep in, but at the moment there is no one else there, including Ya'Ya and Mama.

Rose: I can hear people talking outside the room.
Reena: And what are they saying?
Rose: I can't hear but I am worried. Everybody seems worried ... I can feel it in my tummy.
Reena: And how many different voices can you hear from the outside?
Rose: It's a load of people. Ya'Ya's there ... Deep, calm voice. My mama is there too. [worried laughter] She has a nice voice. Oh! My tummy's so worried ...!
Reena: What are you worried about?
Rose: I don't know, I just feel it. Everybody's acting strange ... Hmm ... not happy like before.
Reena: Any other voice you recognise from outside?
Rose: I can hear an angry voice; I don't know who it is.
Reena: Can you hear what the angry voice is saying?
Rose: No. But [my] tummy's worried ... I'm going to go in there. [cheeky laughter] I think they will see me. I'm going to go in there and I'm going to sit on my Ya'Ya's lap. I think it's a good plan [laughter] ... I go in. Woah! There's a lot of people. There's a light in there that makes my eyes ... [Rose squints]
Reena: Are there as many people there as by the beach?
Rose: No, no. But Ya'Ya looks at me. [He] smiles at me, it's OK. I knew he would do that. Mama's looking a little bit cross at me [laughter] but it's OK...

Reena: … because you're Ya'Ya's little lamb!

Rose: It's OK, I'm all right, I'm sitting on his lap now.

Reena: Does he hold you tight?

Rose: Yeah.

Reena: What else are you aware of?

Rose: I'm looking at the people.

Reena: Anyone you are familiar with?

Rose: I don't want to look at them, I'm just going to look in a minute. It's a very bright light.

After the session, Rose mentioned that Sara did not want to look at things because it was a way of diverting attention away from things that made her uncomfortable and the wriggling went with that escapism that she was trying too hard to master.

This is common when someone is regressed back to being a child – they embody the traits and characteristics of that child. So, it was a matter of directing Rose's focus to someone close and familiar, asking simple questions, to make her feel safe, for the regression to continue and more details to be obtained.

Reena: What we can do is maybe focus on Mama and help describe Mama to me?

Rose: She's a bit angry with me … She's not really, she's smiling at me. Oh, Mama.

Reena: What colour is Mama's hair?

Rose: It's like orange.

Reena: Is she pretty or …

Rose: Yeah. Course! She's wearing green, I think it's green, maybe she has a green blanket.

Reena: Is she slim and slender or is …?

Rose: I can't see. She has a blanket on! [laughing] But I think so, yeah. Oh. No! She's got a fat belly … I know about that, though, it's OK. She's got a baby … I think that's why she has a blanket around her, she's like … [demonstrates the size of Mama's belly using her hands]
Reena: How about Ya'Ya, is Ya'Ya fat as well or …? [Rose shakes head] No. Tell me about Ya'Ya's face.
Rose: It's a beautiful face.
Reena: Tell me about Ya'Ya's eyes.
Rose: They're very kind.
Reena: What colour is Ya'Ya's hair?
Rose: Brown.
Reena: What do you feel about the baby in Mama's fat belly? Do you feel happy, or a bit worried, or …?
Rose: I don't really know. I think happy.
Reena: How do people address Ya'Ya, do you know?
Rose: Yeshua.
Reena: And how do people address Mama?
Rose: My lady. Lady. Mary … Mary. (pause) Yeshua [big sigh]

Once she was comfortable with her environment, we could then go back to the regression.

Reena: Can you focus on the people now?
Rose: I am very shy.
Reena: Just to see if you recognise anyone.
Rose: Well, there's Uncle John, I thought that before but I don't know if that's right, I think so. I know [inaudible] but I don't know their name … Ya'Ya's doing the love thing.
Reena: Tell me about the love thing.

Rose: Well, it's like … it just makes everything feel all right. Everybody's OK.

Reena: The group of people, are there men and women?

Rose: Just Mama, and men.

Reena: So Mama is the only woman, and you of course.

Rose: I'm not a woman! [laughing]

Reena: No. [laughs] Are you a girl? [Rose nods] What happens next after Ya'Ya does the love thing?

Rose: I think I fall asleep.

[In the next significant event she sees things in her mind.]

Rose: I don't think I'm very good at it yet but I see a lot of colours and then I'm seeing … I think I'm dreaming because I feel like I'm in a crowd of people but I'm not really in a crowd of people but I can see the people … because I don't feel any emotion. I just see the crowd of people … lots of people … I feel like I'm below them looking up at them … but I don't feel like I'm there. It's really interesting in my mind.

Reena: So what is your mind sharing with you?

Rose: I see patterns and … I like to do this a lot I think.

Reena: When you see patterns what happens to the people?

Rose: There's no people now.

Reena: How do you feel when this happens?

Rose: I feel good.

Reena: What is the significance of seeing these images in the mind for you?

Rose: It's just something I do.

[Intrigued by what she was experiencing, I wanted to explore more. I wondered if this was something unique to the child Rose had regressed back to, or whether all

children experienced these visions. So I directed her to
the most significant part of the images of her mind.]
Rose: It's so bright. (squinting) I'm not seeing anything;
I'm just feeling a funny … a funny feeling here. Can I
show you? Here, here … [pointing to the area between
her eyebrows – traditionally known as the third eye]
Now I see an eye … [takes deep breaths]
Reena: Are you OK with this eye? [Rose affirms] So
what is happening with this eye now?
Rose: I'm seeing now this beautiful blue and white Light
and the Light tells me everything is going to be OK … I
can't see the eye now.

I was rather startled by this revelation of a blue and white light
communicating with Rose, as Maya too remembered that a
blue light had approached Mary Magdalene and had given her
messages when she was a girl. Was this a familial connection
or was it a specific Consciousness that held and guided these
two ladies, as their paths were so connected? The regression
continues.

Reena: What happens next?
Rose: I can hear screaming.
Reena: How does that make you feel?
Rose: The Light told me everything would be OK.
Reena: Where are you when the screaming happens?
Rose: I'm in my bedroom.
Reena: Who's screaming?
Rose: I think it's my mum …. My aunt is with me and
she's crying.
Reena: Do you understand what is happening? [Rose
shakes head] … just tell me what happens next.

Rose: I think I don't want to tell you. I don't think I want to remember.

Rose was clearly upset and in trauma, and thus did not feel safe remembering the event. As a child, this is understandable, where they would rather not face what is clearly very difficult, just to cope. So, as part of the therapeutic process, I just got her to fire off a pre-set anchor of love and joy, which would make her feel safe to continue.

Rose: He left me ... Ya'Ya.
Reena: Tell me more about Ya'Ya leaving you. Where did Ya'Ya go?
Rose: He went to be with his father ... and he left me. [sobbing]

She was understandably upset with what had happened, and so I just gave her space and time to allow all that suppressed emotion to come out. This too is a therapeutic part of the regression, as it enables the gentle release of pent-up and suppressed emotions that are unhealthy for people to hold and carry. After the regression Rose admitted that the strength, depth and intensity of the emotion took her by surprise, which is what happens where someone is experiencing memories as opposed to making something up. The regression continues.

Rose: The voice in my head said that everything will be OK, it's not OK ... [long pause, upset] I'm very angry.
Reena: You're angry because Ya'Ya left to be with his father ...
Rose: Yes.
Reena: How old are you now, sweetheart?

Rose: I think I'm five.

At the debrief, Rose mentioned that this was the most significant event for little Sara. She felt an enormous sense of betrayal because she was assured that everything was going to be all right, but immediately after, she was told that Ya'Ya had left her to meet his father. So she felt some strong intense emotions that she, as a five-year-old, could not articulate too well.

This is consistent with Maya's recollection as Mary Magdalene, that Sara (or Tamar) was indeed alive, and a mere child, at the time of Jesus' crucifixion. She also confirms that her mother was pregnant, which is consistent with Maya's regression. Whilst some scholars speculate that their first child was born after the crucifixion in AD33,[1] these regressions are more in line with the speculation that the crucifixion took place in AD37,[2] when Sara (or Tamar) was a mere toddler and Mary was pregnant with their second child.

On another note, I found her turn of phrase 'Ya'Ya left to meet his father' an interesting one to communicate his passing. The Zadokite priests, who were prevalent within the Essene Community that Jesus was part of, belonged to the division of 'Abijah', meaning 'my father is Yahweh'.[3] Yahweh is the Hebrew name of God. So, by saying that Ya'Ya had left to meet his father, she was expressing that he left to meet God. The regression continues.

Rose: Mama's very sad.
Reena: Are you still in the room, in the house? [Rose shakes her head] No? Where are you?
Rose: Outside. By my tree.
Reena: Are you alone there or is Aunty Mara and ... [Rose shakes her head] no. Mara and Mama are not

there [Rose nods] ... by yourself. [Rose nods] ... Where are Mama and Mara?

Rose: Inside. I don't want to talk to the voice in my head. It told me everything would be all right.

Reena: And it's not ... [Rose shakes her head] And just tell me what happens next.

Rose: [long pause] All the women are there. Everybody is crying.

Reena: You've gone into your house now?

Rose: Yep.

Reena: Mama's crying as well? ... [Rose nods] And who else is there?

Rose: I'm going to Mama ...

Reena: You're going to Mama ... and what happens next.

Rose: The light came ... It's Ya'Ya's Light.

Reena: And what is Ya'Ya's Light doing?

Rose: It's making everybody stop crying. I can see Ya'Ya and he says everything is going to be all right ... I can see him.

Reena: What happens next?

Rose: We have to eat, we're hungry.

Reena: Can Mama see Ya'Ya? [Rose nods] And what's Mama doing when she sees Ya'Ya?

Rose: She's smiling. We're hungry. We didn't eat for a while.

Reena: How did Ya'Ya leave to meet his father? Did you see him do this or did someone tell you?

Rose: Mama told me.

Reena: Did Mama see Ya'Ya leaving to be with his father?

Rose: I think so.

Reena: Was she in the house when she saw Ya'Ya?
[Rose shakes her head] No. She was somewhere else?
[Rose nods] So did someone stay in the house with you?
Or did you go with Mama?

Rose: I think I went with Mama ... I see my grandma.

Reena: Tell me about your grandma.

Rose: She's beautiful. She's very sad. Everybody's very
sad but I can hear Ya'Ya saying it's going to be OK.

Reena: Where are you? Are you inside or outside?

Rose: Outside ... I feel OK.

Reena: But Grandma is sad ... is Mama sad? [Rose
affirms, hands twitching]

Reena: Is someone holding your hand or ...?

Rose: I have my head in my hands ... I'm not looking.

Reena: What are you not looking at?

Rose: There's people.

Reena: What's stopping you from looking at the people?

Rose: My Mama. She is carrying me.

Reena: Just tell me what happens next.

Rose: [upset] I sing to myself. There's lots of noise. I
don't like it so I'm just going to sing to myself.

Reena: OK, you can sing out loud if you want.

Rose: No ... La la la! [singing]

Reena: Where did you learn the song from?

Rose: I'm just making it up.

Reena: How do you address your grandma?

Rose: I don't know. I think she's Mary. We call her
Mary.

Reena: You call her Mary, OK. Is that how you address
her or is that her name?

Rose: It's her name ... I have a secret name; I can't tell
you. [smiling cheekily]

Reena: Oh, you have a secret name you can't tell me ... well, go on then.

Rose: No. I can't remember it.

Reena: Oh, that's all right. [laughter] What's the significance of the secret name? Is it special?

Rose: Yes, it's a secret!

Reena: What makes this secret name special?

Rose: Just for her and me.

Reena: When she's not calling you by your secret name how does she address you?

Rose: Sarah ... Sara ... I call her Sarey. I told you!

Reena: Is that the secret name?

Rose: Shhh! [giggling] She calls me Sarey too.

Reena: [whispers] We won't tell anyone, it's just our little secret. All right then, so, you're outside ... what happens next, you're singing to yourself ...

Rose: Yeah, I don't want to hear them. The crying ... Somebody takes me.

Reena: Do they carry you?

Rose: [affirms] Think I'm going home.

Reena: What do you do when you're at home?

Rose: Everybody's talking, I don't really understand.

Reena: Where's Sarey, is she there? And Mama and Mara? [Rose affirms] And what are you doing when everyone is talking ... can you hear everyone talking? Are you in the same room?

Rose: Yes, but they're not talking loudly ... I'm with Mama. It's not our house, I don't know where we are.

Reena: Is your cousin there?

Rose: [affirms] They're going to go out.

Reena: Who's going to go out? You? [Rose shakes her head] Everyone? [Rose nods] Do you go with them?

[Rose shakes her head] No … Is Mama going? [Rose nods] And just tell me what happens next.

Rose: I don't want them to go out … It's not my house.

Reena: Did someone stay with you? [Rose affirms] Who stays with you?

Rose: I can't remember … it starts with 'L' … I go to bed. I'm waiting for Mama.

Then, I took her slightly forward to just after she finished waiting for Mama, and when I asked her to tell me what she was aware of, she cheekily laughed and said 'No'. I persevered.

Reena: What's happening with Mama?

Rose: She's happy! She's hugging me.

Reena: How are you feeling?

Rose: Happy.

Reena: Does Mama tell you what is making her happy? [Rose shakes head] No … OK, so tell me what happens next [Rose smiles, a big smile] … What's making you smile?

Rose: Ya'Ya. He's there.

Reena: Ya'Ya's there?! I thought Ya'Ya left to see his father.

Rose: He did.

Reena: But he's there now. Can you see him?

Rose: I feel his light. I can see him. He's smiling at me. He says everything is going to be OK. He's right behind Mama. He's touching her … Mm … he's very light. [deep breaths]

Reena: Is he in light form or body form?

Rose: I think he's in a body … and he's touching Mama … So much light! [Rose moves about]

Reena: How is this light affecting you and your body?

Rose: It's OK.
Reena: What's the significance of this light? [Rose is still moving about]
Rose: I don't know.

At the debrief, Rose, with the consciousness and language of a grown woman explained that what she felt was love – divine love. 'And so, trying to explain it as a little girl, I couldn't really describe it very well but it was really like … the feeling of it … my God, it was just so amazing,' she explained.

She also said that her body was wriggling so much as Sara because she felt like a little child holding too much energy in the body.

The next significant event found Sara in her head again, where it is all golden, bright and beautiful this time.

Reena: What's the significance of this golden light, do you know?
Rose: Mm … it connects me.
Reena: Connects you to what?
Rose: God.
Reena: And when you are in your head and the golden light is there connecting you to God, what's happening around you, do you know? [Rose shakes head] You don't know, OK. That's it, really feel this connection now, this deep connection with God …
Rose: I see God. He's smiling at me. He's blue.

This again startles me because the consistency with what Mary Magdalene's spiritual experience was as a child is just so palpable.

Reena: Does he have a face?

Rose: Yes! [laughs] He's smiling at me! Doesn't God smile at you?

Reena: I'm sure God does [laughing] … so just describe God's face to me …

Rose: I can't see him now. It's just a face and it's blue … it has an eye. He has one eye and a smile. God is showing me pictures … I can't see yet, I just see that it's opening into pictures. Ooh, it's so pretty … I can hear God's voice.

Reena: What is God saying?

Rose: 'Just wait' – I'm getting impatient. [laughs] I want to see. I'm just seeing a load of colours and I'm seeing a lot of swirling and it looks like it's clearing. And I'm seeing a brilliant light, like a flashing diamond light.

Reena: What's the significance of this flashing diamond light?

Rose: I don't know.

Sara stayed experiencing the Light for a while, so I navigated her to the end of it.

Rose: [after a long pause] I'm feeling very, very, very peaceful. I'm not seeing anything.

At the debrief, Rose explained that Sara had spent a lot of time in that state of connection, with God, and with the Eye that she visualised. Sara did not realise, nor could she understand, that not everyone experienced this state of connection. This was a Consciousness unique to Sara. From a navigation perspective, it was interesting breaking her out of that connection to move her down to the timeline of her physical existence. Rose echoed the sentiment: 'It just did seem that she was in quite a lot of that space … like when you would say, "Go to the next thing", almost it was like "What? What next thing?" It was almost confusing in there, going, "Well, what do you mean because I'm still here?"'

The next significant event took us to the point of the birth of the baby in Mama's fat belly.

> Rose: It's funny. The belly, it's very fat. [giggling] … [I'm] happy.
> Reena: You're happy. Tell me more about happy, what's made you happy?
> Rose: Baby.
> Reena: Where are you, indoors or outdoors?
> Rose: Indoors.
> Reena: And where's Ya'Ya? [Rose shrugs] Don't know? OK. Mama? She's there? [Rose nods] What is she doing?
> Rose: She's got the baby … [She's] happy.
> Reena: Does she show you the baby?
> Rose: Yeah.
> Reena: Can you tell me if the baby is a girl or a boy?
> Rose: A boy.
> Reena: Does Mama tell you the baby's name? [Rose shakes her head] No. OK, is anyone else there besides Mama?
> Rose: Aunty [Mara].
> Reena: And what's Mara doing?
> Rose: Working.
> Reena: How old are you?
> Rose: Maybe six now.

It was revealed that Ya'Ya was not around at the birth of this child. Sara did not have an awareness of where he was.

The next significant event moves us on to when Sara was either thirteen or fifteen. She has a plait and she sees water and a mountain far away. The air is colder, and she had long sleeves. She confirms that she is not at the same place that she was at the age of five and six. Her feet are cold and they have rough-looking sheepskin boots to keep them warm.

Rose: I think I am in a boat.

Reena: Are you alone in the boat? [Rose shakes her head] Who else is with you in the boat?

Rose: Mm … boys.

Reena: Who are the boys?

Rose: The baby is big now.

Reena: How old is that baby boy that's big now?

Rose: I don't know … maybe six or something.

Reena: How do you address him?

Rose: David. I think. Davey?

Reena: How about the other boy?

Rose: It's James.

Reena: So who is this James in relation to you?

Rose: He's my brother.

Reena: And how old is James?

Rose: I think he's about nine.

Reena: So Davey's the youngest? James is nine, second, and you are the eldest … is that right?

Rose: I don't remember him very well.

At Sara being thirteen, James being nine and Davey being kind of six, Rose's account of age is very similar to Laurence Gardner's theory that all three children of Jesus and Mary Magdalene were born by AD44, with Tamar being the eldest (born AD33), the second son that he calls Jesus Justus being four years younger, and the youngest, that he refers to as Josephes, being eleven years younger.[4]

Reena: OK, what emotion do you feel being in the boat?
Rose: Nervous. I don't know where we're going.
Reena: Who else is there in the boat besides you?
Rose: Mama's there. Uncle.
Reena: How do you address Uncle?
Rose: Uncle.
Reena: Is it a big boat or a little boat?
Rose: A little boat.
Reena: Is Ya'Ya anywhere around? [Rose shakes head] Where's Ya'Ya?
Rose: He will come.
Reena: So it's just you, the boys, Mama, Uncle … anyone else?
Rose: There are eight people.
Reena: Do you recognise any of the other three?
Rose: [pause] Simon.
Reena: Anyone else you recognise?
Rose: There's John, but a different John.
Reena: Do you recognise that last person?
Rose: Aunty. [Rose's face softens visibly and she smiles softly]
Reena: You're very close to Aunty, aren't you? [Rose nods emphatically.

This deep love that Sara had for her Aunty Mara is consistent with Sally's account as Marta, where she felt as though Sara was her own, due to the closeness she felt towards her. This does make sense, because Sara does admit that her Aunty Mara (Marta) took care of her a lot.

At this point, I thought it was prudent to bring the regression to an end as we had been at it for a while. So, using the deep love she felt towards her aunt, I anchored that trance depth and event for us to revisit the next day.

Completely associated within the body and personality of the five-year-old, Sara could only communicate with me what she perceived in the words and behaviour of a five-year-old. Her voice was soft and young, her language was sweet and charming, and her body wriggled a lot. Whilst this provided great insight to her personality at the time, I also wanted more of a detached observer's perspective to understand her experience better. So before bringing Rose out of trance, I disassociated her from her personality and body as that sweet, charming little girl and took her to a safe place to have a debrief of that aspect of her five-year-old life.

Reena: So, what is the significance of the diamond Light? For little Sara?
Rose: It was the beginning of her opening of her connection to God, All That Is.
Reena: I just want to find out about that bathing that happened at the start, was that like a bathing ritual?
Rose: It was the baptism.
Reena: Ah, it was the baptism, OK.
Rose: She was hearing voices but she couldn't explain … she was able to speak the words and the tongues, she didn't want to do it, and she didn't want to do it then and she didn't want to do it now. [laughs]
Reena: What was stopping her from doing it then and now?
Rose: Persecution, ridicule … she was a lot of time in that space. She was able to bring a lot of information through but at that age she couldn't write it down. So

there was a level of frustration in trying to explain what it was.

Reena: Those pictures that were coming through that God asked her to be a bit patient with, what sort of pictures were they?

Rose: It was before the pictures were clear.

Reena: As she got older did the pictures become clearer?

Rose: Yes.

Reena: So, if you can, give me a sense of when it started to get clear ... was she a teenager?

Rose: Yes.

Reena: OK. Could she speak of this to Ya'Ya and Mama?

Rose: Yes. They understood.

Reena: Did she speak of it when she was a little child or only when she was older?

Rose: She did speak of it but she thought it was normal that everyone could do it so it wasn't really ... she would not really speak about it ... it wasn't something she thought was interesting ... that's the only way I can explain it.

Reena: That makes sense. OK, was there anything I missed that we need to revisit?

Rose: Yes. Crucifixion. Something was missed.

Reena: Is this when Ya'Ya went to be with his father?

[Rose nods]

This was interesting because it was in line with Mary Magdalene's account that she was pregnant and had her daughter for a tiny while at the crucifixion, before Sara was handed to a relative. I also wanted to gather a few more details from Sara's memories as a five-year-old, when Ya'Ya left to be with his father, so it was perfect to go back there. Earlier there was a shutdown, when Sara, completely associated in her body, as her five-year-old self, could not remember. This is understandable as this is the point of trauma for this little girl, where, in her mind, her daddy whom she loved so dearly, and who loved her so much, had left her. So, to make her feel safe, I built in some safety mechanisms and allowed her to watch what was happening from a more disassociative state – separating her mind from her emotions and fears.

> Rose: I did look. It didn't look like Ya'Ya.
> Reena: Who didn't look like Ya'Ya?
> Rose: Ya'Ya.
> Reena: Ya'Ya didn't look like Ya'Ya. So just describe this [Rose shakes her head] No? [fidgety, nervous movements] When did Ya'Ya not look like Ya'Ya?
> Rose: When he was there on the thing. [hands stretched out as though on the cross]
> Reena: Just describe what he looked like.
> Rose: It was like ... [sigh; pause] I looked and it was like, when I look all I see is light so I can't see when you tell me to look.
> Reena: Ah, OK, OK. But that person didn't look like Ya'Ya. When you did see this person who didn't look like Ya'Ya, what was his face like?
> Rose: I couldn't see his face.
> Reena: Because of the Light ...

Rose gestured to her eyes, that were squinting as though a big bright light was shining at them. So, I asked her to imagine having a really strong pair of sunglasses that can see past the light. Creative metaphors like this are a therapeutic technique to get more information about what is happening in a traumatic situation.

Reena: And what is it you are aware of now?
Rose: It doesn't look like Ya'Ya. [laughing]
Reena: Does he look hurt?
Rose: Yeah.
Reena: And the face doesn't look like Ya'Ya's face?
[Rose shakes her head] No. OK.

As the five-year-old girl, though Sara could recognise that the man on the cross was not her father, Yeshua, she could not identify who the person was who was there. This is independently consistent with all the accounts given by James and Mary Magdalene – those who were privy to the first-tier information – that Jesus was indeed substituted on the cross.

Rose's take on the end was telling, as to how much trauma little Sara actually felt when seeing her Ya'Ya, who did not look like Ya'Ya, on the cross: 'It was very intense, so towards the end I was actually feeling like I just wanted to come out of it. I don't know if it's because I didn't want to see or whether it was because the energy was just really strong, but I was kind of like, you know, "OK, OK, enough, enough".'

What she experienced are classic signs of someone not wanting to remember the most traumatic part of their experience, so they employ diversionary tactics. Children especially cannot verbalise trauma so well, but their body language is a great indicator of what they are going through. Not wanting to see, turning their heads, wriggling, running away, crying – these are all signs showing that their pain is great and they would rather ignore it to be able to deal with their pain. So, it is imperative to give them tools and resources to help them feel safe to remember to heal their wounds therapeutically, and in this case, to also get the details of the timeline.

The regression ended here for the day.

11

REMEMBERED

It takes courage to grow up and become who you really are.
– E. E. Cummings

The next day, Rose slipped back easily into a memory of when Sara was nine; her hair was in a plait and she was forced to leave her homeland on the first boat. They were in hiding, and she was scared, because no one had explained exactly what was happening. They just had to hurry and get on a big boat and go somewhere, though she did not know where. It was a long journey that took many months. Although they stopped at many places, and stayed in many houses, none of them felt safe, though the people loved them. Some of these places seemed to be in Egypt or the Middle East, Rose disclosed later. So they travelled for four more years before they arrived at a place that both felt safe and where people loved them.

The next significant event was when they arrived at this safe place. Sara is now thirteen years old and she is aware of being on a small boat wearing a long skirt, of the brown woollen boots covering her feet, and of her torso wrapped around by shawls. Her long brown/red hair is plaited to one side, and her hands are holding another shawl, as it is unnaturally cold to her. The boat lands on a beach in an unfamiliar, new place. There is nobody around and it is very quiet. She does not want to get into the water, as it is cold. So, her big, old, kind uncle, with a grey beard, carries her out of the boat. I ask if this uncle is related to Mama or Ya'Ya in any way and she replies, 'Ya'Ya'.

Next, Sara is aware that everyone is busy unloading. She recognises her two younger brothers there. She guesses that they are aged eight and five, but she is unsure.

> Reena: The baby that came out of Mama's fat belly, how do you address him?
> Rose: David.
> Reena: How about the other?
> Rose: James.
> Reena: Your two brothers are there, are they helping with the unloading?
> Rose: No.
> Reena: What are they doing?
> Rose: Running.

She then goes on to recognise Mama, Aunty Mara and two other men – one that she recognises as their friend, that she addresses as Simon, and another man that she could not quite place at that time as she did not know him very well. This is again consistent with Mary Magdalene's and Marta's accounts that on the boat were themselves, Mary's daughter and first son, and James (who to Sara would be 'Uncle'). Neither could identify with clarity the other men who were with them.

Once they had unloaded, they started walking on the beach. It is night and it is cold, and they were heading to a specific place, which they entered. That's when Rose felt warm.

Reena: And what is it that is making you warm?

Rose: A blanket. I can't see anything. I feel safe ... It's a big room.

Reena: Are you aware of your brothers being there with you?

Rose: We're all there.

Reena: Is Mama there too?

Rose: Maybe. Maybe it's like a church or something. Not a church but like a place where people come. Empty, no chairs, like a big room. But we're sleeping there.

Reena: What is it that made you and your mama and uncle and your brothers go there?

Rose: I don't really understand any of it ... I feel Ya'Ya's light. (big smile on her face) ... I think I mean my mind.

Reena: What's the significance of Ya'Ya's light at this time?

Rose: I just feel the love. I know everything will be OK.

Reena: What happens next?

Rose: Ya'Ya is there. He is hugging everybody.

Reena: Have you woken up or is this in your mind?

Rose: I have woken up.

Reena: How do you feel about Ya'Ya being there?

Rose: [smiles] Happy.

Reena: What happens next?

Rose: Everybody's so happy.

Reena: Are you still in the big room? [Rose affirms] Did Ya'Ya come in the same boat?

Rose: I don't think so.

Reena: So how many days were you in the big room before Ya'Ya came?

Rose: I think only one day. I just woke up.

Reena: Is there anything else of significance?

Rose: There are people helping.

Reena: Do they look familiar to you? [Rose shakes head] Do they speak your language? [Rose shakes head] They don't speak your language. Do you recognise the language they speak? [Rose shakes head] No. OK. Does that affect you at all?

Rose: I feel safe.

The next significant event took Sara back to her mind. There, she revealed that before she went into her mind, she was angry about hiding.

Rose: I don't understand why we are hiding.

Reena: Are you still thirteen? [Rose shakes head] About roughly how old are you?

Rose: Sixteen … We always seem to be hiding.

Reena: And just tell me a little about the place you're in when you're feeling this anger about hiding.

Rose: It's a house.

Reena: Is this your house or someone else's house?

Rose: It's always someone else's house.

Reena: Is this where you are hiding, in this house? [Rose affirms] Is it in the same place? [Rose shakes head] It's a different place now … Is it a different language they speak?

Rose: Mm … Yes. Maybe, no. No.

Reena: Could it be the same language but a different dialect maybe? [Rose affirms] Have you ever clarified with Ya'Ya and Mama about this hiding to make it clear for you?

Rose: The people don't understand … the teachings.

Reena: Whose teachings?

Rose: Ya'Ya's, and Mama ... Yeah, but we don't have to hide! Why do we have to hide?! Just because people don't understand.

Reena: Has it been explained to you what happens when people don't understand?

Rose: We just love. And hide. [laughs] We just be with the people who understand, because then we can keep our message.

Reena: With all this hiding, what happens to the friends that you make?

Rose: I don't have friends. I just have my head ... All mind.

Reena: When you do not hide, what do you do with your time?

Rose: Study.

Reena: Do you go to school to study or ...? [Rose shakes head] ... No. What do you study?

Rose: Teachings ... Ya'Ya's teachings.

Reena: Who teaches you?

Rose: Mama.

Reena: How about your brothers, do they do the same thing?

Rose: We learn to write and we read.

Reena: Does Mama teach anybody else or just you and your brothers?

Rose: Sometimes.

Reena: Sometimes she teaches others. OK, so the people in the place send their children to her?

Rose: [nods] Yes.

Reena: What makes you go into the mind, do you feel safe there?

Rose: They talk to me; they tell me to come.

Reena: Who are they?

Rose: My helpers, my friends ...

Reena: Do you have one main helper and friend or do different ones come all the time?

Rose: One main one.

Reena: Tell me about this helper.

Rose: It's just like a voice ... It's the blue face, but I don't see the blue face, I just know it's them ... He's saying that everything will be OK.

Reena: Do you ever share your anger and fears with Mama and Ya'Ya?

Rose: No, not really. I know they're trying.

Reena: Do you share it with the blue face? [Rose affirms] And does the blue face console you?

Rose: [nodding] You're funny!

The next event saw a coy Sara at nineteen, meeting a boy. Again, this is consistent with Laurence Gardener's claim that Tamar married at the age of twenty in AD53.[1]

Rose: Love.

Reena: Is he a handsome boy?

Rose: Yes.

Reena: Describe this boy to me.

Rose: He's taller than me. He believes in the teachings. He has red hair. He's funny.

Reena: Are you still in that place where they speak that language?

Rose: Different. Yes, but different place.

Reena: Can you speak that language now?

Rose: Yes.

Reena: What is the name of that language, do you know? [Rose shakes head] No. Does he speak that language? [Rose affirms]. Tell me more.

Rose: He loves me.

Reena: Is he about the same age?

Rose: Maybe a little bit older.

Reena: So how did you meet?

Rose: In the teachings.

Reena: Did he come to listen to them? [Rose nods] And who was giving the teaching?

Rose: Mama. I try sometimes to do the teachings.

Reena: What about your brothers?

Rose: They're still a bit younger.

Reena: Do they go with you and Mama to teach? [Rose shakes head] Does Ya'Ya go to all the teachings? [Rose shakes head] No. Does he stay at home?

Rose: I don't think he's there. Maybe sometimes there.

This is consistent with Maya's account as Mary Magdalene where she too said her husband, Yeshua, was not always with the family.

Reena: So how do you address this boy with the red hair?

Rose: I can't remember his name. I should know his name. I'm thinking Simon again, I thought it straight away ... Stefan, Stephen ... hmm.

Reena: OK, and does Stefan/Stephen's family know about the love you share? [Rose affirms] Yeah? Do they understand the teachings, the family? [Rose affirms] And how do they feel about your love?

Rose: Happy.

Reena: Tell me about the family situation of Stefan/Stephen.

Rose: Hmm. They're not farmers. Maybe like merchants. I think they are wealthy.

Reena: Does he have any siblings?

Rose: Sorry, I'm very distracted because I am in my head. And I'm seeing this big eye again.

Reena: Oh, OK. And what is the significance of this eye?

Rose: I don't know.

Reena: OK, so what we're going to do is go back to the point when you could feel the love between you and Stephen, can you feel that in your heart? [Rose affirms] Good. [Rose giggles] What is making you giggle?

Rose: The love. [laughs]

Reena: Just stay in that love and just let me know if he has any brothers or sisters.

Rose: He has a sister.

Reena: How do you address her?

Rose: Starts with a K. Kerron … Karren.

Reena: Tell me what happens next.

Rose: I'm going to marry him.

Reena: Are you still nineteen? [Rose affirms] Tell me about the marriage.

Rose: Ya'Ya is there. Ya'Ya does our marriage.

Reena: So how does Ya'Ya 'do' the marriage?

Rose: He just speaks and we are holding hands. It's just love. There are lots of people.

Reena: What are David and James doing? What role do they play in this marriage?

Rose: They're just there. It's just simple.

Reena: Is it indoors or outdoors?

Rose: Indoors.

Reena: Does Mama play a role?

Rose: She's just there. She's happy.

Reena: Is she a bit emotional? [Rose affirms] Her little girl is getting married. And are you happy? [Rose affirms]

The next significant event finds Sara in her mind again. There is a lot of pressure in her head as though something was trying to show itself to her.

Reena: How does that make you feel?
Rose: I like being in my mind … [long pause] I'm just feeling a great peace. I'm hearing God talk to me. [long pause] … I think God wants me to share his words. He tells me that I'm ready to do it.
Reena: Are God's words similar to Mama's and Ya'Ya's teachings or are they different?
Rose: I don't know yet.
Reena: Has God told you the words yet? [Rose shakes head] OK. And how do you feel that God feels that you are ready to start teaching his words now?
Rose: I feel ready.
Reena: What role does Stephen play in this?
Rose: He understands.
Reena: Are you still nineteen?
Rose: Twenty-two. Hmm … Maybe … write. Maybe write down.
Reena: OK, and do you tell Mama and Ya'Ya about this message you've received?
Rose: Yeah.
Reena: What do they say to you?
Rose: OK.
Reena: Just tell me what happens next.
Rose: Mama and Ya'Ya know it's my plan. They all feel the energy.

Reena: Including your brothers?

Rose: Yeah, sometimes … Everybody has a plan. This is my plan. I feel very happy that I'm going to be doing my plan. I feel very at peace.

Reena: Do you still have to hide?

Rose: Mm … yes, but we are in a community so we're safe.

Reena: OK, is there anything else of significance in this place?

Rose: I have a baby … A girl … Anna.

Reena: How old is this baby?

Rose: Maybe one.

Reena: Ah, so sweet. What colour is her hair?

Rose: Yes, kind of blonde. Like dark blonde. She's cute.

Reena: Does Ya'Ya see Anna a lot?

Rose: Hmm … No. Ya'Ya is always with us, but he's not always with us.

Reena: OK, so could I say he is always in spirit but physically maybe not always there? Does that about sum that up? [Rose affirms]

Rose: But I see him, even when he's not there.

Reena: Oh, right, you see him … is it a strong connection? [Rose nods] How about Mama, is Mama there physically all the time?

Rose: Mama loves Anna.

Reena: What does Stephen do to bring back food, does he do some work?

Rose: Yes … I think he's some kind of teacher … I think like school.

Reena: He teaches in a school?

Rose: I think so.

Reena: And do you still keep in touch with Karren? [Rose affirms] What does Karren do?

Rose: I think she has a baby ... Just a little baby boy.

Reena: Karren and Stephen's parents must be happy. [Rose nods] Yeah. And how about your brothers?

Rose: I think maybe one of my brothers is not there, maybe James is not there. Maybe James is with Ya'Ya? Maybe.

Reena: So James is the younger one? [Rose shakes her head]

Reena: Oh no, James is the older brother. OK.

This is consistent with both James' and Mary Magdalene's account that Jesus and Mary's second child left and went away from the family. Also, in his book, *The Grail Enigma*, Laurence Gardner did mention that it was Jesus Jr (the son of Jesus Sr and Mary Magdalene) who travelled with his uncle, Joseph of Arimathea (who was really James, Jesus' brother according to the accounts of our regressees).[2]

Reena: So your youngest brother is with you. What's his name again?

Rose: David ... He's still studying ... with Mama.

Reena: Do other people still come to be taught by Mama? [Rose affirms] Is she more like a spiritual teacher than a subject teacher?

Rose: Yes, but she can teach lots of things, she's very clever. She knows a lot of things. She learned a lot of things when she was younger ... and [her teachings] are new for the people.

Reena: Are they accepting of them?

Rose: Yes.

Reena: So just her spiritual teachings or her worldly teachings are new as well?

Rose: It's more spiritual teachings ... and her worldly teachings.

Reena: So what is the most significant new spiritual teaching that she teaches then?

Rose: Ya'Ya's. It's Mama's teaching too!

Reena: What is her most significant new worldly teaching?

Rose: It's kind of like sex. [laughs] Because Mama teaches people that sex is good and OK.

Reena: Before that people were uncomfortable about sex?

Rose: [nods and smiles] It's powerful ... in its energy. Mama's teaching, it's not just like teaching you understand, it's like feeling, like being an energy ... She's giving energy, it's not just about the words that comes out (and this is what God tells me too). It's not just about the words, it's about the energy. That's not the right word, but it's about that. It's about the feeling. When people come to the teaching it's beautiful. It's beautiful.

Reena: Because of the transmission of the energy?

Rose: Yes. Yes, it's so beautiful.

Reena: So Mama transmits it orally and you transmit it written. Is that about right? Or is there an overlap?

Rose: She just is *it*.

Reena: She *is* the energy.

Rose: And I am just *it* too.

Reena: You *are* the energy too.

Rose: We don't have to write it or speak it ...

Reena: Ah, you just *are*.

Rose: People are healed by it; people are touched by it. Like Ya'Ya's energy.

Reena: So do you work at just being the energy or does it come naturally?

Rose: No, it just comes naturally. And the more that we are together, the more it expands and we can be in it and this is what I was trying to explain before, but I didn't explain very well, about 'they understand'.

Reena: Are your brothers part of this energy circle as well? So they are *it* as well?

Rose: I'm feeling anxious about one of my brothers but I don't know why ... Oh, it's because he's away ... I miss him.

Reena: Were you there when he got sent off? [Rose affirms] Who did he get sent off with?

Rose: I think he went with Uncle. He wanted to go.

Reena: But the other brother David is still with you, isn't he? [Rose nods]

In the next significant event, Sara is aware of a stream of light that's just flowing down from above.

Rose: I don't know, I don't think I'm in my head but I think I'm actually sitting somewhere and seeing it.

Reena: Was it flowing through you? Or are you seeing it just outside of you?

Rose: No, I'm not seeing it any more ... Maybe it was a sunset, I think maybe I'm seeing scenery and then there was the Light and now it's dark. I think it's just a place that I like to go to Be. I don't really know ... Maybe I go here to talk to God.

Reena: Ah, OK, I see. And how old are you now roughly?

Rose: Maybe thirty?

Reena: Is Aunty Mara still with you and Mama?

Rose: No.

Reena: What happened to Aunty Mara?

Rose: I think she died, before my wedding. [Inaudible … 'with pain'?] I talk to her too.

Reena: How about Mama?

Rose: Mama's still there.

Reena: OK, and just tell me what is the strongest most significant message God sends through to you?

Rose: To write my words, to share my words, to keep so that they are on Earth, to be recorded, to be physical, to not think, to just write my words, to trust …

Reena: And it was eight years ago when you were twenty-two that God first asked you to do this. Have you done any yet?

Rose: Yeah, I come here to do it.

Reena: What is God's strongest message that you need to write down?

Rose: Love. When I write, I write love, I write with love in my words, I *put* love into the words.

Reena: So that when people read it, they feel the love? [Rose affirms] Can I ask what language do you write in? Do you write it in your home language or in the language of this new place? Or a different language?

Rose: I'm looking at it … It's not … It's maybe my old language …

Reena: The language from home?

Rose: Maybe.

Reena: Is that the language which God talks to you in?

Rose: Hmm, maybe I just feel it's easier to interpret it …

Afterwards, at the end of the session, whilst Rose was still in an altered state, she mentioned that the symbolic language that she wrote in looked like Aramaic. What was especially interesting here is that when Rose came out of trance, she wondered what Aramaic was. This does happen in a heightened state of awareness – it is incredible how much our subconscious knows without the conscious being aware of it.

Aramaic is a family of languages or dialects that is part of the Northwest Semitic group, which also includes the Canaanite languages such as Hebrew and Phoenician. The Aramaic alphabet is ancestral to the Hebrew, Syriac and Arabic alphabets. It was the language of Jesus, who spoke a Western Aramaic language during his public ministry, as well as the language of large sections of the biblical books of Daniel and Ezra, and also the main language of the Talmud.[3] The regression continues.

Reena: So you are in this beautiful place and you are sitting and you are writing God's words. You've been writing for eight years? Are you close to completion or ... [Rose shakes head] No. Do you write once a day or just as and when God speaks to you? [Rose nods] Just when God speaks to you? [Rose nods again] OK, and within those eight years you have a baby girl, Anna. Do you have any other children?

Rose: Yeah! I have four!

Reena: Tell me about your children.

Rose: We have a boy, Joseph. I have a Yeshua. Yeshua, then Joseph.

Reena: So let me get this right: Anna, Yeshua, Joseph ...

Rose: And I have Mara.

Reena: Mara, for Aunty Mara. [Rose nods] Is Ya'Ya still around physically?

Rose: He comes to the place.

Reena: Is Ya'Ya still around physically?

Rose: No.

Reena: But he's still connected to you energetically?

Rose: [nods] He's so beautiful. Well, he just went. I don't know where he is.

Later on, Sara explained that she had a very strong connection with Ya'Ya so she was able to feel him energetically. She did not miss him when he wasn't there, quite so much, because she always felt very strongly connected in this field with him. However, he was there physically from time to time, when he was not travelling or teaching. It still had to be a secret he was alive and he could teach. Whilst it was known amongst select communities, they still had to be careful. This account is consistent with Mary Magdalene's about Yeshua also travelling and teaching to stay inconspicuous, and not spending much time with his family.

Reena: OK, but Mama's still there? [Rose nods] Can I ask what's made you stay with Mama?

Rose: She teaches me, and it's just what you do. It's traditional to stay with Mama. I love my Mama and Mama is my teacher.

Reena: When you say it's traditional ... it's traditional from your homeland?

Rose: There are many of us, we're like a family and spirit ... We're like a community.

Reena: Ah, OK, I understand. And James, he left with Uncle? How did they leave?

Rose: I think they went by boat.

Reena: And Uncle, has he stayed with you the whole time or does he travel in and out by boat occasionally?

Rose: In and out.

Reena: This is Ya'Ya's brother?

Rose: I'm not sure …
Reena: Did James go off permanently or will he come back?
Rose: I think he won't come back.

Whilst Rose's account was patchy on the details, it is still consistent with what Mary Magdalene and James said about the eldest son travelling with Joseph of Arimathea (i.e. James the brother of Jesus), having left for good.

Reena: And what happens next?
Rose: God shows me visions … I don't really understand them … I'm seeing colours, I'm seeing the world and I'm seeing … I don't really understand them … Maybe I'll understand one day.
Reena: Oh, OK. Does God explain the rationale behind these visions for now? [Rose shakes head]

The next significant event, Sara is in her thirties, and is aware that she spends a lot of time in her head. She gets a sense of just moving and flying, and she sees a lot of shapes in her mind.

Rose: Just keep writing. Always writing.
Reena: Is it one book or many books?
Rose: It's not a book.
Reena: Sorry, what is it then?
Rose: It's just pages.
Reena: Can you just tell me about these pages? What is it made of?
Rose: It's kind of thick, yeah, and it's like creamy colour, thick. Quite big.
Reena: What do you use to write with?

Rose: It's like a black ... chalk.

Reena: Do you make the writing material or get it from somewhere?

Rose: I get it from somewhere.

Reena: And does the black chalk stay permanently on the creamy pages?

Rose: It's not really chalk, it's ... maybe like charcoal.

Reena: Are the pages made of cloth or string or ... leaf?

Rose: Parchment, like thicker, but long. I have a lot.

Reena: Where do you keep your written parchment?

Rose: I keep them safe. I think I have a place, like a hole ... Deep in rocks. It's near where I talk to God.

Reena: So tell me about these rocks, are they on a cliff or a mountain or ...?

Rose: Yeah, where I talk to God is near a mountain.

Reena: This hole, is it a cave or is it a hole?

Rose: Like a cave.

Reena: Are you hiding it?

Rose: Yeah! God told me I have to keep it.

Reena: Do you not share it and teach it with your community?

Rose: No ... well, sometimes.

Reena: And what did God tell you to keep it for?

Rose: Because it needs to be on Earth.

Reena: So how many of these parchments have you got?

Rose: Oh, lots!

Reena: More than a hundred?

Rose: Oh, yeah.

Reena: Well, you have been writing for more than ten years ...

Rose: A long time ...

Reena: Have you got another child by this time or still the same as before?

Rose: Six.

Reena: So you've got Anna, Yeshua, Joseph, Mara ... who are the other two?

Rose: Stephan, David. Cute.

Reena: Is David the baby? [Rose nods] And tell me about your brother David. Is he still with you or has he left as well?

Rose: He's still there.

Reena: What does he do?

Rose: He's a teacher ... He's not there all the time.

Reena: Oh, he moves around as well. Does he move with Uncle or in some other way?

Rose: Some other way.

Reena: Does he go by boat?

Rose: I don't think so.

Reena: How is Mama?

Rose: Hmm ... I think she's sad.

Reena: Is she healthy?

Rose: Yeah.

Rose revealed later that this was when Ya'Ya had physically passed away. Although Rose did not recall that he was with his family at this time, she says that he came to visit in light form. This is different from Mary Magdalene's and James' recollections that Yeshua died in her arms.

In the next significant event, Sara moved to when she was forty-something and she is with Mama, teaching. Sara is taking over Mama's role as the teacher.

Reena: Is she sort of mentoring you to take over her role?

Rose: Yes. I'm not her though.

Reena: So what's made Mama mentor you to take over her role?

Rose: For when she's not there, and it's important for women to have a teacher and she wants me to understand that.

Reena: What is the importance of women having a teacher?

Rose: This, it's not in the world. In the world there's no women teaching ... spirituality.

Reena: Oh, so there's mostly men teaching spirituality.

Rose: Yes, yes ... In our group women teach men and men teach women ... [I sometimes teach] just to women.

Reena: Is the teaching different if you teach to just women as opposed to when you teach men and women?

Rose: There are some things that are just for women ... like sexuality. But the teachings are for everyone.

Reena: What is the importance of teaching sexuality particularly to the women?

Rose: It's the priestess training. It's energy, it's alchemy. It's healing in sexuality. My Mama, she learned this, and women don't know this. So we teach the women.

Reena: Do you implement this within your own marriage?

Rose: Yes!

Reena: What is the difference when you implement the alchemy and the healing and the energy and the sexuality versus not doing so?

Rose: It's hard for me to explain in words. I will try. I'm hoping you are feeling the energy as I am speaking, how different it is to be in this energy in a relationship ... more of a unity. Children born [are] 'called forth' from

[such] a union, as I was called forth by my parents ... It is a calling-in of a soul, almost from the sexual act of creating the energy for this being to arrive in this loving space. It is a totally different way of creating life ... a much more conscious way of creating.

Reena: And how will this impact the child?

Rose: As with me, I came forth knowing my purpose, bringing my gifts, being nurtured to bring this forth into the world. It's the alchemy of love. It's alchemy of transformation of eternal youth; this is the message that we bring forth in the writings and the teachings for the future when more people can hold this energy.

Reena: So it is safe to say that because of this conscious creation of this other, the living being, that the sexual acts are performed between two people who pledge to live their lives together and to take care of children almost. Does that make sense?

Rose: Yes. But it's not a pledging of obedience, it's a conscious pledge of ... it's souls that are meant to be together, souls who know they are meant to be together. It's not about the forever. It's the knowing, it's the being whole, coming to relationship in wholeness.

Reena: Only in this wholeness can you implement this sexuality to consciously create and call in the other soul. That makes a lot of sense. Is this what you teach the women?

Rose: Yes. We teach the women to be whole. We teach them that their sexuality is part of who they are ... that God's energy is sexual energy. It's alchemical. We came to experience this love in human form. It's sexual.

Reena: Do prostitutes come and listen to your teachings?

Rose: [shakes head] I have to explain this. There are people who use their sexuality as a healing gift to teach men about loving sexuality. We don't call them prostitutes. In the teachings they are priestesses, not prostitutes. It's a sacred sexuality. Not so much where we are now, but in the teachings that my mother has brought forth to me.

Reena: I understand. With these priestesses, do they call in a soul …

Rose: Sometimes … Everybody can learn the teachings, not everybody will apply the teachings.

Reena: Fascinating.

Rose: Yes.

Reena: Thank you for teaching us.

In the next significant event, Rose is still in her fifties and is feeling very hot in the body … burning. She is not well.

Later, Rose revealed that at this point, Mama passed away. Though she was with Mama at this time, Sara lost her will at her loss, hence her body burning. She revealed that Mama chose to die in a cave in the mountains, which was her sacred place, altar, where she talked to God and Ya'Ya. It was a conscious choice for her to pass away, for she had completed passing her knowledge to Sara, and she missed and wanted to be with Ya'Ya.

Rose: Anna is here … Anna is a teacher too.

Reena: Are the teachings passed down from mother to the first daughter? [Rose nods] Is that a cultural traditional thing to do or is that something that is established by your family?

Rose: We called her soul forth … In our lineage … that's how we carry the information forward. We always call in the soul who will take on the work, which will take on the Remembering.

Reena: Do you share with her the writing?

Rose: Yes.

Reena: So she knows the place? [Rose affirms] Does that mean that you and Anna have to stay in that place, guarding the writings? Or can you move around quite a bit?

Rose: It can be where we stay in the place. We stay close to the place.

Reena: Is Stephen around?

Rose: Mm ... where [is] Stephen? ... He's not here ... She's so beautiful, Anna. So beautiful. It's her heart.

Reena: Is Anna married or is she single at this point?

Rose: She's married.

Reena: And does she have a child? Is it a girl?

Rose: Yes, she has two children, two girls.

Reena: What are their names?

Rose: Sara.

Reena: After you. [Rose nods] And?

Rose: Lara. Lira or Lara.

Reena: And is only Anna there or have you got other children ...?

Rose: She's taking care of me ... I think I can leave my body if I want to leave. I want to leave but I need to finish my work.

Reena: The writing?

Rose: Anna. Teach her.

Reena: Mentor her? [Rose nods] Have you finished your writing work by now? [Rose affirms]

Rose: That is why I can go.

Reena: So when did you finish your writing?

Rose: Just finished.

Reena: It's like thirty-odd years writing.

Rose: [laughs] Not every day, sometimes … It's my life's work.

Reena: What is your decision about your life's work? Do you just keep it in that hole in the rock?

Rose: There are others with plans. They'll find it.

Reena: Oh, it's meant to be found?

Rose: We trust in the divine plan.

To get more information on this place, I chose to disassociate Rose from her past life of Sara and spoke to Rose's subconscious to identify this place in current terms. The mountain was in southern France. She also identified a white church with a single spire, dedicated to Mary Magdalene, as a landmark by this mountain.

The regression continues. In the next significant event, Sara finds herself back in her head/mind, where she is experiencing expansion. She is in her sixties. She is aware that her body is frail, and she is sitting with her family.

Rose: I'm really in this space a lot.

Reena: Are you aware if Anna goes into her head a lot or not aware?

Rose: She does … I'm actually happy, very happy. I think it is time to go. I'm ready … Anna is fully mentored; she can take over the lineage … Our community is strong, but it is small.

Reena: I'm just curious, and you may or may not have this, but does the community have a symbol or a sign?

Rose: It's like a cross. It's like that. [air draws it with her finger]

Reena: It's like two infinities crossing. And what is the meaning of this sign?

Rose: As above, so below.

The meaning that Sara gave of this cross is consistent with Mina's Thomas description of the ritual of connecting with the energy – above, below and with one another – thereby creating an Energetic Cross. He called it connectedness.

Sara was navigated to the point after her heart stopped beating, and then moved to the Realms of Light, where she was greeted by Ya'Ya and God, who manifested to her as Blue Face, when she was young.

The first insight that she received was around all the visions and experiences she was feeling whilst she was in her mind. It was about energy opening up to bring more information and light; and whilst the human mind wants to attach significance to experience, sometimes the experience is a healing, an activation, a level of initiation which Sara was going through. Through their lifetimes she, Mama and Ya'Ya went through many levels of initiation in the human body, and not within a temple teaching environment. So their initiations and annointings were performed by their Spirit Guides, teachers or Higher Selves on the other side.

Rose then elaborated that whilst Sara was in her mind with these energies, a lot of it was very vague and she was in that other space so much of the time. However, she really was just going through these levels of energy shift the whole time that she was here, to bring herself up to that level, and she almost knew that she had that direct connection and guidance, so she was being guided through it.

Reena: Sara kept going into her mind because she had all these experiences in the mind. I don't know how to say this without putting a label, it's not what most children go through.

Rose: No. There are people who have come to bring a new energy to the planet and you think in this time we have a lot of children that are doing that. Had she been alive now she'll be [perceived] a very odd child. She was probably even then, but she was very connected and she was learning to manage the energy and connection and still be here in her body, which I think wasn't really true for a lot of people now, a lot of children. So it's very interesting.

Reena: Are there children in this place that's bringing this energy down, especially during this time?

Rose: Yes, yes.

Reena: Are they Savants? Or …

Rose: Or autistic children even. There are those on the autism spectrum who really connect more with energy than the world sometimes.

This struck a chord because during the regression Sara had to consistently be asked to connect to the body, because otherwise she connected straight to the mind and she was in that energy space. Rose illuminated that, for Sara, the 'most significant event' was to be in the energy, and not what was happening in the body.

Rose: You know the thing for Sara was that she was surrounded by love and understanding, which made it OK. There was no sense that she felt that it was not OK to be doing that. She really felt that was what she was supposed to do.

Reena: What is the significance of Sara's story for now? For the people reading the book?

Rose: It's Sara's time. She left her imprint hidden on Earth. It's time for the energy to come forth – it was

264

suppression of the hiding. She didn't like the hiding then, she knew that it wasn't right and in history she does not exist. But she does exist because she left that imprint behind, which was part of the divine plan. It's time for the teachings to come forth again ... the teachings that she wrote, that she passed down, that her mother taught her, the conscious relationship, the conscious conception, sexuality, the female as Christ. She carried the Christhood energy. She went through all the initiations on Earth. She had a strong energy, whereas Anna had [a] very pure, soft one ... Eventually the teaching is not to be taught the same way but the energy of the Christhood female has been held on the Earth plane, and it has been done, the blueprint is there – in Mary Magdalene and in Sara. That is what's important.

Reena: Did Mother Mary hold this as well?

Rose: It's a different energy.

Reena: All these pages, have they been found yet? [Rose affirms] Is it out then in the Consciousness or is it still hidden?

Rose: The information is in the Consciousness but it is not attributed to Sara, but that's OK.

Then the insights moved on to Sara's relationship with her father and his love, and the different love she felt with her mother.

Rose: It is a very special love, maybe it's the archetype of Father, but he wounded her, he did. She felt very betrayed and let down by him right at the beginning. I think we sometimes think of male/female betrayal in relationships as just between loving partners but this

was a … it was a very, very big wound for her until she
learned that really she could connect with his energy. I
think it's just the soul's resonances, it's like we have
strong resonance with souls, which can play different
roles in our life. Maybe what she is really just also
showing is his effect on people in general. He brought
that love, what that felt like to be bathed in that … and
she was really the object of so much focus of that. It is
very special. In the relationship with her mother it was
total trust, total love, total solid safety.

It was also revealed that Sara has been hidden from existence
because her presence changes everything, especially the
balance of power. Rose emphasised that there was no need to
hide; and who knows what would have happened if they had
not.

These last statements made by Sara are especially pertinent
in the context of Laurence Gardener's research around the
Succession of the Church, as he writes about in great detail in
his book *The Grail Enigma*. He states that from the first to the
third century, the Judaeo-Christian Church was dynastically
governed by hereditary leaders, starting with James, Jesus'
brother. However, in the fourth century, the Church compiled
the Apostolic Constitutions, to dislodge the hereditary leaders,
in favour of Apostolic Succession, starting from St Peter and
carried on by Popes, selected by leaders of the Church.
According to Gardner, whilst there is no record of Peter
heading the Church in Rome, this choice was made by a single
Gospel entry in Matthew 16:18 stating, 'Thou art Peter, and
upon this rock, I will build my Church.' According to
Gardner, the accurate translation of the Aramaic language is
that, for Peter, his mission was to be founded upon the 'Rock
of Israel'. He claims that the reason why the Gospel of

Thomas was excluded from the New Testament at the Council of Nicaea is because it states that Jesus bequeathed his personal leadership to his brother James: 'Wherever you are, you are to go to James the Just'. The claims the Church made that Mother Mary was indeed a virgin, that Jesus was the only child born to her, that Mary Magdalene was merely a prostitute who was healed by Jesus, and that there was no bloodline to continue the traditions of Jesus' ministry, upheld this claim of Apostolic Succession.[4] So Sara and every other descendant of Jesus was wiped clean from history.

There are not very many mentions or books written about Sara or Tamar. However, there are a satisfactory number of historical accounts that do concur that Jesus and Mary Magdalene had a daughter, called Tamar (the Hebrew version of Sara). There are murmurs that when the Pope and the Inquisition wiped out the Knights Templar, a movement that was said to protect the bloodline of Christ, and the Cathars, a branch that practised Gnosticsm in southern Europe between 12th and 14th centuries, they wiped out the branch that stayed true to the teachings of Mary Magdalene and Sara. So, by Rose's account, she was accurate in saying that Sara's story and teachings were kept quiet or secret.

This account was key in giving us a perspective into the continued bloodline of the Davidic Line. It also showed Sara to be a sweet, charming lady, who may have demonstrated savant/autistic symptoms, whilst actually having a very close connection to Source or God. Her loyalty to her mother and her teachings, as was Sara's soul plan, was strong and a determining factor in her dedication for carrying the teachings down the ages.

12

HIDDEN

Government is an association of men
who do violence to the rest of us.
– Leo Tolstoy

Jane, who lives in Australia, is a graduate of the Past Life
Regression Academy. During one of the sessions in the
course, Jane spontaneously dipped back to a life of what we
assumed was the Disciple John in the biblical era. Andy
Tomlinson, who was teaching at the time, told me about this
event. So, the next time I went down to train the group, I got
in touch with Jane to ask her if she would participate in this
book. Jane kindly agreed to help, on condition of anonymity.
When we explored this life more thoroughly, we were
surprised to find that she was not John the Disciple, but
David – the hidden son of John the Baptist.

Jane entered the life as a blue-eyed male child of about four
or five, being aware of bare feet, legs and arms that were raw,
wearing a tunic like a sack cloth. His hair is light-brown, quite
straight and fringed, quite long. It is daylight, and he is
outside, playing in the street with his sister, whom he
addresses as Viv-yen. There are lots of buildings, and it is
really dusty.

Reena: What are you playing?

Jane: I think we are playing 'Tiggy' … There's a drain in the middle of where we are, where all this … something goes, and we're not allowed to step over it. We've got to run around it and we're going to try to touch each other but we're not allowed to jump over this drain thing in the ground.

Reena: Is that an exciting game for you?

Jane: It's all we've got time for at the moment … We're going somewhere and we're just waiting for Mum and Dad to be ready … I'm scared of Mum, actually … she's very sad and I can't really see her face … It's like she has cloth over her head and her hair and I can't really see her. Mum looks really sad … I don't think she is my mum; I think she's just the lady that brought me up. She's not my mum, she's my dad's sister. But we're supposed to call her Mum and I won't.

Reena: I see, so what do you call her?

Jane: She's got really … she hides because she has really expensive stuff on underneath and she has to hide it. And I call her … if it's Louise, we call her Lou … but she doesn't like it when we call her that because we're not supposed to.

Reena: Do both you and your sister call her Louise?

Jane: No, my sister calls her Mumma.

Reena: It's just you that calls her Lou?

Jane: Yes, I defy. I don't like being told what to do.

Reena: Tell me about Dad.

Jane: He is away a lot. He's not home a lot so we're alone a lot. We're looked after by a lot of people, a lot. But this rich lady, who's our aunt, comes down and looks after us … when she can.

The boy (as yet unnamed) describes Dad's hair as being light-brown and curly, rather wiry. He has a beard. He wears a tunic and has sandals to protect his feet. His dad has really kind hands. He also mentions his dad's immense love and respect for water.

Next, he is told to go inside because the soldiers are coming. Whilst they are just doing their daily routine, the children are not allowed on the street.

Reena: Tell me more about the soldiers.
Jane: The soldiers ... you can't hardly look at them on a sunny day because they're so bright as they've got metal and it's really bright and really hurts your eyes. Some of the soldiers are really nice and they drop us food when they're not supposed to ... a lot of the soldiers were people from where I live. So that's why some of them from behind the wall, give us food and bread.
Reena: Do you get the food? [Jane nods] Is there a difference between the food that the soldiers are dropping to the food you get?
Jane: Yeah, yeah. The bread's really crispy and really fresh, it's just ... [deep breath in through nose] Ah, the bread is so good. Ours is just a bit stodgy and it's not nice but the bread they give us is really, really fresh; it's really good ... Sometimes they give us apples, red apples, and they are huge. And black grapes that are just massive, really big. Ours don't grow like that.
Reena: So what's making it so different, the food, then?
Jane: It's the (better) water they have that we don't ... and they are allowed to water their crops, we're not ... We can't afford the water.
Reena: What happens next?

Jane: We're walking down. The soldiers have gone and we have to walk quickly behind this aunt and [my sister and I] have to keep up and we're going down some side streets … There's other people walking with us, there's other people joining us now, we're all going to a meeting … Children aren't really meant to go and have to stay outside, but because our dad's there, we're allowed to go, sneak in and sit at the back. It smells really sweaty inside. It's really hot.

Reena: Tell me more about the inside.

Jane: There's lots and lots and lots of men in there. It's really sweaty because it's so hot and it feels like you can't … you can breathe but it's stale, real stale, smelly. But it's comforting as well because my dad's there and I know that it's OK and he's up the front.

Reena: So what is it about your dad that enables you and Viv-yen to go into the hall and not the other children?

Jane: Because our aunt lets us just sneak in at the back and our dad knows, everybody knows, but nobody minds because we're really good children.

Reena: I see, and your dad's in front. Is anyone else in front with Dad?

Jane: Yeah, there's a few people. I know this meeting is really secret. It has to be kept really quiet.

Reena: Can Aunt Louise go in?

Jane: No.

Reena: No, because it's a meeting for men …? [Jane affirms] But Viv-yen can go in, because she's just a child. [Jane affirms]

This account is consistent with the patriarchal old Judaean societies, where women take the back seat to men at important political, economic and leadership meetings. This is consistent with Sally's account as Marta, as well as Rose's account as Sara. However, after the session, Jane gave an interesting take on why this was so, that we have not heard from anyone else. 'Because they didn't want women to lie … The women were pure-hearted, to bring love and light into the world with the children, and if the women were asked to betray and lie it wasn't a strength that a woman carried well. Also the men didn't want the women suffering if they were caught and tortured. They really did know nothing … most of them,' she said.

Whilst many see this aspect of the patriarchal society as an act of disempowerment and suppression of women, Jane illustrates that from the perspective of men it was done as an act of love and consideration. The regression continues.

Reena: So tell me more about your experience with this meeting?

Jane: I can see all the feet, so they're all … they're not sat on chairs but they almost are and I can see lots of feet and lots of dust. There's no carpet or anything like that, it's just a hut, sandy. There's rows and rows of men, I don't know, for a child there looks like there's thousands but there's probably about fifty or a hundred. And then right up the very front there's quite a few people, a few men, standing together, and there's one in particular who's talking. Well, I don't know, all the other men seem to talk and this man seems to stand and he's just there and everybody is just there.

Reena: Tell me about 'He's just there'.

Jane: It's almost like he's not even real. When you look at him, it's like he looks different to everybody else … To me he looks like he glows, and he looks so clean, but he's not, that's just how he looks. That's how he feels, compared to everyone else. And he's got really long fingers, beautiful, really long hands. But you can see all his veins, so he's definitely worked, his hands are strong but they're long. He's got long fingers.

Reena: Is this man in any way familiar to you?

Jane: I'm not sure yet. I just know that my dad will do anything for him, would lay down his life for this man. That's how much he believes in him ... and so would the other men who are with my dad.

After the regression, Jane mentioned that this was a young man yet he seemed so old. She saw so many people living within his soul, which was so peaceful yet so busy. More souls connected to him, making his light just so bright. However, he was just so humble and so peaceful ... and so clean. Everyone else looked dirty, with their skin being tarnished with the weather, and looked like they'd had a hard life. He did not. He also did not seem to have any wrinkles, scars or dirt under his fingernails or abrasions on his feet. He just seemed pure and clean, yet walked with two feet like everyone else did. The regression continues.

Jane: There's someone called Samuel that I know, that's up there beside my dad ... Samuel has really blond hair, and he is supposed to be in the army but he's not. So he's to be hidden because he ran away. He didn't want to do what the soldiers were doing and what they were plotting. Yet he seems to know what is going on, on both sides, he knows what is going on behind the big walls and he knows what's going on here too.

Reena: So he plays quite an important role.

Jane: Yeah, yeah.

Reena: What role does your dad play?

Jane: Well, my dad seems quite close to this … he seems to be up there beside this other man. He seems to be right beside him as if … they both have very different roles to play but yet they have to come together. They've got the same intention. I know they're trying to … it's to make the poor people not poor.

Reena: Anyone else that you're aware of that you're familiar with there?

Jane: There's somebody with a name that begins with 'B' but I don't like him. He's … I don't trust him, I don't trust him at all, and he looks at me and always looks angry. He's got dark hair and a dark beard with white bits in it. And I think he wants to hurt my dad.

Reena: What is it that makes you feel that B wants to hurt Dad.

Jane: It's his eyes, it's like I can see into his soul and his soul's not good. But my dad doesn't want me to talk about my ability to do that … because if too many people find out, they might take me away and try to knock it out of me.

Reena: Tell me more about your ability to see souls of people.

Jane: I can see whether they are good or evil. I can see when their heads are connected to the rainbows and when their heads are not connected to the rainbows. And when they are not connected they are lying and when they are connected they are telling the truth. I can see that. I can see the rainbows coming down into their bodies … They can do so much good. But sometimes if the rainbows are too bright, the soldiers kill them.

Reena: So tell me about this man with the beautiful hands. Does he have rainbows or not?

Jane: [affirms] He glows, he just glows.

Reena: And what about Dad?
Jane: Dad's heart is massive and his hands just glow.
Reena: And how about Viv-yen?
Jane: I don't want to talk about Viv-yen.
Reena: OK. Is there anyone else there that's connected to rainbows? I'm guessing B is not?
Jane: He used to be, but his son was killed, which is why he then came over to our side.
Reena: So he was a soldier.
Jane: Yeah.

Later on in the regression, it was revealed, to David's shock and dismay, that eventually his father killed B. Apparently there had been an argument between B and John. B wanted to move ahead faster and make more progress with their mission, whilst John insisted that they had to wait for the glowing man's return. B did not agree and threatened to tell the soldiers that the glowing man was away and could be captured. After this, John and B fought and, out of self-defence, John drowned B. The regression continues.

Reena: How about Samuel?
Jane: Samuel's always white. He just always looks white. In a good way.
Reena: So you like Samuel?
Jane: I do, yeah. Samuel brings us eggs. He's not supposed to. Samuel's not very old.
Reena: He's not as old as Dad?
Jane: No.
Reena: Is anyone talking to Dad at the moment?
Jane: Yeah, they're all talking in the room, they're talking up the front.

Reena: How do they address Dad?

Jane: I want to say John, but my heart's palpitating.

Wondering what made him anxious about saying his dad's name, I navigated to the source of his heart's palpitation. He went back to when he was three and his mum was dying in childbirth.

Reena: Did she give birth to your sister? Or someone else?

Jane: Someone else. The baby didn't make it. The baby was a funny colour and was strangled. [Upset and starts to cry] ... But I can see [mum] her leaving her body. And I'm a bit scared, but I'm not because she's just doing this [gestures putting fingers to lips, a shushing sign] and smiling at me ... I know I'm going to be OK. But I'm worried about Dad because he's just so distraught.

Reena: How did Mum address you?

Jane: David ... [whispers] David, my name's David. Wow ... I'm a healer. I'm a healer like Y'seu. I'm a healer like him.

Reena: Who's Y'seu?

Jane: He's the big man ... With the beautiful hands. My dad's really scared because my mum was too and my dad's really special too. Dad's a healer of the land. The water and the land, he's a healer. And he can heal people. But differently.

Reena: What happens next?

Jane: My sister and I have been taken away to another part of the room while Mum's being taken out of the house and Dad is trying to breathe and bring himself together. This is the first time I meet Y'seu. He's in our house and he's bringing comfort to my dad. And he's bringing all this light and energy without touching him. He's just bringing all this energy into my dad ... over his head and down over his shoulders and into his heart. [gesturing with hands]

Reena: Is he using his hands like you're using ...?

Jane: This is what he is doing, he's doing this with his hands [gesturing with her hand] and then he goes round to Dad's heart ... because Dad's got such a beautiful heart ... and he tells Dad that he has a lot of work to do and that he must let Mum go. He is almost telling him that Mum would've got in the way and Dad's a bit cross, but he gets it as well.

Reena: How does Y'seu address Mum?

Jane: Mum's name begins with 'G'. Sounds like he calls her Genevieve or something like that, I don't know ... But I'm scared because I can do what Y'seu can do.

Reena: What's making you scared about that?

Jane: Because nobody seems to touch him. He seems like such a loner. Nobody seems to touch him and I don't want people to be like that with me ... because he seems peaceful but he seems sad. I think he's sad at what's happening to all the beautiful people, but he seems very alone. Yet he's so peaceful, he's peacefully alone. [laughs]

Reena: When you're around Y'seu, how do you feel?

Jane: Like I'm ten foot tall. And when he looks at me I know he's looking right into my soul like I can look into his soul. But it frightens my dad ... that I do it back, because my dad knows.

Reena: And Y'seu is aware as well, is he?

Jane: He doesn't need to talk, it's like I know his thoughts.

Reena: So what are his thoughts about your abilities?

Jane: That there's lots like me.

Reena: So how does he feel about your abilities?

Jane: He just makes me feel so peaceful, and makes me feel so calm and just makes me feel like I'm OK. 'You're OK, this is exactly who you're meant to be. It's OK.' We're all capable of feeling like this but there's a few of us who have to stand in our rainbow and help everyone's rainbow become alive ... He calls [Dad] the Son of John. He doesn't just call him John.

Being called 'Son of John' by Jesus is particularly significant within their community. 'Son of Man' is an accolade experienced by Ezekiel in the sixth century BC, for someone who must be separated from his fellows and his carnal, ego self, to be entrusted with the responsibility of warning people what is to come, and to leave all sense of identity and self to ensure the love of God endures and prevails.[1] So, being acknowledged as 'Son of John' is key here, where it gives John the direction to devote his life more completely to their joint mission, after the death of his wife.

Reena: OK, so let's just go by that name for now, Son of John. So go to the most significant part of him addressing Son of John and just tell me what it is you are aware of that he says.

Jane: He is telling him his gifts are many and he mustn't fear. He must surrender ... surrender his fear.

Reena: Does he give any advice to Son of John about you?

Jane: No, not at the moment.

Reena: So it's just about him then.

Jane: It's about him surrendering his fear and being able to help continue the work he's doing. Cleansing all these people so they can follow, and they can believe. The more they can get from behind the walls the more crops will grow, the more land will come back, the more we will be able to give back instead of taking it all away, and putting up brick walls that don't need to be there, that separate us when we're all the same. We're all one. We're all flesh and bone. [speaking passionately] We're all the same.

Reena: So tell me how Y'seu heals people and how you heal people, as you said he heals differently?

Jane: Well, I don't yet. I know I can and I know that I've got lots to do but my dad ... It's all to do with water.

Reena: So how does Dad heal the land and people with water?

Jane: He heals the people who work on the land and by healing the people who work on the land, the land heals. Because then they can connect to the rainbows and then they can connect to the earth and then it heals.

Reena: How does he use water to help with the healing?

Jane: There's a big queue of people and he's got a big metal bowl. I know it is metal because I can hear the noise, it makes a funny kind of scraping noise. When his hands are in it he does something with his hands in this bowl. I think he's putting light with the water ... and his hand and he's mixing it round. I am watching from over here and when he does it, I can see sunlight going into this water. The water's really clear and sometimes these people drink this water and sometimes they just put it over their head. It's different for every person.

Reena: How are you feeling watching Dad do this?

Jane: I'm feeling really alive and buzzing because I want to go and help. But if Dad got caught, his throat would be cut ... he'd be beheaded. He's healing the land so we have better crops. He's healing the people to heal the land. He's not doing anything wrong.

Reena: While Dad's doing this, where's Y'seu? Is he with Dad or is he somewhere else?

Jane: No, he's somewhere else. Dad does this on his own.

Reena: So you're allowed to watch.

Jane: I'm older now ... sixteen.

Reena: Are you allowed to help him?

Jane: No, because then I'll be taken by a soldier to either be killed or so they can burn it out of me ... if I don't do as they say.

Reena: How does it feel that you want to help and Dad doesn't let you help?

Jane: I understand because he doesn't want to lose me and I understand, and I love him. I'm not angry at him but I want to fulfil my own purpose. I want to fulfil what I am here to do, not just watch what he's [doing] and learn. I want to fulfil my destiny too.

In the next significant event David goes to a point where he witnesses a man being burned.

Jane: There's a man strapped to a cross. Strapped to wood. And he's not on the hill where others go. He's down in a ... it's like ... it's not up on the hill because not everybody sees this, it's like it's hidden. This is done secretly but yet only certain people can watch. It's like a teaching and a learning as well. So it is like there's a circle and there's people around watching but it's not very big. There are these wooden structures in the ground that they're strapped to so they can't move. There's a big, long wooden pole that has a cloth on the end and rope, and it has oil on it and it's set [on] fire. It's like they brand them until they say they're not ... they can't speak, they can't hear angels and God. They brand them until they say they're lying. So they burn them with this hot [brand], all over their body.

Reena: How old are you now?

Jane: I think I am sixteen.

Reena: Are you familiar with the man they are branding at the moment?

Jane: No, no. But he looks the same age as me. I am hiding, because I want to go back and tell the others what's going on. I'm not supposed to be doing it, because Dad won't let me help. He doesn't want me to get caught. I won't get caught ... The smell's horrible.

Reena: The smell of the branding?

Jane: It's awful. It hurts your nostrils, it's almost like there's an ammonia smell, as I breathe in. It's like they use something, ammonia, to keep the smell of the burned flesh away so that people don't know what's going on. So it's ammonia that's burning my nostrils, something like ammonia.

Reena: What's happening to the rainbow when this man is being branded?

Jane: The ones that die, they go up into the rainbow, the ones that don't make it. And the other ones, the rainbows are there, right into here [points to her solar plexus] ... right into their core. Almost trying to help them, support them. But a lot of them that's straight and a lot of their bodies are like this [moves body so it's crooked] ... So it doesn't work because they are in so much pain and moving that the rainbow can't be straight so it can't connect them. So the ones that die can't feel the connection. The ones that survive and are strong are the ones that feel the connection, so the rainbows are straight through them. But the ones that die are the ones that fight it too much ... I just want to tell everyone to keep their rainbows straight.

Reena: I know you said you don't want to talk about Viv-yen earlier. Are you comfortable talking a little bit about her now?

Jane: Well, she's left now.

Reena: Oh, she's left, OK. How old are you now?

Jane: I still feel like a teenager ... I'm begging her not to leave to be a prostitute.

Reena: How old are you?

Jane: I'm fifteen.

So, it is evident here that David spontaneously regressed to revisit what is clearly a painful time for him.

Reena: How old is she?

Jane: She's older than me. She must be eighteen.

Reena: Can you see the rainbow in her?

Jane: No, she's shut it down ... Yeah, I am crying and I'm begging her with my blue eyes, I'm begging her not to leave and she tells me I'm killing her ... My big blue eyes. She would've done anything for my big blue eyes but she's begging me to let her go. She doesn't want to stay and live in poverty. No, she doesn't want to do that.

Reena: When did she first shut her rainbow down?

Jane: It's when Mum died ... Mum was so kind and so loving and so supportive and Mum was so ... she was just constant, she was just there and it gave her something to believe in because she didn't believe in Dad's gifts …

Reena: She didn't believe in Dad's gifts …

Jane: No, she didn't, but she knows now. She used to watch Y'seu telling Dad how to cleanse the souls so that they could heal the land and heal the Earth. And she was sad that she didn't feel like that and she couldn't do that. And she just had no self-worth, no self-confidence, nothing. She didn't see herself as special.

Reena: Is that why she shut down as well?

Jane: She couldn't do what I could do and what Dad could do. But it was her life and she did what she had to do … to bring pleasure to others because times were hard and horrible.

The next significant event took David to when he was sixteen. He was hiding in the long grass and watching his father servicing a queue of people with the cleansing water.

Jane: There's soldiers at the very end of the queue. They're coming for him. They're just going to slit his throat and that's it. And then all the water goes red, from his blood … They're telling him that he is evil and that he's done bad things. I'm shivering with disbelief and fear and pain … [I'm] helpless.

[The other interesting account here is about the place where John the Baptist was executed. According to Tobias Churton, he theorised that John was executed in Macherus Castle, across the water from the Qumran Caves,[2] which was the epicentre of the Essene Community, that John cleansed with water, and where the Dead Sea Scrolls were found. So it makes sense that

John was still cleansing people just before his execution.]

Reena: Tell me about his rainbow?

Jane: It's funny, he's beheaded. I can see his soul coming right out of his body, almost like coming out where the head should be ... Yeah, it's just coming right out and he's just ... it's like he's just gone. [big sigh] There's all this ... more light, more rainbows come down, like raining down on everybody – as if killing him just makes his light grow even stronger. It's like killing him was the right thing to do because he can do even more now. So they can take away his physical [body] but they cannot do anything about his soul. And now his soul can do even more work.

Some of the soldiers that can see, because we all can, it's like they've got it and they've realised that they've actually done a really good thing – although it's a horrible thing – they've done a really good thing as well. But those that are not in the rainbows don't see that. There's just about three of them that do. They can see him as well as I'm watching, but there's so much light just coming down out of the sky. The more he's out of his body, the more the place is just filled with light. I have just never seen anything like it ... And he's dead and there's blood in the water and yet all this light is cleansing the water. So the water is still cleansed for the people. It's like his blood is good.

Reena: What's the Light doing to the people that the Light touches directly?

Jane: It wakens them up. They get a moment ... a 'wow' ... It's like they've been asleep and they've been awakened. And it's only a drop of light and it just [Jane makes an explosion noise]. He was amazing! He was a

cleanser of evil, a cleanser of the evil that was around.
He cleansed people of the evil.

Reena: So in a sense he was like water himself?

Jane: Yeah, yeah!

This account was particularly interesting. In Mark 6:16, Herod Antipas is convinced that 'John, whom I beheaded: he is risen from the dead' after hearing about the miracles performed by Jesus, because he believes that Jesus is actually John in the risen state and, being in that state, John can perform miracles.[3] However, according to David, his father John did indeed perform miracles after his execution – however, via his spirit and light touching everybody, and not going into the body of Jesus, as Herod had assumed. I also find this interesting because one of the cornerstones of the Christian belief as we know it, is that Jesus shed his precious blood to cleanse the sins and transgressions that everyone had committed ... however, according to this account, it seemed that John the Baptist played that role, where his blood flowed into the water, but his light cleansed the water for the people.

The other fascinating point is that during the reign of Herod Antipas, beheading was reserved for people with rank.[4] Whilst from young David's perspective, his father was killed for his cleansing work, politically he was seen as a liability for standing up against Herod Antipas's campaign to divorce his wife in order to marry his half-niece, who was also his sister-in-law. This would have led Galilee and Perea to war with the neighbouring King Aretas, whose daughter was married to Herod.[5] This shows John's enormous influence over the minds of his followers and positions him as being a leader of his community. This is consistent with him being the Zadok priest, which Laurence Gardner hypothesised and these accounts by Jane illustrate.

I asked if Y'seu was alive or dead at the time of John's beheading, to be told, 'He's still alive.'

This is historically accurate. In his book *The Mysteries of John the Baptist*, Tobias Churton puts a convincing historical argument that John was executed in AD36 CE and Y'seu later, in March AD37.[6] At this point, David reveals that Y'seu is of similar age to John, who is slightly older. This is consistent with historical accounts that John the Baptist was born six months before Jesus; and also is consistent with John dying before Jesus as well.

The next significant event sees David wanting to go to a burning on the hill.

> Jane: I want to go to the burning on the hill. I know there's burning on the hill and I've not been there before and I know this is the night of the crucifixion and I know there's a burning on the hill … I feel as if I'm dead and I'm watching this from above because I'm actually dead but I'm watching what happens.
> Reena: Oh, you are dead?!
> Jane: Yeah, I died, the night this happened. It was like I died when he died. So it's like I can watch it like when my dad left, and when my mum left, it's like I can watch.

As David seemed to have rushed through his own death to witness another, he was navigated to the events that led to his own death.

> Jane: I've just come back from a meeting. There's been more [secret] meetings and I've been going … They're getting bigger all the time, sometimes they're outdoors, they're not always indoors.

Reena: Tell me more about this meeting. And what's discussed in these secret meetings?

Jane: Y'seu has been away and he's come back. He's telling us there are lots of people around, lots of followers, who wish to join and help us help the King see how wrong what he's doing is. I think he's a king, I don't know, there just looks like there's gold, when we talk about him ... He's telling us that there's lots of followers who believe, that he has shown and helped. They're all coming to support us. We're all going to turn the land back to the peaceful land that it used to be and we're now going to grow crops. The water has been blessed, and it's all going to grow our crops. When the people behind the wall try to grow their crops it will be tainted and their crops won't grow and ours will. He's talking about all these followers, all these people that are coming. There are more and more coming to join us and we need leaders. One man would head up five hundred people, another man would head up another five hundred. There are all these people working in the Light to help shift the energy on the Earth, it is sad and oppressed and he's talking to us about that. Some of the men don't understand at all and others understand and are switched on. As I look around the crowd I know which ones get it because I can see their connection and I can see their rainbows, as can Y'seu. And he has fifteen people behind him. There's fifteen of them and him.

Reena: Who are these fifteen men behind him?

Jane: They are people who are like him that he has chosen.

Reena: Was your father one of these fifteen?

Jane: Yes, yes. At the time of his [Y'seu's] death there are not fifteen. There are thirteen. Three are gone. But initially there have been fifteen plus him.

The number fifteen here is especially significant. Within the Dead Sea Scrolls, found at Qumran, is an extract called 'Community Rule VIII: 1–15', which states that 'In the Council of the Community, there shall be twelve men and three Priests, perfectly versed in all that is revealed ... an Assembly of Supreme Holiness for Aaron'.[7] This would account for fifteen being in the team, including the twelve known disciples, John the Baptist, the enigmatic B and the mysterious Samuel.

Reena: Is Samuel there?
Jane: Yes, he's there. But even though they have gone, their souls are still there. So as I am looking at fifteen of them, it's all fifteen of them, the three souls and B's soul is there. But not everybody can see that. Wow.
Reena: Is your dad there?
Jane: Yes, right behind Y'seu.
Reena: If you are looking at B's soul, what do you notice about his soul?
Jane: It's young. It's filled with bubbles. It's golden and there are lots of bubbles in it.
Reena: How about Son of John, tell me about his soul, is his soul young too?
Jane: His soul is just straight up and down, beautifully connected and massive. His soul is complete. It's middle-aged, but it's evolved as much as it needs to, like he's evolved quicker than he ever expected to. It's like he's had nine lives, like a cat, in this one lifetime.
Reena: What happens next?

Jane: Everyone starts running away. Everyone's leaving and I have to run back to my house. Because the soldiers are coming ... so we all have to run for safety.

Reena: What happened to Y'seu?

Jane: He's just standing there like this ... [demonstrates the 'I am here' pose – with arms straight down the side, palms facing outwards, chest out] He's willing, it's his time and he knows. He's telling everyone else to go. He's done as much work as he can do and he's left it all exactly how it's supposed to be and all his, I'm going to call them his Followers, have to ... take off ...

Reena: What were they called?

Jane: He's calling them Followers and he's calling them Followers because we're all equal and it's really important, his message was that we're all equal. And to give them a glorified title is to not treat people as equals and it feels like it's really important that that is said.

Reena: So the fifteen were also Followers?

Jane: Yes ... Those Followers I guess are more evolved, they're more practised, and therefore they can show their gifts to each group they all lead up, not because they're better but just because they are more practised in it. Their souls are more evolved.

Reena: OK, right. What happens next?

Jane: It's the weirdest thing ... I still know his thoughts. Even though I've run away, it's like I'm still looking through his eyes and I know what's happening. So it's like he's ten feet tall, which he's not, but it's like he is and he's covered in all this light, which the soldiers do not see. I can see him and he has given his soul just to spread the Light but his body now has to be dealt with and man – the soldiers – think that by maiming and crucifying and burning ... and [demonstrates crossing, hammering in the nails, nailing him] … They think that that controls. They think that keeps the soul in the body. If they burn it and then they put the nails through it there's no way his soul can leave the body, so there's no way his soul can do what it's meant to do … But it's not true, because his soul's already doing what it needs to do.

Reena: That's why they nailed his hands?

Jane: Yes, they were shutting down his energy centres, but they didn't know that was what they were trying to do. There was a wise woman, who spoke to the person who told them to do this, and said that this is what you have to do to this one, because it shuts down their energy centres and the crown.

There were lots of reasons why he had this crown on his head, including to show that he was making a mockery of the crown, which he wasn't. It was also to shut down his crown chakra. But they were only hurting flesh and bone – they weren't doing anything to his soul. At all! Nothing to his soul. All this is going on and I'm hiding behind my door whilst the soldiers are looking for me to kill me. His soul's too big.

Reena: At what point did the soul leave the body?

Jane: I think at that meeting. He was still connected but it was like that meeting was when he truly left his body and then it was like he just left the physical, they could do whatever they liked with the physical. But he still had things to finish off but he … because the silver thread hadn't left. That doesn't leave until the crucifixion. But they're burning people as well. As well as him being on this hill being crucified there're fires going on as well. It's like they're trying to burn everything that he stood for and flush it out. They are setting fire to everything to get rid of everything that he did. But what they don't realise is that it's only things – they don't get it – and that's the message that he was trying to leave. That it's not about the physical, it's never been about the physical.

Reena: With the burning, is this an actual burning/branding or burning as in …?

Jane: Oh no, there're buildings burning down, there's flames everywhere. There's smoke, there's fire … some of the houses have got wood put on the outside of the doors so [people] can't escape as well. They've been prisoners in their house. But what I know and what I can see, whether I'm dead at this point, I can just see above it all and I can see all the souls just coming out of the houses and it's like we're all just going, 'Well, do what you like, who cares, we're all still here.'

Reena: And just check to see whether your heart stops beating.

Jane: Yeah, I think I'm definitely dead. I was stabbed … by a soldier.

So David was navigated to the point where he was stabbed.

Jane: I'm hiding behind the door and the soldiers have come in the house and they are looking for me and they run upstairs to the roof. They go up a ladder and they come down and one soldier's seen me and he knows me but he's not going to tell. Then the other mean soldier works out what's going on and he just puts his spear right through the door and it gets me.

Reena: What was it about you that made them go for you?

Jane: I was the son of John ... and I had to be killed, because I was way too bright. I was too much of a threat ... they had to make sure, they couldn't have just barricaded my door because I would've got out, they had to make sure that ...

Reena: You were dead ... [Jane nods] Were they given orders to find you?

Jane: Yes ... [by] the man behind the wall. He stayed behind the wall all the time. He was not very tall, he was very gluttonous – in taste and in appetite. He was a glutton for everything. He had to have too much of everything because he was trying to fulfil his soul, but he couldn't, he was empty. He thought that by having soldiers and women and food and people – that made him heroic, that made him important. It didn't fulfil. He was empty inside.

Reena: What role did he play in this land?

Jane: He wasn't supposed to be the ruler, his brother was, but his brother either died or didn't make it. I'm not sure but he wasn't meant to be the ruler, but he ended up being the ruler. Or he got that title.

Reena: How did the people normally address him?

Jane: I know he was an emperor.

This account is consistent with history. After Herod the Great died in 4BC, and subsequent ethnarch (not king) rule by Antipas's brother, Herod Archelaus, Herod Antipas was named to the throne by Augustus, to rule Galilee and Perea as a client state of the Roman Empire.[8]

David's description of Herod Antipas being gluttonous is also accurate – an example is the drama that ensued in the pursuit of him marrying his half-brother's wife, and his own half-niece, Herodias, whilst divorcing his own wife, who was the daughter of a wealthy Arab king, Aretas (who led his kingdom, Nabataea, and his capital Petra through a Golden Age; the carving of a temple out of rose-red rock is a still-standing monument to his rule). According to historical accounts, John was vocally opposed to this marriage, because it would lead Galilee to war with Nabataea, which was one of reasons why he was targeted for execution – for his political stance.[9]

The next significant event took David to the point after his heart stopped beating.

Jane: I still can't get past the crucifixion; it's like I have to watch. I have to watch him leave.
Reena: So, tell me what it is that is happening?
Jane: So I'm aware that I'm dead and I feel free and I feel light. And I'm watching in the distance and there are fires all over the place, there's chaos beneath me but I'm very peaceful. There's so many people weeping at the physical of Y'seu being taken, and yet he almost is passing with a smile on his face and peace – because he knows it's the beginning, he knows it's not the end. But there's … a whole circle of us waiting for him, and I seem to be one of them. There are all these souls waiting for his silver thread to come away from the body as well. But I don't feel any pain and I'm really close now to watching the crucifixion. I feel sorry for the people who are alive thinking he's in pain when he's actually being freed and … knowing that we're all going to touch as many people as we can that are left behind, and help them see the Light because when all these people, that think he's in pain, see the Light then they'll get it. The message was never to worship him. It was never to see him as someone untouchable … it was to

say he is one of us, we all have this light within us and that message has not been carried forward properly. But it's time that message was carried forward.

Reena: That he was just like one of us ...

Jane: Yes, and we all have that light within us. We all have the connection and the ability to heal ourselves and one another because we're all the same. And having 'things' don't make us better. They make us weaker.

David's references to the 'silver thread' is the 'silver cord', a well-known feature of astral projection and out-of-body experiences, not only amongst mystics who are trained in these skills but amongst people who have come close to death and then been revived. This silver cord is our spirit body's 'lifeline' to our physical body in the same way that our umbilical cord is our 'lifeline' to our mother's body during the birth process. Just as the baby's umbilical cord must be severed for the baby to experience life, the silver cord must be severed for the spirit body to experience spiritual life.[10]

The existence of the silver cord is even mentioned in the Bible: 'Remember him – before the silver cord is severed, or the golden bowl is broken; before the pitcher is shattered at the spring, or the wheel broken at the well, and the dust returns to the ground it came from, and the spirit returns to God who gave it.' (Ecclesiastes 12:6–7)

It is interesting that both of these images, the symbols of water and light, are used in this biblical scripture, which is similar to how David and John the Baptist viewed the world – through water, light and rainbows (light refracted and dispersed by water).

What has been inconsistent with all the other regressions in this book though is that even though David was a soul watching the crucifixion, he identified the person and soul on the cross as Y'seu, and not the substitute.

It is a commonly held view that once the soul leaves the body, the soul has access to the ultimate truth, and has clear vision of what is happening. However, as shown in countless Between Lives Regressions that immediately after leaving the body after death, the soul still holds all the memories, personality and perspective of the life. Only once the soul travels to the Spirit Realms, will the soul clear remnant energy from the life and proceed in its pure form, attaining clear vision and ultimate truth. In this case, the soul of David was still hanging around on Earth as he perceived the crucifixion and thus was holding onto his personality, memories and perspective. So because he saw a form that looked like Y'seu, he surmised that the soul leaving that body was Jesus too. The regression continues.

> Reena: Just tell me what happens next. His soul's joined the group?
> Jane: There's a lady down at his feet. She's down there, and he loved this woman, she's a younger woman.
> Reena: Is she the mother?
> Jane: No, I don't think she's the mother … there's two women and he's coming down to this woman that he loved and he's just putting his arms around her and he's just placing his hand on her chest and just giving her some love. And she just gets it and she lifts her head and she gets it, and she gets it. And his mother gets it, she sees him. This woman looks like she is pregnant.

When asked if David had any contact with this pregnant lady, he answered he had not, though he thought his sister might have. His father had told him that this pregnant lady was sold as a slave and a prostitute so that her family could survive. However, she managed to escape to be healed and cleansed by John. David did admit that he found her to be beautiful and have really beautiful energy. Whilst this story is not consistent with the actual regression on Mary Magdalene, it is consistent with the rumours that were being spread about her through the grapevine about her first marriage, where she was forced to share her life with an awfully abusive man. The regression continues.

Reena: Is your dad there?

Jane: Yes, I think so. My father thinks he has to be forgiven (for) sins, anything that he's done wrong. It's like he did something wrong for Y'seu, which he didn't, but he thinks he did ... Y'seu said that everyone's soul is already cleansed. Everyone's already pure. My dad's trying to say that he has to cleanse them first before their souls are clear – but he's actually cleansing the physical to help release the Light that then goes to heal the land. But it's almost like chicken and egg, they can't decide what comes first. But of course, Y'seu's right and my dad knows that, but he wants his job to be just as important and just as cleansing. But he doesn't believe it, it's my dad's stuff, he doesn't believe it.

Reena: How does Y'seu address your dad at this point?

Jane: He knows he's a Son of God and 'thou shall be called John'. But he was christened something else ... not christened ... When he was born he was called something else but it was Y'seu that said 'thou shall be called John'. Y'seu renamed *all* his followers to make us all the same so that there was no distinction between whether if it was Hebrew, and where you came from, because we were all the same. So he renamed them all.

[At the end of the regression Jane revealed that the word 'baptise' was not used at that time, and she did not know where it comes from. John just thought he was performing cleansing. They were simple people, doing amazing things, and through the centuries they have been built up to be magnificent. John was just a simple man 'cleansing' souls – but civilisation and control had just got hold of it to manipulate it to how they wanted it to be.]

Reena: Can I just ask about your father, John ... he had a big heart and workman hands, but lovely, beautiful. What other temperament did he have?

Jane: He was very fiery, because he wanted to do the right thing all the time, but he was also very angry at his wife dying. He was very fiery. He was very hard-working.

Reena: With the secret men meeting, because he was sitting in front, can we say he was almost one of the leaders?

Jane: Yes, he was, he was sat up there. When Y'seu was in front my father was always right behind him to his right, always. He wouldn't sit down like the others, he stood very closely behind him. The others would be behind. When they had to say something they would get up and speak but my father never sat, he always stood right behind him ... It was like he was Y'seu's right-hand man.

This description was very telling and in line with how Laurence Gardner describes it in his book *The Grail Enigma*. He says that John, being the eldest son of Elizabeth and Zacharius, was the prevailing head of the Zadokite (priestly) line within the Essene community, and Jesus, being the eldest son of Mary and Joseph, was the rightful dynast of the Davidic (kingly) bloodline.[11] In fact, Tobias Churton states that it was Zacharius, as the High (Zadokite) Priest, that sought God's guidance and paired Joseph and Mary, to continue the Davidic lineage.[12] So, given they were the inheritors of these key succession lines with their community, it does make sense for Y'seu to be the leader and John to be the right-hand man.

This unexpected regression gives us a very good perspective of the massively unstable political landscape that John and Jesus played such a crucial part in, under the rule of Herod Antipas. Jane's accounts show how closely Jesus and John worked together, comrades in a unified mission to galvanise the fulfilment of transformative spiritual promise and knowledge in an environment where even temples had become corrupt. One soul was not more important than the other. John seemed equally influential as Jesus amongst his followers, and equally rebellious to the rulers. Again, it shows how the entire biblical history is born on the shoulders of all, and not just The One. Also, it shows how the Divine Light was in everyone, enabling ordinary people like you and I to perform extraordinary feats.

Whilst history has no mention of David, it is consistent with Jane's account that he was kept hidden, for his own safety, not only due to his spiritual gifts, but also for political purposes, given the role his father played. Jane's account of the history and the political quagmire around John and Jesus is eye-opening and consistent with historical accounts of that time.

13

SUBSTITUTE

Someone has to die that the rest of us should value life more.
– Virginia Woolf

I have to admit, whilst I was facilitating all these sessions, I was blown away by some of the extraordinary stories that I was hearing. Although I did not know much about Jesus, the disciples and the events that took place in those times, I was aware that Jesus' death and resurrection were the lynchpins of one of the world's biggest religious beliefs, Christianity. At the time of these sessions, I did not do any research into the matter, again to maintain objectivity and integrity whilst facilitating these regressions. I was flummoxed hearing these consistent accounts that went against popular tradition and stories, and questioned them ... until Anna came along.

Anna (not her real name) was another student of the Past Life Regression Academy in the UK. An American lady, living in mainland Europe, Anna has a healthy curiosity, and some knowledge, about biblical times. One evening, whilst working with another student, Anna spontaneously slipped back into a past life where she too was living in those times.

Knowing my interest in this subject matter, the student told me about Anna's experience, and I thought it would be fascinating to explore this further. With Anna's permission, we entered into her memories of a seventeen-year-old girl.

Anna: I'm near a port, near some water.

Reena: And do you know where on the Earth you are?

Anna: Near an ocean. I just see the boats. There are some boats.

Reena: Could you describe the boats?

Anna: Most of them are sailing-type boats. They're big.

Reena: Big sail boats?

Anna: Mm.

Reena: Are there any oars on these boats?

Anna: There are oars coming through holes. They are coming out of the sides of the boats, like the bottom part. It's closed on the top but the oars are down.

Reena: And what are you doing?

Anna: I'm getting fish. There's a market or someone's selling or something. I'm just there for a bit.

[During the debrief, post-regression, Anna acknowledged that she was somewhere in the Middle East, and by an inland sea where there was plenty of fishing activity. In Judea, during those times, according to the Talmud and Gospels, the Sea of Galilee was a main hub for the fishing industry. So one could assume that this is where Anna first found herself upon entering the past life.]

Reena: And just tell us what happens next.

Anna: I'm in a hurry. I'm late.

Reena: And what are you late for?

Anna: I don't know. I'm just slow. [chuckles] Yes, I'm just taking that home for a meal or something.

Reena: OK. And when you get home, just tell me a bit about your home life.

Anna proceeds to inform us that she lives with her family. When she gets home from the market, she sees her aunt, whom she identifies as Rachel, and two other grown women. She also finds her two younger brothers, her older sister, who calls her Mimi, some little kids and an older man around. They are all relatives of hers. Her mum and dad are not home. She also finds one of her sister's friends there.

> Anna: There's someone there named Sarah. And I don't know who she is. She's not my sister, but she's with her.
> Reena: And who is Sarah?
> Anna: My sister likes her.
> Reena: Is she friends with your sister?
> Anna: Yes. Very close. They know things that they don't tell me.
> Reena: How does that make you feel?
> Anna: Angry.

As we move to the next significant event, Mimi, now eighteen, finds herself in a town, and there is a lot of shouting in the streets.

> Anna: I'm indoors … watching from upstairs.
> Reena: And what are they shouting?
> Anna: The army or something is coming. I don't know.
> Reena: Can you see the army coming?
> Anna: They are there. They're just going through the streets – some soldiers, ordering, telling people what to do … I'm not very scared of them. They have a lot of shields and funny weapons. And they've got funny headgear on. I've not seen it before.

Mimi goes on to describe the soldiers' attire. The helmets are part metal and pointed, with some having the metal close to their heads. They have metal on their bodies, across the chest and hips/groin areas, with some having a short cloth beneath, from which their legs can be seen. Dark, thinnish leather covers their feet to their shins, whilst some of them just have sandals on.

Reena: You say you are not afraid of them?
Anna: No. They don't care about me. I'm just watching from upstairs.
Reena: And what's making the other people in the streets yell and shout?
Anna: They want them to go away. The soldiers [are] just trying to scare us.

Moving to the next significant event, Mimi finds herself at home. It is a little house, with dirt floors, wooden furnishings and a big courtyard. She reveals that her family members are packing up their possessions ready to move.

Anna: We're going somewhere, my family's moving. We're wrapping everything up and leaving … It's just that we have to move.
Reena: And what's making your family move?
Anna: My father says we have to move. We're not safe.
Reena: Does your father explain what you're not safe from?
Anna: No. But we have to listen.
Reena: OK. And what happens next once you've finished packing up your house.
Anna: We're going. We're travelling … walking … We're going further away from the sea. More inland.
Reena: Do you understand why you're going inland?
Anna: It's safer.

Reena: Does anyone explain to you what you're safer from?

Anna: No.

[The next significant event sees Mimi at the front door.]

Reena: Tell us a bit about the front door.

Anna: There's someone at the door ... A messenger ... He has something to tell my father.

Reena: Do you know what he's telling your father?

Anna: No. I can see my father's agitated.

Reena: What role did your father play in the community by the sea before you went away?

Anna: I think he had some political ... I don't know. He had some position. Yeah, he made decisions ... Political-type decisions.

Reena: How did people address your father?

Anna: I don't know.

Reena: So he's received a message that's got him a bit agitated. What happens next?

Anna: Nothing for the time being.

Reena: The messenger ... does he look like the soldiers?

Anna: He's got some kind of uniform ... a longer dress on, skirts. It goes down. And on the top he has a vest or something. He did not carry a weapon.

At the next significant event, the regression took an unexpected turn.

Anna: No.

Reena: No?

Anna: No. I'm not saying anything.

Reena: What's stopping you from saying?

Anna: No, I don't. I don't know ... what to do about it ... No, I'm not ...

[long pause] I can't do it.

Reena: What can't you do?

Anna: I'm not going to. I will not say it. It's not the right time.

[Anna was getting visibly distressed, wringing her hands, growing pale.]

Reena: Oh, it's not the right time to say this. OK. Shall I move you forward? How are you feeling about this?

Anna: No. It's not good for Todd. I have to look after him. It's dangerous.

Reena: OK. Is there anything we can do to help you feel safer?

Anna: Todd is not supposed to know.

Unbeknownst to me, Todd (not his real name) is Anna's son in this current life. When she revealed Todd's identity during the post-regression briefing, this unexpected turn became clearer.

Reena: OK. Do you want to sit with that experience and get all the information you need? Would you like a moment to do that?

Anna: Yes [pause] … No, I don't want to.

Reena: Do you want to come out, then?

Anna: I feel dizzy. I want to come out.

When she came back to conscious awareness, Anna and I continued our conversation about Todd, and what caused the dramatic shutdown during the regression.

Anna: I got to this point where I was watching the crucifixion and everything was so clear. I was so shocked. I didn't know what I was looking at … To suddenly see the cross … My reaction was to look at other people, to look at their faces and to see that they didn't see it. Suddenly that recognition went through my body: that's not him! I just saw the replacement, who looked a lot like Jesus, but I knew it wasn't him. Don't they see it? Can't they see it? Can't anybody else see it? And there was so much noise. People were screaming, people were shouting. There was so much confusion and so much noise. I was shouting: 'Can't you see? Can't you see?' No one was listening. It was very vivid.

I saw Todd again and what was going to happen just freaked me out. All I got was a feeling that I was related to Todd. That was the feeling I got. Not that I was related to Jesus or anyone else, I was related to whoever that other person was.

Reena: Do you know what the relationship was?

Anna: The replacement. He was related to me as well, I fear. He was my father! That was why he was agitated, that's why he wanted to run away, that's why he got agitated with the messenger.

During the post-session debrief, what came through was that Anna did finally recognise that it was her father who replaced Jesus at the crucifixion, and the soul of her father then came back as her son, Todd, in this life. As she had not had a chance to work through the shock and trauma of this teenage girl seeing her dad die, it triggered the emotional memories within her, and made it traumatic for her to go through the session, with not just the memory of seeing her father crucified, but also carrying the soul understanding that her father in that life is her son in this.

Anna explained, 'So then of course the energy started to just merge and more of me started to surface, you know, around that, and that became the priority really. That's why I couldn't really see any more, I started to just blank out on all the other things that were happening.' And so the regression ended.

So, which biblical character could this mysterious replacement be? There are a couple of candidates that we could look at, the first being Simon of Cyrene, and the second Judas Iscariot.

Simon of Cyrene is mentioned in three of the four Gospels in the Bible as the man compelled by the Roman soldiers to carry Jesus' cross out of Jerusalem. Cyrene was situated in modern-day Libya, on the northern coast of the African continent. Settled by the Greeks in 630BC and later infused with a significant Jewish population, Cyrene was the capital of the Roman district of Cyrenaica at the time of Jesus' crucifixion. By then, Cyrene was home to a large number of Greek-speaking, or Hellenistic, Jews.

Many Jews from Cyrene had returned to their native Israel and were part of a community in Jerusalem called the Synagogue of the Freedmen, comprising Jews from many other provinces including Alexandria (Egypt), Cilicia and Asia (Acts 6:9). Luke records men from Cyrene being amongst those converted at Pentecost (Acts 2:10). After the martyrdom of Stephen (Acts 7), believers from Cyrene were amongst the first to be scattered by the persecution in Jerusalem; arriving in Antioch, they preached to the Gentiles there (Acts 11:20). These believers were instrumental in the formation of the church at Antioch, where, for the first time, 'the disciples were called Christians' (Acts 11:26).[1]

Simon of Cyrene is mentioned in Matthew, Mark and Luke. Matthew only records his name and place of origin (27:32), but Mark and Luke say that he was 'on his way in from the country' (Luke 23:26). Mark, uncharacteristically, provides the most information about Simon, adding that he was 'the father of Alexander and Rufus' (Mark 15:21), men obviously well known to Mark's readers. It is speculated that the Rufus mentioned here may be the same man Paul greets in his letter to Rome, whom he calls 'chosen in the Lord' and whose mother 'has been a mother to me, too' (Romans 16:13). Paul's knowledge of Rufus's family indicates that at some point they lived further east.[2]

Very little is known of the life of Simon of Cyrene before his mention in the Gospels, or even after. The only thing we know is that he was the father of two sons,[3] and Anna did mention that, in that life, she'd had two brothers. Because of Cyrene, there are questions about his descent – was he of African descent (therefore was the colour of his skin darker) or did he emigrate from Judea (therefore was his skin of olive tone)? No one knows, as no records exist.

Could the replacement have been Simon of Cyrene, who instead of helping Jesus carry the cross to the execution site, actually volunteered to take his place to be crucified? Was that why the guards, who were bribed by James, chose him, as opposed to the hundred others who were watching? Was that also why Simon and his sons had special mention in three Gospels and Paul's letters – to immortalise him for his sacrifice? Could Simon of Cyrene have been the father of Anna in that life?

There is another document, the Gospel of Barnabas (a little-known and controversial writing, copies of which go back to the fifteenth century), that claims that it was Judas, not Jesus, who was crucified on the cross. This work, that many claim contains remnants of an earlier record, states that Judas' appearance was transformed to that of Jesus' when the former, out of betrayal, led the Roman soldiers to arrest Jesus, who by then had ascended to the heavens. This transformation of appearance was so identical that the masses, followers of Christ, and even the mother of Jesus, Mary, initially thought that the one arrested and crucified was Jesus himself,[4] which was in line with Maya's regression in a previous chapter.

This Gospel then mentions that, three days after burial, Judas' body was stolen from his grave, and then the rumours spread of Jesus being risen from the dead. When Jesus was informed in the third heaven about what had happened, he prayed to God to be sent back to the Earth, and descended and gathered his mother, disciples and followers, and told them the truth of what happened. He then ascended back to the heavens, to come back at the end of times as a just king.[5]

It is very interesting that the latter part of the account in this Gospel is in line with the accounts of most of the regressees, who experienced the time after the crucifixion. According to Mia's account of James, the replacement's body was 'hurriedly moved' from the cross, and while those who were privy to the third-tier information thought he did ascend, his disciples and followers (second tier) were privy to a little bit more knowledge.

Again, there is very little information that records Judas' life before becoming one of Jesus' followers. Texts such as John 6:71, 12:4 and 13:26 mention that Judas was the son of Simon Iscariot and perhaps a native of Kerioth. He was considered to be Jewish.[6]

There is no information about his family life, or his work, other than being the treasurer for Jesus and his ministry, so no definite conclusion can be drawn from Anna's regression if Judas was the replacement. Was Judas the father of four? Was he actively involved in politics during that time? Did he sacrifice himself on the cross for Jesus, rather than betraying him (or because of the betrayal), thus deserving our respect as opposed to vilification?

Apart from the accounts of the regressees who participated in this book, there are few records mentioning the substitution. Given that it was such a deep secret, as Jesus' and (possibly) James' lives depended on it being kept, this does make sense, and thus cannot be conclusively affirmed or denied. However, the 1945 discovery of Gnostic texts at Nag Hammadi, Egypt, unearthed a book called *The Second Treatise of the Great Seth* that does record Jesus implying that he was substituted at the cross.

'I did not succumb to them as they had planned. But I was not afflicted at all. Those who were there punished me. And I did not die in reality but in appearance, lest I be put to shame by them because these are my kinsfolk. I was about to succumb to fear, and I suffered according to their sight and thought, in order that they may never find any word to speak about them. For my death, which they think happened, (happened) to them in their error and blindness, since they nailed their man unto their death. But in doing these things, they condemn themselves. Yes, they saw me; they punished me. It was another, their father, who drank the gall and the vinegar; it was not I. They struck me with the reed; it was another, Simon, who bore the cross on his shoulder. It was another upon whom they placed the crown of thorns.' [7]

From my perspective, after having conducted quite a few regressions, I think that it was an absolute act of synchronicity that Anna, who was the daughter of the replacement, emerged, to not just pull these other accounts together, but also enigmatically divulge fleeting details about the mysterious replacement that leaves a lot of food for thought ...

14

Consciousness

Knowing yourself is the beginning of all wisdom.
– Aristotle

During the explorative journey of this book, whilst I believed that these were indeed genuine past lives, I began to question a few things. Firstly, I thought it was an extraordinary act of synchronicity and serendipity that so many people who had experienced significant lives during biblical times were drawn to either my therapy or training rooms. So, I wondered, were these souls experiencing their genuine past lives or were they tapping into a Collective Consciousness to bring these stories through?

Secondly, I started to think about the large number of different people who have claimed to have experienced lives of Mary Magdalene or Jesus – and wondered if there was a greater energy that moved through the people who lived in those times, or whether Jesus Christ and Mary Magdalene were living, breathing higher Consciousness in physical bodies.

Thirdly, as I began to do more research into this subject matter, I was quite intrigued with the arguments over the Trinity concept of the Father, Son and the Holy Spirit, as well as the controversy over the divinity of Jesus Christ. Was he truly divine, or was he like every other man who embodied and lived the seeds of divinity?

Using the process similar to navigating between-lives spiritual regression, I asked Jane (who regressed to the life of the son of John the Baptist) if she would be willing to participate in an experiment to access a higher Consciousness to help answer my questions. Jane is highly psychic intuitive, yet has had limited exposure to and knowledge about Jesus Christ and biblical times. This made her the ideal candidate for this session. She, very kindly, was totally game for it.

So I guided her into deep hypnosis and made the intent to link to the Christ Consciousness. Please note that during this session I used the term *Christ Consciousness* to label the divine energy. The term Holy Spirit is used by the Church to define this energy. *Christ Consciousness* is just a term or name that we used and is not to be taken as absolute.

The following is what was communicated to her:

Reena: So just let me know what happens for you to be able to get to the Christ Consciousness.

Jane: Leaving the physical body behind and floating up above my body.

Reena: What colour is your energy?

Jane: White, but I am connected to the body and that's OK.

Reena: … maybe you can tell me a little bit about your journey as well if you can.

Jane: It's just so peaceful, so peaceful and so light. It's like I'm just floating, floating with purpose, and it feels like there's humour and curiosity surrounding me. There's lots of other people too, lots of other lights who look like me. Some of them are dead, returning, and some of them are meditating.

Reena: Interesting ... The ones who are meditating –
how are they different from the ones that are dead?
Jane: The ones that are dead are much lighter, the ones
that are meditating are heavier, still weighed down a
little. The ones that are dead are just so light.
Reena: And just tell me anything of interest ...
Jane: There's a Buddha energy. It's amazing! It's
amazing. There's all these monks and Buddha and it's
like they've got their own little section and it's amazing,
it's amazing! They're amazing people, their hearts are so
pure. It's amazing! Some of the people who are
meditating connect to it because you can see the wires
or cords connecting them but it's just energy, I could
put my hand right through it and it wouldn't break it.
It's just ... it's light, it's all light and I can put my hand
right through it.
Reena: How beautiful. Can I ask if that's Buddha or
Buddha Consciousness?
Jane: Buddha Consciousness ... because it's all the One
Consciousness. It's all connected to the Main
Consciousness. It looks like a giant brain. It's just ... I
quite like this - everything's connected.
Reena: That Main Consciousness, is that the Christ
Consciousness or is it the Christ and Buddha
Consciousness making up the Main Consciousness?
Jane: Yes. The Christ Consciousness was the awakening
of humans, reminding us of our purpose in life. It was
to awaken love, because love was dying. Wherever
there's a birth there's always love and there was no love
around this birth.
Reena: Jesus' birth?
Jane: Yes.
Reena: There was no love around Jesus' birth?

Jane: On the planet. His birth was very difficult, very difficult.

Reena: Really?

Jane: Yes. For Mother Mary.

Reena: What was making it so difficult for Mother Mary?

Jane: He was just laid really, really awkwardly and his shoulder was stuck. When his little head came out his shoulder was stuck, but he had to fight to come into the world.

Reena: And was Joseph there helping him?

Jane: Yes. And someone, feels like a sister to Mary. And so much light, it was like when he was born a nuclear bomb of light went off … in terms of the energetic vibrations.

Reena: Beautiful, and what did that do?

Jane: Shifted everything on the Earth. It made even more hatred and evil, and it made those that loved determined to love and determined to do the right thing and overthrow any evil. It awakened everybody.

Reena: Can I ask whether Jesus was a soul that agreed to carry the Christ Consciousness into the body or whether Jesus *was* the Christ Consciousness?

Jane: Jesus was connected to the Christ Consciousness in a big way. You can't birth the Christ Consciousness. He was connected in a big way, in a really big way … like the Pharaohs.

Reena: So did the Pharaohs connect to Christ Consciousness as well?

Jane: Yes, yes … I'm watching all of this from above.

Reena: And what are you watching?

Jane: Everything you ask me just appears in a picture.

Reena: Gorgeous ... Just to clarify, is there a Magdalene Consciousness or is there not one?

Jane: When you say her name she feels much heavier than Jesus, she just feels different, when I look at her she feels different ... She feels like she had to try to connect like the meditating people.

Reena: So she was trying to connect to the Christ Consciousness?

Jane: Yes.

Reena: OK, the reason I wanted to ask is that there is talk that there is a Magdalene Consciousness, but it's nice to know that it was a soul within a body that was connecting into the Christ Consciousness. OK, got it. The Christ Consciousness, does it have a Feminine or Masculine energy or is it a balance of both?

Jane: It's a balance of both ... but it's a light energy and a dark energy as opposed to male and female. I think it means the same.

Reena: It means the same and it's just a balance? OK, is the dark energy the one that brings through fear or is it something else?

Jane: There's no fear there at all.

Reena: So you have the Christ Consciousness and the Buddha Consciousness ... are there any other Consciousnesses around?

Jane: There's lots because man has created lots to try and control it. Man has tried to control this Divine Consciousness by creating its own little parts of it.

The revelation that man can create different Consciousness came as an absolute surprise to me. As this session continued, little did I know that there were more surprises in store. With these surprises came clarity.

Reena: So was Christ Consciousness created by man or the Divine?

Jane: The Divine.

Reena: And Buddha's Consciousness?

Jane: [Created by] Man.

Reena: OK, what other Consciousness did the Divine create?

Jane: There's one in a language I don't know but if I had to understand it [pause] ... I don't know ... it feels Sanskrit-ish.

Reena: So it feels Sanskrit-ish. Is that where the tantric learnings have come from?

Jane: Yes.

Reena: Got it, OK. Any others?

Jane: There is a One, it's behind all the others.

Reena: What is the significance of it being behind the others?

Jane: It brings birth and when you have birth you have love and the man-made ones tried to eradicate it. I can see lots of shoots growing through the ground and I can see lots of baby animals being born. I can see lots of birth in springtime ... It's like the Divine Mother.

I found this particularly fascinating. Laurence Gardner, in *The Grail Enigma*, explains that within the Gospels of Nazarenes, the Holy Spirit was a feminine aspect of the Divine, known to the Greeks as Sophia. Whilst making no mention of Mary or the birth of Jesus, the Nazarene Gospel emphasises that it was at the baptism of Jesus in the River Jordan where Jesus was said to have been empowered by the Holy Spirit, which he recognized as the Divine Mother.[1] Could this be the Consciousness he tapped into during baptism?

Reena: Any other divine-inspired Consciousness?

Jane: Not on this planet.

Reena: What are some examples of the man-made ones? You've got Buddha … anything else?

Jane: There's a lot of singing … there's another one and there's a lot of singing that belongs to it.

Reena: Is that the arty one that inspires artists or something?

Jane: Dunno, there's lots of singing, chanting, it's an Indian female. This is created by man.

Reena: And what does this one 'do'?

Jane: This one doesn't feel very good. This one feels very greedy. It's a much lower vibration to the others. The Buddha Consciousness really wanted to be created by the Divine like the Christ Consciousness but birthing that energy into a human soul is not something that is done lightly.

Reena: So what happened to it to make it man-made?

Jane: Tried to hurry the process, tried to hurry it up, souls trying to evolve too quickly. But this big, huge white brain that I can see would scoop them all up and take them all into it with love, but they are not ready for it yet.

Reena: Is there Consciousness there to do with material gain at all?

Jane: It feels very connected to the chanting and singing one, that's a material-gain one.

Reena: We found out what the Christ Consciousness is about, which is love, and the Feminine Consciousness, which is about birth. How about the Sanskrit Consciousness? Is there a name for it, that we're aware of?

Jane: No.

Reena: What is the purpose of the Sanskrit Consciousness and the Tantra?

Jane: It works on the vibration and the energy of the people who understand it and connect with it. It doesn't work for everyone; it depends on their soul journey. Someone who understands that level of Consciousness would never understand the Christ Consciousness.

Reena: Oh, is that right?

Jane: Yes. It's a different vibration for them.

Reena: But it's still the Earth vibration?

Jane: Yes.

Reena: Interesting. So that's why they can't combine on Earth, because they have different vibrations?

Jane: Yes.

Reena: So the people who work with the Feminine vibration, can they understand the Christ Consciousness?

Jane: Yes.

Reena: So the Feminine can work with both?

Jane: Because Feminine is about birthing and it's about love, and love exists in all the Consciousnesses in lots of different shapes and forms, so therefore the Feminine can embrace *all*.

Reena: OK ... Just focus on the Christ Consciousness again ...

Jane: So many people are trying to make it into something that it's not. It's just simple. The simplicity is that it's love in balance. It's love. Jesus was born to bring love but when you bring so much love, so much hatred is also brought.

Reena: What is the learning or the relevance of bringing in so much hatred with so much love?

Jane: To balance the hatred and eradicate it. But each of these souls are dying and learning their lesson and then coming back to live a life in love and bringing back love where there was once hatred. Healing the land where much blood has been spilt. Teaching souls when they pass through and bringing in the love.

Reena: And how can they embody the love? When souls embody the love of the Christ Consciousness?

Jane: The quicker they get through their soul's journey, the quicker they can then live love in their life. The more people who help the souls to get rid of the pain and suffering from past and present, the sooner they can move on in love and it's not happening fast enough … Everyone is born with an equal balance [of] love and hate. It's up to us and our free will to keep that balance. And man has still got it wrong.

Reena: And this is just an intellectual question … does it mean Divine Consciousness is benevolent? With all these man-made Consciousnesses, could there be one that is malevolent?

Jane: I want to say yes, but it will never overtake. It's man-made and it's people believing in something that's not real, creating an energy of something that doesn't exist.

Reena: Yet in man's creation of it, it is enabling the existence of it. OK, thank you. The other question I'd like to ask is, do all these different Consciousnesses interact? For example, do the Feminine and Christ Consciousness interact or can the Sanskrit interact with Christ Consciousness?

Jane: Well, no, they connect through the Main Consciousness.

Reena: Otherwise they have people just tap into them individually?

Jane: Yes.

Reena: Are there any plans for allowing the different energies and Consciousness to come through at the same time? For example, Feminine and Christ Consciousness or Sanskrit and Feminine or Sanskrit and Christ, you know?

Jane: Well, no, when they connect through the Main Source together, they then connect together. They have to come together up there to come together down here. [pause] I am just being taken through the Christ Consciousness.

Reena: Just tell me your experience of being taken through the Christ Consciousness.

Jane: I feel as if every cell in my body has had a blow-dryer put on it, but it's cool, it's not hot, it's like it's just blown through me like a wind. When the Native American Indians talked about the wind the conscious energy was blowing through them and directing them and guiding them. And that's what it feels like, it's like it's just blown through me and left parts of itself all over me. It's just amazing … It's so light. It feels like it's got really messy with people trying to understand it – monsters for knowledge, when all that knowledge is inside of us. It's got really messy, hence all the different Consciousnesses. I can see so many souls, so many people, souls everywhere in the Main Consciousness. There're so many souls.

Reena: Are they souls that are meditating or souls that have passed?

Jane: These have passed. Some of them still look asleep, they are the ones that have to be reincarnated, the ones that are not truly awakened.

Reena: So it is those that are not truly awakened that need to be reincarnated. What happens to the souls that are awakened?

Jane: They are helping to dissolve all the extra Consciousnesses that have been created. Healing work, helping balance that.

Reena: Man didn't create all Negative Consciousness, they did create Buddha. That's quite positive, isn't it? [Jane affirms] So how did that happen?

Jane: He was able to connect to the big brain and because he connected to the big brain he bore in the same energy that Jesus was born with.

Reena: But that's via his connection and opposed to being born with it?

Jane: Yes, he was able to raise his vibration, truly connect.

Reena: Was that his plan?

Jane: No, it surprised Buddha. He tries hard to help others to do the same, he allows others to work at doing the same.

Reena: He allows others to ... work to do the same?

Jane: Feels like he was meditating one day and he drifted out of his body and when he came back into his body he brought down this big 'plop' of energy in his head, like a massive raindrop. And that's what happens to all the brilliant inventors in this world and artists and musicians. They all have a big plop of the Consciousness put within them when they are born. Because before the human skull closes there's spaces for this plop to go into those who are chosen. But Buddha just got it a bit later and got heaps of it.

Reena: So with this access to this 'plop' (with the great inventors and artists and musicians), their life seems to be quite drama-filled, quite difficult and challenging. Does this plop exacerbate all that?

Jane: Yes.

Reena: So it exacerbates the talents and their shadow selves?

Jane: Yes. But the shadow selves can't cope with it, it's too much.

Reena: Can I ask, just on a different note, what Consciousness did all the Native people tap into, like the Aborigines, the Native American Indians …?

Jane: The Divine, the Main, always, because they tapped into the planet, the planet's connected always.

Reena: The planet is connected to the Main Consciousness …

Jane: Always.

Reena: So then they were destroyed by the Europeans who carried quite a lot of the Christian teachings, isn't that right?

Jane: Yes.

Reena: So what Consciousness were these people carrying then?

Jane: Their man-made god.

Reena: And who started the man-made god?

Jane: Jesus, because he knew that he was part of God, he knew that he was connected. But other souls weren't evolved enough to understand.

Reena: So they misinterpreted his teachings.

Jane: Yes, they did. And this brings him much sorrow.

Reena: So wasn't it in the divine plan for the … for the church to obliterate the religious practices of the Native people? For example, when they went to Peru they made the Incas demolish their own temples and put up churches.

Jane: Because the Europeans knew they were already connected and they couldn't have that because the Natives were mere savages. This 'mere' people had more than the Europeans people had and they hated that … the Europeans couldn't have that because they would lose all value. They'd lose all faith and the faith that thousands of others had been practising, connecting in their own individual ways for centuries. It would make them all look silly.

Reena: So what Consciousness is that, that they (the church) were tapping into or creating?

Jane: The man-made god. God is not a man, yet they wish him to be. Jesus was not a God, yet they worship like he was.

The discussions around the Trinity doctrine (of the Father, Son and the Holy Spirit) centred around establishing Jesus as a divine being. Whilst there are 45 entries in the New Testament which state that Jesus was called the Son of God by others, there are 90 mentions of him being the Son of Man, the majority made by Jesus himself.[2]

Reena: So Jesus is a man that brought lots of Christ Consciousness with him.

Jane: Yes, of love. And there is much love because of his birth and there is much greatness because of it. There was much energetic shift because of it, but there was also much harm.

325

Reena: Was this a plan that had gone wrong or was it just part of the plan for the evolution of souls?

Jane: Part of the plan for the evolution of souls.

Reena: OK, I'm just wondering how the misunderstanding of the love and Christ Consciousness and the development of the man-made Consciousness can help with the evolution?

Jane: The more these powerful souls are being allowed to hold the Light from being on the planet and being above the planet, the more that it helps restore that which was undone. I'm being shown everybody holding the planet.

Reena: What was undone?

Jane: The love that was intended by the birth of Christ.

Reena: So the love was undone. Was that a mistake?

Jane: Yes. To rectify it, just trust and ye shall find the love within, it is not hidden and when we find the love within: illuminate, share and connect.

Reena: Thank you.

During the first Council of Nicaea in AD325, convened by Emperor Constantine, some tradition holds that an elderly Libyan priest called Arius was punched in the face by Nicholas of Myra, for arguing that as Jesus had been physically born of a woman, he was not eternal, but earned his way to the divine status of Son of God, as other people could. Arianism, as it was known, gathered much support, and even the sympathy of Emperor Constantine. In AD381, however, his successor Emperor Theodosius decreed (for his own political gain and advantage) that all must uphold the doctrine of Trinity. The greatest repository of Arian texts was said to be in library of Alexandria, which, in AD391, Theodosius instructed Bishop Theophilus to raze to the ground, destroying not just the

Arian texts but half a million documents representing the finest minds in the ancient world.[3]

The information that Jane accessed supports Arianism – that Jesus was not *the* Christ Consciousness, but he embodied it on Earth. This too accounts for why Mina's Thomas spontaneously referred to Jesus as 'Christian', as reflected by Flavius Josephus in his first-century *Antiquities of the Jews*, which made two claims that Jesus was called Christ (or Christos).[4] If Jesus can embody the Consciousness, so can every soul on Earth, and live as Jesus and his followers can. As we saw from Greg's regressions to Paul, it was Paul who started raising Jesus to a divine being, as a vehicle to get the message out. The Church continued to perpetuate this perception, which Jane referred to as man-made God.

Through Jane and all the other people who participated in this book, the version of the story that has emerged is that Jesus and his followers were ordinary people, embodying the Christ Consciousness, doing extraordinary things. They had a strong realisation that they all held the divine energy within them – which made them no different to God or one another. This does not diminish their stature in any way – rather it augments them, in my view. They showed that we are all divine and connected. Jesus' role was to embody love and share it with all, and he showed us this by his example. If he is the same as all of us, we can do this too – embody our own Divinity and the love of the Divine and share it with all, regardless of the faith and religion we follow, or do not.

Conclusion

1. The Spiritual Story:

Ancient Hellenistic mythology speaks of Moirai – three white-robed incarnations of Destiny, weaving the Mother Thread of Fate of every soul. Sitting by their looms, weaving their rich tapestry of life, it is said that these three sisters predetermine the destiny of a soul – and only the mighty Zeus was excluded from their cycle of spinning.

One cannot help but wonder about the intricate tapestry of the life of Jesus, and all those around him. The shimmering rainbow bouquet of threads of destinies interlacing, warping and wefting across 2,000 years, woven meticulously, everything connected, to create one of the richest, most ornate and opulent works of fate – around one incredibly inspirational figure.

In *Shrouded Truth* we clearly see Jesus as the man, an ordinary soul, doing extraordinary things. He was married, had children, and was frail of body. He taught that all souls are equal. He was surrounded by people who loved and believed in him so much that they sacrificed unconditionally, in their own ways, for him and the cause he led. We see how the lives of his blood brothers, his wife, his daughter and his spiritual brothers weave with his, creating the figure that he is known as today. Everyone has played a role, individual threads woven into the Fabric of Whole.

It is a very different story than what has been commonly portrayed. Whilst common perceptions portray Jesus as the Son of God, the memories in this book portrayed Jesus as being a normal man, performing divine-like feats.

Whilst common perceptions portray Jesus acting alone, the sole deity on his mission of peace, these memories have portrayed the tight unit of selfless individuals around Jesus, working with and helping him through the tough times to ensure the success of the mission he led.

Whilst common perceptions paint Jesus as being divine, these memories tell a tale of Jesus embracing and embodying the divine energy of Christ Consciousness – a Consciousness that is there, readily available for everyone to embrace and embody in the pursuit of their own paths.

The basic principles of these memories digress wildly from the more accepted tale of Jesus. To move forward in clarity and to be able to combine various historical references with spiritual doctrines, there needs to be clarity without reliance on superstitions.

Whilst the Bible is taken by many Christians as the Word of God, there is equally strong support for the argument that it was created by man. Tom Paine wrote eloquently in a letter on 12 May 1797, 'But by what authority do you call the Bible the Word of God? For this is the first point to be settled. It is not your calling it so that makes it so, any more than the Mohammedans calling the Koran the Word of God makes the Koran to be so. The Popish Councils of Nice [sic] and Laodicea, about 350 years after the time the person called Jesus Christ is said to have lived, voted the books that now compose what is called the New Testament to be the Word of God. This was done by yeas and nays, as we now vote a law. The Pharisees of the second temple, after the Jews returned from captivity in Babylon, did the same by the books that now compose the Old Testament, and this is all the authority there is, which to me is no authority at all. I am as capable of judging for myself as they were, and I think more so, because, as they made a living by their religion, they had a self-interest in the vote they gave.'[1]

Stories have been dressed up and told to create a reality that does not always accurately portray reality. Greg's regression to Paul highlights this. There have been agendas behind a lot of the great religions, and though they may not have started that way, they got hijacked and rewritten with aspects being left out and other aspects being added, sometimes to create what is necessary to portray the message that those wanting to maintain their power want to convey. And so vital information which helps in the understanding of the spiritual connection to one's own eternity both within and without is lost.

The basic fundamental spiritual practices of all religions state that the connection starts from within ourselves and then connect outwards. However, if this information is manipulated, the connection becomes severed or distorted. In time, each and every individual will have the ability to reconnect to themselves. This is their given birthright. It's the Remembering.

It is the remembering of the connection and that individuals do not necessarily need somebody telling them there is a right or wrong way to connect. Each individual will have a unique blueprint so, although there are techniques, each connection is unique to that individual, just like their fingerprints.

It is the misguided manipulation of many religions to control, and this can sometimes prevent people from finding their unique way both through life and their connection. This does not mean religion is wrong. The Church has been vital in spreading important spiritual messages and creating a community – as we've seen in the memories of Paul. This is to not disregard all aspects of religion.

But as more evidence of the spiritual message is stacked up, it is harder to hide that evidence, and it comes from so many different sources. New historical evidence has come to light, more and more academics are delving into these religious stories; and this is just another means of carrying a message to those who may not hear it in a different format – that religions have clouded spiritual messages for control, and power.

In the last 2,000 years, a superstition of Jesus – the Son of God – was created. We have to remember, Jesus was not a Christian. Much like our time now, the era in which he was born was clearly a time of change – of revolution – where the common men armed themselves with both word, deed and weapons, to fight against their oppression by those in power, be it the Romans, the Pharisees or the Sadducees. Jesus was not a Christian as we know Christians to be now. Jesus rose up against the power and control of the social and religious leaders of his time. Jesus did not believe in his death and resurrection at the time of him teaching his spiritual principles. He believed that all men and women are divine in their own right.

Two thousand years ago, it would have been very hard to move from the kind of very superstitious, mystical way in which people viewed the Earth, viewed the world. People then needed a hero, to break through the status quo and fill them with the spirit of change. They wanted gods, and they created these gods. And so Jesus and others have become the bridge. They are the man-gods. It doesn't make the story wrong or irrelevant. It is just what was needed at that point in time. As Rose reminded me, astrologically, 2,000 years ago was the start of the Piscean Age.

At this time of change, the end of the Piscean and the beginning of the Aquarian Age, status quo, power and control is once again being threatened. Similar to what we are experiencing today, they were experiencing a transition to a new way of Being. The crucifixion was a dramatic occurrence that facilitated the teaching of breaking through established structures. Those who participated in that change were all sons and daughters of God, who saw past the establishment, and performed incredible acts of courage and made devastating sacrifices to enable these changes to occur.

We too are all sons and daughters of God. *Shrouded Truth* illustrates that we too can be like Jesus – that the Superhero we seek is within us. Yes – we all have physical limitations, but *Shrouded Truth* shows that Jesus Christ was no different. However, his life's gift is the inspiration that we can all be ordinary people doing extraordinary feats, that we all have and can embrace and embody Christ Consciousness and be and live as he and those around him did.

Shrouded Truth urges us to overlook the cloak of superstition and religion, and return to the essence of the spiritual message. The truths of Christ can still be followed, but without all the traditions that were built around it. Ultimately, we are all Connected – to the Divine within us, in one another, the Christ Consciousness, and the Main Consciousness.

2. THE METHODOLOGY:

Whilst it is interesting debating the theological and spiritual elements of the stories that have emerged in *Shrouded Truth*, it is imperative to examine the methodology used to get this information.

Are these memories genuine? Also, did they all genuinely experience these past lives?

While most past-life regressions take clients back to ordinary lives, some souls go back to their genuine past life of people who are considered famous, like Jesus or Mary Magdalene.

One question that is asked is why didn't the soul Mary Magdalene, for example, be incarnated as another great soul in this life – for example, Mother Teresa. Why is it Maya? I then ask back, why can't Joe Blow have been Joseph or Sheila Smith been Mary Magdalene? After all, our project has shown that the biblical characters were all ordinary people, doing extraordinary things under extraordinary circumstances. Also, the hierarchy of the evolved soul is judged by our ego selves – in the realms of the spirit and divine, there seems to be more equality and mutual respect between the souls.

For those whose souls recall but have not genuinely experienced these biblical lives, there could be several explanations.

Collective Unconscious

In 1916, Carl Jung introduced the concept of the Collective Unconscious in his article 'The Structure of the Unconscious'. This is an idea that we all share instincts and Consciousness from collective memories of the past and can all tap into it. He went further and talked about it containing 'archetypes'. They are aspects of basic human behaviour and situations that are explained simply to give meaning to the generalised instincts and behaviour of people. Jung says that the Collective Unconscious does not develop individually but is inherited. The Collective Unconscious distinguishes from Freudian's Personal Unconscious, where the latter represents an individual's personal repressed memories.[2]

In an altered state, regressees are able to tap into both their own Personal Unconscious and also into the Collective Unconscious. Sometimes the regressees tap into the past-life experiences stored in the Collective and re-experience a life as if it is their own. Why? It depends on the individual – for some, it is for their own soul's growth and development to learn different aspects of emotions; for others it could be to just experience and gain insights on the archetype they are exploring.

How do we tell the difference between lives from the Collective Unconscious or genuine past lives, almost from the Personal Unconscious? It is a general rule that it is very difficult to create an emotional reaction from the Collective. It's almost like having an emotional reaction from watching an emotional scene in the movies versus actually experiencing the emotional scene. The more intense the emotion and body sensations, the more likely it is to be a personal memory.

Projection of Therapists' Thoughts

The experience of direct communication between two minds has been reported frequently. Sometimes we do it on a daily basis – knowing who's on the other end of the phone before picking it up (before the days of caller ID), thinking of someone and suddenly getting a text from them.

These days, quantum physics has taught us that nothing is solid, and that everything is continuously vibrational energy. Quantum physicists refer to this as String Theory – when physicists have broken down matter to the tiniest particle thus far, they realised that it is just energy that vibrates so quickly, it looks like string.

Based on these quantum theories, our thoughts are also energy vibrating. Whatever thoughts we choose, they vibrate at a certain frequency that is drawn to and attracts elements (including other thoughts) that vibrate at the same frequency. This can manifest in different ways in people's behaviours, including thought transference.

British physicist Sir William Barrett conducted one of the first 'thought-transference' tests between distant hypnotised subjects in 1883, in which he examined the correlation between what thoughts hypnotised subjects at a distance were sending and receiving. His experiment was reported to be successful and encouraged others to investigate on either side of the Atlantic.[3]

People are particularly susceptible to thought transference when their minds are in the alpha state, which is the state they are in under hypnosis. If the therapist has preconceived ideas and notions about the subject or story that the regressee is even beginning to tell them, then the therapist can inadvertently project these thoughts and the regressee can pick them up and reflect those thoughts back to the therapist as if it's their own experience.

Could I have transferred my thoughts to these regressees? There are three reasons why I don't think this would have happened.

Firstly, I have been trained to suspend judgement and not have any preconceived thoughts as a regression therapist.

Secondly, this mammoth project needed the regression of eight souls, spread all over the world, mostly with no knowledge of one another, with different levels of individual biblical knowledge. The only link between them was myself, who was born and brought up a Hindu before moving on to the spiritual path. I had no prior knowledge of the biblical characters, story and context until I regressed the subjects. I had no prior knowledge to transfer to my subjects in the first place. All my research was done at the end of collecting all the accounts from clients to minimise bias during the sessions on my part.

Thirdly, I did not set out to regress people back to biblical lives. This project came about when several clients, around my professional sphere of either being a therapist or trainer, spontaneously accessed biblical lives. As a regression therapist, it was fascinating to observe multiple clients experiencing lives of that same time, and also know that 80 per cent of the recollections matched one another, even with clients who had not met, much less conversed, with one another.

Reflection of Souls' Deepest Desires

Sometimes the soul can manifest its deepest desires to experience or assume the role of one they have idolised for many years – in this case, centuries. This can then be played out in the client's psyche and take the form of having experienced the life. As an example of this, I have included a regression in the Appendix of a soul who clearly idolised Jesus and his teachings, and dedicated many lives devoted to the cause – including as a Cathar and Knight Templar.

Of course, under this topic, conscious mind confabulations are possible. The souls are merely remembering something they have read, seen or heard. The desire to assume the identity is so great that the mind creates scenarios and experiences that feed into the regressee's own desires. Even though I personally have only regressed one Mary Magdalene, for example, I have colleagues who have regressed multiple people who have experienced the lives of Mary Magdalene and Jesus Christ.

How can we tell the difference between a confabulated story and a genuine memory recollection? Again, it is the intensity of emotions and body sensations felt. Deep emotions and spontaneous body sensations and physical movements cannot be imagined – only recollected.

Cryptoamnesia

Cryptoamnesia is the condition where a forgotten memory returns to someone, who believes it is something new and original. It is a memory bias whereby a person may falsely recall experiencing a memory as if it were a new inspiration. So some critics could say that these regressees may have seen, heard or read accounts of the story somewhere else and, under hypnosis, regurgitated what they had received as second-hand information, as opposed to experiencing genuine memories.

Whilst it is feasibly what has happened here, this argument does not take into consideration three vital aspects of this methodology:

There were eight people, men and women, spread across the world, who experienced these lives. These clients had minimal, if any, connection to one another – and had not discussed matters of private regression sessions with one another. 80 per cent of these independent accounts corroborate with one another. I was careful to ensure that clients were not told of the details of the story that had been gathered beforehand. The accounts included many tiny details that the clients would normally not have access to in second-hand accounts.

Name Anomalies

In collecting information from the regressions for this book, one of the most glaring challenges was the anomaly of names, given for the same character by the different regressees, and frankly the historical references. How do these affect the validity of the information gained?

When we, in our current lives, recall details that we have watched in films, read in books, or even our own memories from ten or so years ago, our strongest memories are the emotional situations that we are in. Names and things of that nature are far less important. For example, when you think back to your childhood you will remember the most highly charged emotional memory of the seventh birthday party but you may not be able to remember clearly all the names of the people who attended. Confusion is created when you try to get several people to name all the people who were at that seventh birthday party, thereby creating errors. That type of information isn't recalled in the greater detail. As Rose admitted, accessing names is hard in regression, typically because a different part of the brain is being accessed, and the regressees then consciously second-guess the name.

Some of the memories aren't quite what a lot of people think they are – the recall in absolute minuscule detail of what happened. Soul memories are of the major events that occurred, the emotionally inspiring events, positive emotion and negative emotions. Those are the ones that are remembered in more detail.

Also these memories will be filtered by the perception of the person in that life. For example, Paul's language and Mary Magdalene's language are very different, and attest to their personality and perception filters that they hold – just like us these days. Three people could witness an accident and give three very different accounts of it, based on where they were standing, their relationships with those involved, the amount of emotional shock they felt, and the snippets of conversation they were privy to beforehand.

Final Thoughts

Within *Shrouded Truth*, the core story of all eight regressees is the same. In matters of Law, when interviewing suspects, the Police never expect secondary details to be consistent, if the core of the account is the same. In fact, if the accounts are too similar then they are suspected to be manipulated. If we apply this same principle to *Shrouded Truth*, it makes the accounts that much more authentic.

Ultimately, *Shrouded Truth* is the story and messages of Jesus, told through the memories of those who were closest to him. It is a story of love – the love that Jesus had for all around him, as well as the love they all had for him. It is a story of man – with a wife, with children, with siblings – who fought, with every fibre in his being, for a mission. It was really the feeling of just the beauty of the love and the connection, and when that group was together, enjoying the womb-like embrace they shared. The energy is so real and so beautiful and it is what we could have and Be at this moment.

At some point, we have to plant a flag on a mountain of uncertainty where not every question is answered. The human mind will not get to the bottom of every mystery in the Cosmos. Source, God or Consciousness has no name, apart from the ones we have given, yet so many of us believe through our faith, our intuition, our gut feel. Those are the best ways to determine the authenticity of these accounts – does it feel right for you? Do you resonate with the accounts? Do you resonate with the messages presented in *Shrouded Truth*? How did the energy of the book make you feel?

The feeling, when something is in true resonance, creates a vibration and in remembering that vibration, there is just Joy and Peace.

It is up to you to decide.

APPENDIX 1

PAST LIFE REGRESSION – THE PROCESS

Past-life regression is a technique that uses hypnosis to recover memories of past lives or incarnations. It is typically undertaken either in pursuit of a spiritual experience, or in a psychotherapeutic setting to resolve trauma or related difficulties in the current life.

Hypnosis – Getting People into Past Lives

The first step of guiding clients into past lives is to allow them to go into a deep state of relaxation – also known as hypnosis. There are so many misconceptions and definitions of hypnosis – but our focus here is therapeutic hypnosis. It is a process of deep relaxation that shifts a person's brain waves into the alpha/delta state. This is the similar state to when a person is meditating or is in deep sleep. In this state of focused attention, the client can access the subconscious mind a lot more easily than in the normal state.

Why do we need to access the subconscious mind?

One of the main jobs of our subconscious mind is to store everything that has ever happened in a huge memory bank. Its capacity is virtually unlimited. Under hypnosis, older people can often remember, sometimes with perfect clarity, events from fifty years before, and even beyond their current life. It is by hypnosis that we tap into this inexhaustible memory bank to gather information needed for the session.

How do we get in touch with the subconscious? Using the analogy of the car – in our normal wakeful state, the conscious is driving the car, and the subconscious is in the passenger seat. Under hypnosis, the conscious mind is so relaxed, it drifts to the passenger side, and the subconscious mind takes over driving the car. Having more access to the subconscious, we can work with the deeper part of a person's psyche. The function of the subconscious mind is to store and retrieve data. The subconscious memory is virtually perfect. It is the conscious recall that comes into question. Just to add – the conscious mind that is in the passenger seat is not asleep. It is just relaxed. So, it is aware of everything that is happening around it, and what is being said. It is just so relaxed, it does not filter and interfere with the flow of information from the subconscious.

Have you ever been so deeply engrossed in an activity that you lose track of time? How about when you drive: do you sometimes get to the end destination without being aware how you have got there? In these states, you are experiencing light hypnosis. Athletes, musicians and artists regularly enter this state whilst they are performing. A common term for this is being in the 'zone'.

Regression and PLR Therapy

The function of our subconscious mind is to store and retrieve data. Its job is to ensure that we respond exactly the way we are programmed and it makes everything we say and do fit a pattern consistent with our programmed beliefs and patterns. It makes our behaviour fit a pattern consistent with our emotionalised thoughts, hopes and desires.

The subconscious mind has what is called a homeostatic impulse for our basic survival. It keeps our body temperature at 37 degrees Celsius, just as it keeps you breathing regularly and keeps your heart beating at a certain rate, without you even consciously thinking about it.

Our subconscious mind also practises homeostasis in our mental realm, by keeping us thinking and acting in a manner consistent with what we have done and said in the past. All our habits of thinking and acting are stored in our subconscious mind. It has memorised all our comfort zones and it works to keep us in them. Our subconscious mind causes us to feel emotionally and physically uncomfortable whenever we attempt to do anything new or different, or to change any of our established patterns of behaviour.

In the hypnotic state, there is direct access to the subconscious, giving us the direct route to the source of our lives' programming. The source could be in our past life, current life or both. Therapeutically, transforming at this level thus gives us the fastest and most decisive point to changing our programming, thus changing our lives.

To guide someone into a hypnotic state, I first ask them to make themselves comfortable – either in a reclining or lying position. With their eyes closed, I ask them to focus on their breathing and guide them to relax physically. Then, using my voice and certain words, I help them get into a state of both mental relaxation and alertness. As they move more and more inward, they leave external distractions outside, and slowly their brain wave shifts from the beta state to the alpha state – whereby they are able to access their subconscious, thereby accessing deeper and suppressed memories, either of the current life or their past life.

Past Life Regression Therapy works with the content of past experiences and extends the timeline to allow past-life stories to emerge. Clients are guided back and encouraged to relive and resolve the conflicts from the past that have been previously inaccessible to their Consciousness. Often they are experiences that are still influencing and distorting their mental and emotional stability.

In regression therapy other psychotherapeutic models like psychodrama and gestalt therapy are incorporated within the sessions. Also, in most cases, the sessions extend into the current life, especially resolution through inner-child work, where the source issue normally first manifests in the current life. There is no doubt that many people have benefited from and been healed by Past Life Regression Therapy. This is not just based on my experience as a regression therapist but that of the many pioneers and practitioners of this form of therapy.

Areas where regression therapy has had proven results include unexplainable pains (including migraine, phantom pain syndrome), deep-seated emotional patterns (including feeling disempowered, depression), relationship problems, addiction, and also physical challenges that have an emotional issue behind them (including irritable bowel syndrome, inability to conceive).

In the therapeutic setting, it is not important for the therapist to prove that the past-life story is real. The most important thing that therapists focus on is using the experience that the client is undergoing to heal a deep-seated emotional challenge that has been plaguing him or her.

Spiritual Investigation via PLR

For this book, however, the sessions conducted were not so much therapeutic but information-gathering. So the method used to collect details was slightly different to when conducting therapeutic sessions. It is still integral to work with the clients in the hypnotic state – that does not change.

However, there is a refined way of questioning to ensure that the person still remains in the experience and the conscious mind of the person is not engaged.

Let's use gathering names as an example. In the therapeutic sense, the main thread that is followed is the emotional pattern, and experiences relevant to the pattern. The name of the past-life character is not required, for it does not affect the therapeutic experience of the client. Only when the name comes up spontaneously do we take note of it for future reference, if relevant.

However, in the case of this book, it was important to get information like names, dates, names of places, for the purposes of research, cross-referencing and to verify the validity of the stories that emerged. Unless fully embodied in the experience, asking the person under hypnosis, 'What is your name?' will more often than not take the person out of the experience and into the conscious mind, which is not ideal as they may access the information from books or internet as opposed to the experience. What I predominantly do instead is, whilst they are at relevant points of the story, to ask them, 'How are you addressed?' This then keeps the person in the experience of the memory and gets a more authentic response. However, therein lies another problem: how they are addressed may not be the actual name (e.g. Jesus may have been addressed as teacher, son, brother, father, husband, or by a nickname by respective people) and so it was difficult to maintain the consistency of names especially. The way we tried to overcome that was to ask the person at multiple significant points in their regression, 'How are you addressed' and use the 'majority rules' principle to then determine the name.

Age was another difficult detail to obtain. Even in our current life, we normally remember the experience, and we get slightly fuzzy about the age we were when it happened. The same principle applies for past-life recollection. For this we then ask questions like, 'At what point of your life does this occur? Are you a child, a teenager, an adult or an elderly person?' Then we try as much as possible to hone into a reasonably small age range.

In both instances (for information gathering or therapeutic purposes), the most authentic experiences elicit deep emotional responses. So for example, when using the torture of Jesus, most people we regressed felt deep emotions, and expressed them quite visually and audibly ... either crying or a softening of the voice, or silence as they try to manage the emotions to speak. Experiencing deep emotions as a reaction to events is one of the ways that we determine the authenticity of the experience.

Using the example of a child riding a bicycle for the first time as a trigger, let us just think about this. If we do not have a child, and we witness a child riding for the first time, our imagination is triggered at how we think the child feels and we may have a small smile on our face. However, if we have our own children, and we see another child riding for the first time, this will trigger a memory of our own child riding a bike, and the delight we feel will be far deeper and more intense because there is a personal experience we can relate to.

The same applies to past-life experiences. If the experience is made up by the conscious mind, there will be very little to no emotions displayed by the person. However, if they are experiencing a memory via the subconscious mind then the emotions that they exhibit, more likely than not, are deep, intense and totally authentic.

Intense emotion can also explain spontaneously remembering past lives, or any repressed memories in the current life. When there is a trigger of the highly charged emotion, the associated memory will immediately be drawn up to the conscious awareness. For example, I had a friend who was terrified of the dark. She could not stay alone in the dark without becoming breathless and getting a panic attack. One day, she came home late from work, fumbled around to turn the lights on and felt something furry (her cat) brush against her ankle. She immediately had a vision of herself being a man struggling with a giant bear, feeling intense fear and anxiety. When she came to me for a session, she saw herself as a burly hunter, who was so intently following his prey, he did not realise it had gone dark. So, he went to seek shelter in a dark cave, and stumbled on something quite furry and fell. The next thing he knew, there was a almighty roar, and a flash of white teeth, and he was mauled by a bear. In a disassociated state, he realised the cave was home to a mother bear and two cubs. She saw him as a threat and attacked. My friend brought that fear of darkness into this life, not understanding it until the feeling of fur on her in the darkness spontaneously triggered the intense emotion and brought the memory to her conscious awareness.

Memories can just as well be triggered by positive emotions as well. Say you had a fabulous relationship with your grandmother, who always smelled of lavender, and every time you saw her you were filled with joy. She passes away when you are three. One day, in your thirties you happen to chance upon a lavender garden and, as you take a deep breath, you are filled with joy and you see your grandmother's face. The scent of lavender is the trigger of the emotion and the memory.

The same principle applies to a past-life memory. If the experience was so deep and triggered such intense emotions (e.g. rape, torture) a subtle stimulus could trigger the same intense emotion, bypassing all rational filters, and spontaneously bring up the memory from the past life.

SCEPTICS

There is no end to what sceptics say against past-life regression. One of the arguments is that the use of hypnosis and suggestive questions make the subject particularly likely to hold distorted or false memories. They claim that the source of the memories is more likely cryptomnesia and confabulations that combine experiences, knowledge, imagination and suggestion or guidance from the hypnotist, rather than recall of a previous existence. Once created, the memories are indistinguishable from memories based on events that occurred during the subject's life.

There is also the assumption made that subjects undergoing past-life regression indicate that a belief in reincarnation and suggestions by the hypnotist are the two most important factors regarding the contents of memories reported.

However, let's look at it this way. The work of Dr Ian Stevenson, Carol Bowman (in her book *Children's Past Lives*) and many others since who have documented past lives of children, is a strong indication of the existence and authenticity of past lives that has nothing to do with prior knowledge via mass media, suggestions by the researcher or even a belief in reincarnation.

While there are some memories reported during past-life regression that have been investigated and revealed historical inaccuracies, there have also been some where the information is spot-on to actual historical findings. I would ask the sceptics though, if someone gets a memory detail of their childhood wrong, does this mean that all their childhood memories are unreal? So if a detail in the past life is wrong, does that mean all the past-life memories are wrong? And also, who is to say that the research is more accurate than the past-life story?

Historical research is normally based on intelligent deductions of physical evidence found and also stories told – but deductions nevertheless do not make an absolute truth, especially when new physical evidence is found all the time that changes the historical narrative.

Also, psychologically speaking, what we experience is a matter of perception. We will most likely retain the perception that has had the biggest impact on us. For example, let's say my husband and I go to the Formula 1 Grand Prix. The biggest impression that I had was the loud sounds every time the cars drove past, and the searing heat. If you asked me details later, I would not be able to remember the colour of the cars or the names of drivers. My husband, whose background is engineering, was more interested in the speed and corner turns and horsepower. If you asked him, he would not remember the heat, pollution and loud noises, but would give an enthusiastic monologue about the details and mechanics of the cars, as well as the driving strategies.

As for our book, some of the people we regressed had prior knowledge of the commonly told story of Jesus, preached by the Church, and some people went in with very little, if any, information. During the process, I made every attempt to keep the primary questions as open as possible, in the hope that at this level at least I would not be leading the subjects. During the session, the most asked questions were, 'What happens next?' and 'Tell me more about that' – to allow the clients to remember the experience. Even the entry into the experience was very open and did not pre-suppose the entry into the characters of the story. It was left open for them to experience the life authentically. Moreover, as mentioned, all the regressees had spontaneously regressed to these biblical past lives through private therapy or students on the course prior to regressing them for the book.

Another phenomenon that occurs in past-life regression that is very difficult for sceptics to challenge is xenoglossia – or the ability to be able to speak in languages that have not been acquired by natural means in this lifetime. The phenomenon encompasses cases where the subjects speak languages to which they hadn't had any form of exposure to. For example, someone has the ability to speak Swahili when they lived in a part of the world that has no relation to Swahili, nor has the person ever studied it, or read books referring to it, or conversed with someone who spoke it, or had any other form of exposure to it.

Dr Ian Stevenson was one of the most respected academicians in the United States. He carried out specialised research into xenoglossy and his book *Xenoglossy* (Stevenson, 1974) is one of the leading scientific studies in this area. In it he documents a study he made of a 37-year-old American woman. Under hypnosis she experienced a complete change of voice and personality into that of a male. She spoke in the Swedish language – a language she did not speak or understand when in the normal state of consciousness.

Dr Stevenson's direct involvement with this case lasted more than eight years. The study involved linguists and other experts and scientists who meticulously investigated every alternative explanation. Fraud was ruled out for a number of substantive reasons which Stevenson outlines in his study. The subject and her physician husband were thoroughly investigated. They were under extreme and continuous close scrutiny, did not want publicity and agreed to the publication of the study only if their names were changed to protect their privacy. Both the husband and wife were considered by their local community to be honest and decent and their behaviour exemplary. Certainly there was no motive for personal profit.

What makes xenoglossia so important for Past Life Regression Therapy is the fact that it offers direct validation to reincarnation and past-life regression. Often, when we regress our subject, the subject tends to stay sceptical. Even if they see things, their conscious mind so dominates their subconscious mind that they assume it must have been their imagination as opposed to a past-life memory. However, if the subject starts speaking in a language they did not know, it instils a lot more faith in the experience. It also provides a more intimate and intense experiential reliving of the past life, which is tough to dispute.

With regards to sceptics – at the end of the day, there is not one piece of evidence or research done that proves that past lives categorically do not exist or that regression therapy absolutely does not work. Until there are some, this leaves the many doors of possibilities open – including the existence of past lives.

WEBSITES

For more information about past-life regression, please refer to the following websites:

Spiritual Regression Therapy Association (SRTA)
This is an international association of past-life, regression and life-between-lives therapists that respect the spiritual nature of their clients. They are professionally trained by the Past Life Regression Academy to international standards and work to a code of ethics that respects the clients' welfare.
Website: http://www.regressionassociation.com

Earth Association of Regression Therapy (EARTh)

This is an independent association with the objective to improve and enlarge the professional application of regression therapy. It provides internet forums, newsletters and professional standards for the regression therapy training schools that are recognised by it. Every summer it offers a series of workshops for ongoing professional development.
Website: http://www.earth-association.org

The Past Life Regression Academy (PLRA)

The Academy specialises in past-life and regression therapy, past-life regression, life-between-lives regression and hypnosis training in Europe, Asia, India, South Africa, Mexico, United States and Australia. It awards internationally accredited qualifications enabling its graduates to belong to independent professional associations, including the Earth Association of Regression Therapy. The Academy training director is Andy Tomlinson, a graduate in psychology, registered psychotherapist, certified past-life regression therapist, international trainer and author in this field.
Website: http://www.regressionacademy.com

BOOKS

Healing the Eternal Soul, Andy Tomlinson, From the Heart Press

Turning the Hourglass: Children's Passage Through Traumas and Past Lives, Christine Alisa, Author House

BETWEEN LIVES SPIRITUAL REGRESSION

In 1994, Dr Michael Newton caused a stir through the publication of his book *Journey of Souls*. This groundbreaking book documented ten years of research that he had undertaken to navigate souls through the between-life stages, where they can find out the plan that they had agreed to for their current life. This process can be incredibly insightful and poignant as it gives the regressee a spiritual look at different events, relationships and circumstances of their lives, the pleasant and the not so pleasant, which they then gain a deeper understanding and appreciation for. It has been known to be a life-changing experience. Since then, therapists who have been trained in this process have conducted more than 15,000 successful between-lives sessions worldwide.

Part of that process is called the Eternal Now – where clients communicate with their guides and other evolved Spirits of Light to gain clarification and insights into specific areas of their life that they are having trouble with in their current existence. Within this book I used similar process to have Jane access the Christ Consciousness (and a few others, as it turned out).

I must say, when I thought of the idea, I did not know if anything would come out of it. It was just an experiment. This experience has just affirmed to me that there is so much out there that we do not know about. If we close ourselves to the possibilities, we will never know about them. If we, however, open ourselves to the infinite possibilities and trust our more subtle senses, we may be pleasantly surprised by so many forms of experiences. In this case, I am glad that both Jane and I gave it a go.

The first step employed to get the best possible results for this is to make the intent to access the right vibrational frequency or spiritual being before putting the client into hypnosis. I also make sure that the communication will be for the highest good of the people involved and/or for the project. This is done bearing in mind that we are working with really subtle energies and making the right energetic connection is important. It is like dialling the right number on the telephone.

I also conscientiously clear any unwanted intrusive energies that could interfere with the channelling. This is to ensure that the energetic pathway to meeting our intent is clear. Once communication is established via hypnosis, normally the deeper the hypnosis the better, the question and answer session can commence; but all throughout, I am very vigilant of any intrusive energy, and will keep topping up the protection around the session as this needs to be maintained throughout the entire session.

Once the session ends, we politely give thanks to all who helped us and I bring the client out of hypnosis slowly and gently, as they would have been quite deep when this occurs.

A question I get asked frequently is 'Can anyone access these high vibrational spaces?' I refer back to the fact that there have been more than 15,000 people that have accessed higher frequencies during life-between-lives sessions, and many more who access them spontaneously or by intent outside. If all these people can do it, I believe so can anyone, if they are open and trust the subtle energies, and the steps outlined above are followed.

Extra References on Between Lives Spiritual Regression

Exploring the Eternal Soul, Andy Tomlinson, From the Heart Press.

Journey of Souls, Michael Newton, Llewellyn Publications, US.

Destiny of Souls, Michael Newton, Llewellyn Publications, US.

APPENDIX 2

THE REGRESSION OF 'JESUS'

Whether one is a regression therapist like myself, or whether one moves in the New Age circuit, one will encounter many who claim that they are the incarnation of famous spiritual figures. Regression therapists have seen many a Jesus Christ and Mary Magdalene walking through their therapy rooms.

As mentioned in Appendix 1, when someone comes for a therapeutic session, what we see as important is the therapeutic benefit for the client, not so much the information gathered. However, for collecting information for books such as this one, it is vital to understand the reasons for stories to deviate so wildly, namely:

- Confabulation
- Conscious mind interference
- Accessing elements of a life that pertains to a challenge they are facing in the current life just for therapeutic benefits.

So, this then calls into question the validity of all their sessions, as well as the regressions in this book. How can we vouch for the credibility of a session then? Maybe this next regression can shed some light on the matter.

Anthony (another self-chosen pseudonym) is a pleasant, unassuming individual, who was living in the Middle East at this time, with a background of spiritual experiences dating back to the age of five and a working knowledge of the Jesus story and alternative scenarios. He had also previously regressed to lives as a Knight Templar and a Cathar. He was a student of the Past Life Regression Academy.

Unlike all the other candidates, he did not spontaneously relive any memories from the biblical period. This was entirely my doing – in my fervour of collecting more regressions for this book, I had assumed he'd had a past life in biblical times, due to the amount of knowledge and passion with which he spoke of some of Jesus' disciples – Judas in particular. I had observed this behaviour for some time, and thought we should do a trial regression to the time of AD1 and see where we ended up. It was just a very short session - literally just fifteen minutes. He did indeed end up in Judea, and he identified himself as being Jesus.

Although my intuition registered disbelief, I decided to schedule a full regression with Anthony anyway. Sometimes, with a full-blown regression, as with Jane, as more information is revealed, the identity of the characters will become clearer. I was also curious about the intense emotions he had speaking of those times, and wondered where that came from.

Anthony's entry point was in Gethsemane. He had identified it as such, and this was my first clue that this could be conscious mind interference as in the other regressions; whilst the regressees have had vague recollections of the wider regions that they were in, they were not so specific in the use of current names for locations and people's names.

He entered into the body of a man in his thirties with long hair. He was wearing a brown 'gown'-like attire – high in at the neck, that fell to the feet, with no sleeves, with a cord around the waist. He found himself in a beautiful garden on a bright but shady and cool day, and he was leaning against a big tree. There were lots of people around looking at him, as he kept saying 'Gethsemane' to himself. As he got up, everyone still sat there, cross-legged on the floor, as he walked past them, feeling relaxed and happy.

Reena: And do you have a name?
Anthony: Jesus.

The next event sees him on a hot day, wearing white. There are lots of people around in a great big courtyard or square. There are some officials behind a table and he is being pushed towards this table.

Reena: And what happens next?
Anthony: I'm confused. They're talking to me, sort of laughing.
Reena: What is it that's communicated?
Anthony: They're not talking to me. They're just stood there.
Reena: Do you say anything to them?
Anthony: No.
Reena: What happens next?
Anthony: I feel as though I'm being pulled back, taken down ... down some steps. There's many steps.
Reena: Are you going by yourself or are you with anyone else?
Anthony: I'm in the back of a cart. It's got a wooden cage made of branches. I lie in that, waiting.
Reena: What's going through your mind at the moment?
Anthony: Nothing. Just waiting.
Reena: Just move on until something happens and then tell me what it is. What happens?
Anthony: I've been laid out on a cross and they are driving nails through my hands – through my wrists. It

doesn't hurt. I feel as though it's just a dream. I'm not really there. I don't think it's really happening. The cross is lifted up. It jolts and it goes down. It's like a jolt and it's stuck down a hole. It's the first time I sense pain. That's brought me ... What the hell's going on? Why? Why?

Reena: Are you by yourself at the moment or are there other people?

Anthony: There's lots of people.

Reena: Do you recognise any?

Anthony: Some. Some friends are crying.

Reena: These friends that are crying, do they have a name?

Anthony: No. There's an older woman. She's really round. She's giving me ... she's not looking at me, she's really round, but she's giving me something. I feel her presence is very important. She's sat, she's not even looking at me, she's looking away. She's in brown, dark brown. The ones on the right all seem to be in distress and the ones on the left seem to be quite joyous.

Reena: And what happens next?

Anthony: It's dark. People have gone away.

Reena: Are you actually in your body at the moment or ...

Anthony: Yes, I'm still there. It's cold, quite cold.

Reena: And what else do you experience in the body?

Anthony: Pains in the shoulders.

Reena: Anywhere else?

Anthony: My ankles. People have come. They've got ladders to take me down. I fall forward. I'm too weak. I've fallen off.

Reena: Who is this that's taken you down?

Anthony: I don't know. It's very quick, it's very busy.
I'm being carried. I feel so weak. I'm getting feeling
back in my arms. It's starting to hurt all over. I'm being
cleaned. There are people cleaning me. Across my arms,
my wrists and my feet, my ankles. My ankles hurt. Feet
don't hurt.
Reena: Your heart's still beating?
Anthony: Yes.
Reena: Just describe the scene.
Anthony: It's very busy. There's talking. It's like I'm not
there. Like I'm dreaming. It's like I'm not really there.
But I am there.
Reena: Just describe these people who are cleaning you.
Anthony: They're giving me some water. Lifting my
head. They're crying. They thought I was dead and I
wasn't. There's a lot of emotion.
Reena: Tell me the names of the people who have been
tending you.
Anthony: I want to say Barabbas.

According to the Gospels, Barabbas was the Zealot captive
chosen by the people to be spared crucifixion.

Reena: Who else?
Anthony: Everything's stopped. Stopped and just stood
there. I've got no names. Lots of figures with beards.
Hair with plaits. I'm cold.
Reena: And are they saying anything to you?
Anthony: I'm very cold. They are covering me up.
Reena: Do you recognise who these people are?
Anthony: No.
Reena: OK. And what happens next?

Anthony: I'm very tired. Very weak. They are giving me some warm broth or something. It's warm. It tastes good.

Reena: And as they are giving you this warm broth, how do they address you?

Anthony: There's no sound. Lord! They're sweet people.

Reena: OK. What is it that happens next?

Anthony: I didn't hear that. I seem to be drifting in and out as if I'm delirious. I might just keep passing out. I'm not fully aware of what's going on. The talking is all muffled. There seems to be a group of five in front of me on the left. They seem to be trying to work out what to do. They don't know what to do. One of them keeps turning and looking at me and smiling and I feel as though I recognise him but I can't give a name. He seems to be the one that is in charge, trying to ask the others what he should do. He's very tall. He's taller than the rest.

Reena: Let's just check whether you are in your body and your heart's still beating.

Anthony: Yes. I'm lying there.

Reena: And what is the significance of this very tall person?

Anthony: It's somebody close.

Reena: Can you tell me more about somebody close?

Anthony: I feel it's James. Very slim, very tall.

Reena: And tell us more about James.

Anthony: He's listening. But he's only half-listening to what is being said. He's looking at me. His body's facing them but his head is turned to the right and he's looking at me.

Reena: Tell us more about that.

Anthony: I ache all over. Pain in the shoulders. My back aches. Everything aches. I want to sleep.

At the next significant event, Jesus is feeling weak; he is stooped and walking with difficulty, largely hidden by a cloak and supported by James and another person. As James assures him of his safety, they board a small boat on the shore of a lake. It's early morning and a mist rises above the surface. He identifies four people on board, excluding himself: James, two oarsmen and a woman seated at the bow clad in a brown cloak with a yellow belt. She is upset but James urges them forward.

At this point, to get more context to the story, I took Anthony to his first significant event – where he was a small boy watching his father work as a carpenter in an open corner shop. According to him, his father is a round, happy, happy man – full of fun and laughter. I ask if his father has a name.

Anthony: [chuckling] Yes, Joseph. He's so full of joy. He's beaming. He just radiates light. Full of fun and laughter. He is well liked by everybody.
Reena: OK. And what else happens?
Anthony: Nothing. I'm just stood looking at him. I like to watch him work. I like to look at him.
Reena: How old are you at the moment?
Anthony: About five. I like being with him. He doesn't want me too close. It's dangerous.
Reena: And what else happens?
Anthony: I am just stood there. He is laughing. He laughs like Santa Claus – ho, ho, ho. He's a round, happy man. He's got a beard. He seems old. He seems older than I thought at five.
Reena: OK. And what happens next?

Anthony: I'm with some elders. Talking to them about philosophy.

Reena: Can you just describe who you are talking to?

Anthony: My heart is starting to race. It's exciting. It's interesting. It's heated. Not angry, but heated.

Reena: What is the discussion about?

Anthony: They are not angry with me but they're not listening.

Reena: Just tell me a bit more about what you are communicating to each other.

Anthony: It's about what's going on. These are the elders – they should be in control but they're not. They're not doing anything about it. Why aren't they doing something? It's heated. I'm telling them they need to do something. I'm shouting at them. I shouldn't be shouting at them – I'm so young and they are so old. They're telling me to respect my elders. 'How can I respect [you] when you behave like this?'

Reena: Then what happens?

Anthony: I'm stood up and shouting at them now. I'm angry. I'm angry at them.

At the next significant event, Anthony goes to a time when he is a lot older.

Anthony: I've got long hair. I feel serene. I feel marvellous. I feel wonderful. I feel about eighteen feet tall. I just feel it. It's lovely. I feel the connection. There's lots of people. It's like they're so small. It's like I am a giant. I'm not. It just feels that way. Lots and lots of people coming.

Reena: OK. Just continue and tell me what happens next.

Anthony: I'm just talking. There's a group very close to me. Then there's a lot of others. I feel the group who are my close friends. They are with me all the time. I don't know who they are but they come to listen. I'm getting the statements out of … things that I've heard, things that I know are coming out of me rather than it being from memory. I can't decide which is which. I've got things … it's gone dark. Everybody's gone. It's very relaxed. There's a lot of laughter. It seems like a bit of banter with things being said and laughing and …

Reena: OK. Is there anything else of significance before we move on?

Anthony: No.

At the next significant event, Anthony returns to the Gethsemane garden, where it's dark and the same small group of five is with him, including James, a woman and three others he does not know the names of who have expectations of him. Anthony then describes how he and the others in this small group are arrested by Roman soldiers.

Anthony: It seems a very friendly affair. It doesn't seem anything that's aggressive. There was no conflict. It was all very polite and amenable. They asked us to come so I went with them. I'm back in that place again where I was, with the steps.

Reena: Just go into more detail this time. What's happening?

Anthony: A lot of jeering, a lot of shouting. I'm being pushed. My arms are being tied behind my back.

Reena: What's being communicated to you?

Anthony: Insurrection. Trying to organise a revolt. A troublemaker.

Reena: Troublemaker? Is that what they're saying to you?

Anthony: Yeah.

Reena: And what else are they saying to you?

Anthony: I don't speak. I don't say anything. They shouldn't be there. They shouldn't be in our land. Why don't the people realise this? They shouldn't be there. Who are they to say these things? That's not what I say – it's what I'm thinking. I look at them with …

Reena: What else?

Anthony: I'm just taken in the back of this cart. There are three of us … It's a very cobbley road. It's very uncomfortable. It's difficult to stay stood up. We're banging against each other. There are just a few people around, that's all. Not many. It seems funny for some reason. Banging around.

The emotional light-heartedness of Anthony's explanations, compared to the deep intense emotions that the other regressees experienced, was yet another clue that this session did not have the ring of authenticity that the others had.

Reena: And what happens next?

Anthony: I'm back on this cross again.

Reena: Just go through these events slowly and then tell me what's happening.

Anthony: The old woman is there again. She's talking to me now. She said: 'Don't be afraid. Everything is OK.' I said: 'I'm not.' She knows. She knows. She's got very deep understanding. I feel she's very … I like having her there. She's very knowledgeable. I think it's through her I don't feel any pain.

Reena: What is it that stops there being pain?

Anthony: Her words.

Reena: What is she saying?

Anthony: I don't know. She is talking to me. It's very soothing. I don't know what she's saying.

Reena: And what is the significance of this woman to you?

Anthony: I think it's my mother. But she's not upset. She's not upset like the others.

Reena: And what else is happening?

Anthony: Nothing. I'm back ... I just felt that jolt again when they lift the cross. And that's it. Nothing else. It goes dark. And then when everybody's gone some come with ladders and take me down and I fall and James catches me. Over his shoulder.

Reena: Were you tied or attached to the cross some other way?

Anthony: Nails.

Reena: How did they pull the nails out?

Anthony: I don't know. I don't know. I saw the ladders from a distance. I was away looking at it. I wasn't on the cross when I could see the ladders. But when they took me down I was over his shoulder. I could see it both ways. I was over his shoulder but also watching it as well.

At this point Anthony progresses to where he is being helped into the small boat and ferried to a small white house with a bed of fresh straw. He spends the next three months being nursed back to health by two unidentified women. Towards the end he becomes very impatient to leave the house, but the women stop him.

Then James arrives. Anthony sobs as he just wants to hold James, for he has not seen him for so long, and he had so many questions.

James, who is described as 'my little but big brother – he's younger but very big', tells him arrangements are being made to take him away but he has to be patient and stay where he is. 'I laugh and say, "It's all right you saying that – I'm stuck here!"'

James returns to Jerusalem and subsequently a message arrives telling Anthony's Jesus he is going on a journey and needs to prepare.

'Be prepared?' he laughs. 'That's silly. I can just walk out. I have nothing to prepare. What do they expect?'

Again, the levity seems at odds with the flavour of what was actually happening as well as the tone of the previous regressees.

As they leave one night, he enjoys the cool, fresh air taking in the beautiful smells. He is taken to a slightly bigger rowing boat with four oarsmen, which he says is something 'with brass things' that he has seen at the Alton Towers theme park in England. Again, there is some conscious mind interference here because of the modern reference to Alton Towers, that did not exist in the 1st Century.

The only passengers are Anthony's Jesus himself and 'that woman again' – but she is not a happy woman.

Anthony: It's only me and her but she's not with me. She's on the front of the boat and I am on the back.
Reena: And who is this woman?
Anthony: She's very close but we're not very close at the moment. It's not the same as it was. We seem distant. She didn't want to leave. She wanted to stay. But we had

to leave and I think she felt she was obligated to come with me. But she is not happy.

Reena: And just tell me a bit more about this obligation.

Anthony: I don't know what's wrong with her. It's all a blur. I don't know what's been going on. I know it took me a while to recover. I didn't know what was happening at the time. And she wasn't there during the time I was recovering. But she wasn't told. She wasn't there when I was taken down from the cross. She didn't know. She's angry that nobody told her. She didn't know what was going on. It made her angry. She felt like nobody trusted her.

After Anthony identifies the woman as his wife, he then tells us she has a sense of humour and adds: 'When I address her, I'll say, "Hey, you," and she will say, "Don't you dare call me that," and smile. So I call her all sorts of names. Because she doesn't like it. Her name's Mary but I don't use it very often.'

Again, this story does not tally at all with any other of the previous regressees' that had taken place – where there was reverence between Jesus and Mary. Calling Mary 'all sorts of names because she doesn't like it' seemed flippant and prankish and does not also fit in with the historical findings of how the Essenes behave, particularly one who is the heir to the Davidic kingdom towards his wife. The regression continues.

At the point of disembarkation, after 'a few hours' at sea, they find themselves at a big port in what Anthony thinks is the 'north Mediterranean area'. The couple climb a ladder to the quayside and are taken to a tavern-like place for the night. The next day they are given a small wagon and instructed to 'keep going until we find somewhere to settle'.

Anthony: We've got to keep moving a long way away –
getting as far away from Jerusalem as we can.

Reena: And what's the significance of getting as far
away from Jerusalem as you can?

Anthony: Somebody might come from Jerusalem and
recognise me ... The Romans wouldn't like that. There
was a commotion when they couldn't find the body.
They were looking for me. They wanted the body. So
I've got to go.

Reena: And what is the significance of James being in
Jerusalem when they couldn't find the body?'

Anthony: James carried on with the message ... The
message is not what they've told ... the message is ...
the message ... We are all one. The Romans need to go.
They've got to be thrown out.'

After 'lots of travelling', the couple end up in a beautiful land
that is green and silent, in which they decide to stay.

Reena: Tell me what happens next in this beautiful
green land.

Anthony: We settle. We do nothing at first. We just
begin to settle down ... Just Mary and I. There's
nobody else ... We just keep ourselves to ourselves and
learn the language. People are nice.

Reena: Do you speak the language?

Anthony: Not at first. It takes me a while. I find it very
difficult. Mary does it quite easily. [pause] There's
children. Two boys. We've been there a while now.

Reena: What's the significance of these boys?

Anthony: They help us integrate better.

Reena: Into the country?

Anthony: The people. Because of their friends and their parents.

Reena: How do we address these two boys?

Anthony: One is James.

Reena: How do you address the other boy?

Anthony: Peter.

Reena: And how did you get to know them?

Anthony: They are my sons.

Reena: OK. And tell me more about your sons, your children.

Anthony: James is athletic and strong. Peter is more studious and small.

Reena: Which one is the older one?

Anthony: James.

After 'years and years', he decides it's time to tell people about 'truth'. At fifty-five, he starts looking for places where he can talk publicly.

Anthony: The children must have been born in France, by their ages. James is eighteen and Peter sixteen ... I am now known as Henri and [my] wife as Marie ... I begin to get a following again. People listen but this time everybody listens, everybody takes it, and I become quite a celebrity.

Again, the use of the term celebrity shows not so much the passion of what Jesus talks about, but a reflection of his perception of his status. Also, his rationalisation that the children 'must have been born in France' clearly shows that he was not recounting the experience, but was consciously analysing it. More warning bells of conscious mind interference.

Reena: And where do you talk?

Anthony: All over. I walk, talk, and people come and gather. I see myself in a hall. And people just come and we talk and they ask questions.

Reena: And is this any different to what your experience was in Jerusalem?

Anthony: Yes, this is easy. There's no … They absorb it so much quicker. I start telling them and they pick it up straight away. They just understand. There is nobody opposing. They want more and more and more. It grows very fast … It's a beautiful life. It's wonderful. Everybody is so nice. Everybody is so loving. The community is gorgeous. There's lots of beautiful scenery. It's a beautiful country. Everything is nice. I like cheese. How odd! I've got a big plate of cheese.'

Reena: You like *cheese?*

Anthony: Yes, there's a big plate of cheese that has been served to me. And wine. The red wine is lovely.

Reena: What is the significance of the cheese and wine?

Anthony: I don't know. There's just a table full of different cheeses and a glass of red wine and lots and lots of wonderful, loving, happy, kind, people all picking up the message and adding to the understanding. They're connected. They don't need me now. They've got it themselves. It's wonderful to see such acceptance of truth. It makes me feel so good.

Reena: How old are you now?

Anthony: The same. Fifty-five. I'm quite portly. I don't get enough exercise. But it's very clear now. All the scenery is very clear. This lovely house – it's cool in the summer with vines and the energy. It's a beautiful area with a beautiful view of the sea. Oh, yes. It's lovely. But that's it now. I know this is the end. I go.

If, as history and the portrayal of other regressees, are right, that Jesus was a Nazarene, of the Essene community, he would have renounced most material desires and possessions. This again does not sit well with his account of dying a portly man, living the good life.

I thought it best to investigate his relationship with James again, as it was during these accounts that Anthony displayed intense emotions.

Reena: Did you ever see James again?

Anthony: (sobbing) No, I never saw him since. That time he came to see me was the last time I ever saw him. I never saw him again.

Reena: How does that make you feel?

Anthony: [still sobbing] Very emotional.

Reena: Would James have been proud of what you did in France?

Anthony: Oh, yes!

Reena: How does that make you feel?

Anthony: He was an inspiration.

Reena: Tell me more about that.

Anthony: I was so angry with the Romans and the elders and he wasn't angry with them. He could face it more easily.

Reena: And is James your only sibling or are there others?

Anthony: He's the only one I'm aware of.

The next significant event took him back to when he was fifty-five, and at his death point.

Anthony: I know my work is done. They don't need me any more.

Reena: Who are they?

Anthony: The people around there and the facility. It's growing and they are taking it out themselves. They are going out further and further themselves. They don't come as often as they used to [do] to ask. They don't need it and I'm happy because they're doing it themselves. They are connecting with the divine themselves. They don't need me.

Reena: And what is your main message?

Anthony: We're all divine. We're all of it. We are all one. We are all one being of light. God is light … Love all. Have compassion and forgiveness. People do not know what they do. But they are all the same.

Reena: Is this what you were teaching in Jerusalem?

Anthony: James was teaching more of that. I did teach that. I taught love and forgiveness because I know it. But I was so angry with the Romans and the elders so James was my inspiration.

Reena: And is he teaching it successfully in Jerusalem?

Anthony: I don't know.

Reena: And describe James to me.

Anthony: He's tall and strong. Slim but strong. He's not built like a warrior. He's got elegance and grace. And charm.

Reena: How about facial features? Are there any similarities between you and he?

Anthony: We're brothers.

Reena: Yes, but are there any similarities between you and him?

Anthony: I don't know because I rarely saw my own face.

Thus the session ended.

It is pretty obvious that this session deviated wildly from the other sessions in the book. The accounts do not match, nor do the emotions make sense. This session also had a very different flavour or tone to the others. One of the explanations is that Anthony confabulated this story.

In psychiatry, confabulation is the production of fabricated, distorted or misinterpreted memories about oneself or the world, without the conscious intention to deceive. Individuals who confabulate are generally very confident about their recollections, despite contradictory evidence. There are many reasons why a client might confabulate a memory of being a spiritual figurehead.

Firstly, if someone can spend many lives in contemplation and in awe of a certain figure or cause, and also much time in this current life researching that figure or cause, then what is actual and what is delved into can merge quite frequently. If a soul has experienced many lifetimes of devotion as a member of a religious order, like Anthony has as a Templar and Cathar, then the soul yearns to be worthy and become that object of their devotion. It's more about self-perception than absolute truth. This also could account for his passionate recounting of the tales of Christianity and the disciples, as he was devoted to the cause through several lifetimes.

Secondly, much of the information that came across from Anthony did not just deviate from the consistent story recounted by the main regressees within this book, but also was information that is commonly available and taught in Sunday School or in Church. As he was very much influenced by his conscious mind throughout the process, and in his excitement of discovering that he could possibly be Jesus himself through my soliciting him, he may have confabulated the story that he was indeed Jesus.

Thirdly, the type of emotion he displayed during most of the session was more one of levity as opposed to deep, heartfelt emotions. Jesus was a rebel during very trying times, running for his life, trying to keep his family and the cause alive … Whilst some comic humour at some point may have alleviated his main emotional state, the amount of levity that was displayed did not ring as authentic. So, this was another indication that the session was confabulated.

During therapeutic sessions, sometimes the way for healing for a client is to access information from the Collective Consciousness, as opposed to going through a real soul experience, because that is the best platform or story that is needed for their healing. It also could be that they have not put in place coping mechanisms needed to manage their own personal trauma, so that it is safer to access a gentler avenue that is not theirs. In doing so, they can access many experiences that are available. Therapeutically, though, we never talk about the legitimacy of the story – we just focus on the depth and effectiveness of the healing that has taken place.

Ultimately, the best way to ascertain the authenticity of a regression is really by intuition and research. Does it feel right? How authentic are the displays of emotion? Can some of the details be backed up by research? If there are multiple characters within the story, and most of them are regressed, how consistent are their stories? Do you intuitively feel that the regression is genuine? The answers to these questions are the best gauge to establish the credibility and validity of a regression.

BIBLIOGRAPHY

Books

Bridonneau, Yves, 2006, *The Tomb of Mary Magdalene Saint-Maximin-la-Sainte-Baume, Christianity's Third Most Important Tomb*, Compagnie des Editions de la Lesse, Aix-en-Provence, France

Brodie, Renee, 1996, *The Healing Tones of Crystal Bowls – Heal Yourself with Sound and Colour*, Aroma Art Ltd, Vancouver, Canada.

Churton, Tobias, 2012, *The Mysteries of John the Baptist – His Legacy in Gnosticism, Paganism and Freemasonry*, Inner Traditions, Vermont.

Ehrman, Bart, 2005, *Lost Christianity, The Battle of Scriptures and Faiths We Never Knew*, Oxford University Press, USA.

Elder, Isabel Hill, 1999, 10th edition, *Joseph of Arimathea*, Glastonbury Abbey Shop Ltd, UK.

Gardner, Laurence, 2005, *The Magdalene Legacy, The Jesus and Mary Bloodline Conspiracy*, Weiser Books, San Francisco, USA.

Gardner, Laurence, 2009, *The Grail Enigma – The Hidden Heirs of Jesus and Mary Magdalene*, Harper Element, London, UK.

Jowett, George, 2011, *The Drama of the Lost Disciples*, The Covenant Publishing Company, Durham, UK.

Kelhoffer, James A., 2014, *Conceptions of 'Gospel' and Legitimacy in Early Christianity*, Mohr Siebeck, Netherlands.

Stevenson, Ian, 1997, *Where Reincarnation and Biology Intersect*, Praeger Publishers, USA.

Tomlinson, Andy, 2006, *Healing The Eternal Soul*, From the Heart Press, Hants, UK.

Tomlinson, Andy, 2007, *Exploring The Eternal Soul,* O Books, Hants, UK.

Websites

Mansur al-Hallaj, Anal Haq (I am the truth: Aham Brahmo Asmi), Reincarnation in Islam. Retrieved from http://www.adishakti.org/_/reincarnation_in_islam.htm
S. Abdullah Tariq in Islamic Voice, February 2002, Reincarnation in Islam. Retrieved from http://www.adishakti.org/_/reincarnation_in_islam.htm
Johnson, R., The Bible's Ungodly Origins. Retrieved from http://www.deism.com/bibleorigins.htm
How Many People in the World Believe in Reincarnation, 4 March 2016. Retrieved from http://reincarnationafterdeath.com/how-many-people-believe-in-reincarnation/
Carl Jung, 1939 Evanos Meeting Lecture. Retrieved from https://carljungdepthpsychology.wordpress.com
Samad A., Nayeem A. MD, 13 November 1999, Was Jesus Substituted on the Cross? Retrieved from http://www.oocities.org/abusamad/substi.html
Who was Simon of Cyrene? Retrieved from http://www.gotquestions.org/Simon-of-Cyrene.html
Ketchum D., What Did Judas Isacriot Do Before Following Jesus? Retrieved from http://people.opposingviews.com/did-judas-iscariot-before-following-jesus-5530.html
Kareem A., The Crucifixion of Judas. Retrieved from http://www.answering-christianity.com/abdullah_smith/crucifixion_of_judas.htm

Why Do People Believe in Reincarnation, 10 May 2016, http://reincarnationafterdeath.com/why-do-people-believe-reincarnation/

The Silver Cord and The Near Death Experience, Near-Death Experiences and the Afterlife, 2016, http://www.near-death.com/science/research/silver-cord.html

Power Animals, Crystal Links, http://www.crystalinks.com/poweranimals.html

Harrison, R.K., 1986, Background on Leprosy in the Bible, International Standard Bible Encyclopedia. Eerdmans, Grand Rapids, http://ldolphin.org/leprosy.html

The Mar Thoma Orthodox Church, 2014, History of the Mar Thoma Orthodox Church, The Syrio-Indian Roots of Thomasine Christianity, http://www.marthomaorthodoxchurch.com/history.html,

S.G.P., 2002, How the Apostles Died, http://www.prayerfoundation.org/how_apostles_died.htm

Esteves, Junno Arocho, 6.10.2016, Pope Elevates Memorial of St Mary Magdalene to Feast Day, Catholic News Service, http://www.catholicnews.com/services/englishnews/2016/pope-elevates-memorial-of-st-mary-magdalene-to-feast-day.cfm

Reidy, Tim, O'Connell, Gerard, 2 August 2016, Vatican Announces Commission on Women Deacons, America, The National Catholic Review, http://www.americamagazine.org/content/all-things/vatican-francis-announces-commission-women-deacons

Wineyard, Val, http://www.marymagdalenebooks.com/mary-magdalene-and-the-cathars

New World Encyclopedia Contributers, 2015, Saint Thomas the Apostle, New World Encyclopedia,

http://www.newworldencyclopedia.org/p/index.php?title=
Saint_Thomas_(the_Apostle)&oldid=989973

Wikipedia Contributors, 2016, Thomas the Apostle,
Wikipedia, The Free Encyclopedia,
https://en.wikipedia.org/w/index.php?title=Thomas_the_
Apostle&oldid=735219460

Wikipedia Contributors, 2016, Paul the Apostle, Wikipedia,
The Free Encyclopedia,
https://en.wikipedia.org/w/index.php?title=Paul_the_Apos
tle&oldid=735323967

Wikipedia Contributors, 2016, Zacchaeus, Wikipedia, The
Free Encyclopedia,
https://en.wikipedia.org/w/index.php?title=Zacchaeus&ol
did=707525672

Wikipedia Contributors, 2016, Ancient Israelite Cuisine,
Wikipedia, The Free Encyclopedia,
https://en.wikipedia.org/w/index.php?title=Ancient_Israeli
te_cuisine&oldid=724374286

Wikipedia Contributors, 2016, Herod Antipas, Wikipedia, The
Free Encyclopedia,
https://en.wikipedia.org/w/index.php?title=Herod_Antipas
&oldid=732757576

Wikipedia Contributors, 2016, History of France, Wikipedia,
The Free Encyclopedia,
https://en.wikipedia.org/w/index.php?title=History_of_Fr
ance&oldid=742902923

Wikipedia Contributors, 2016, Aquitani, Wikipedia, The Free
Encyclopedia,
https://en.wikipedia.org/w/index.php?title=Aquitani&oldid
=727463309

Wikipedia Contributors, 2016, Catharism, Wikipedia, The Free
Encyclopedia,

https://en.wikipedia.org/w/index.php?title=Catharism&old id=742813826

Documentaries

'Mary Magdalene, The Mother of Christinity?', *Jesus Conspiracies,* The Discovery Channel, Karga Seven Pictures Production Company, USA, April 2012.

'Jesus, The Rebel?', *Jesus Conspiracies,* The Discovery Channel, Karga Seven Pictures Production Company, USA, April 2012.

NOTES AND REFERENCES

Introduction
1. http://reincarnationafterdeath.com/why-people-believe/
2. *ibid.*
3. *ibid.*
4. http://reincarnationafterdeath.com/how-many-people-believe/-in-reincarnation
5. Carl Jung, 1939 lecture at the Eranos meeting

Dutiful
1. Gardner, L., *The Magdalene Legacy*, 2007, Weiser Books, p. 21
2. Gardner, L., *The Magdalene Legacy*, 2007, Weiser Books, p. 58
3. Gardner, L., *The Magdalene Legacy*, 2007, Weiser Books, p. 179
4. Gardner, L., *The Magdalene Legacy*, 2007, Weiser Books, pp. 122–3
5. *Jesus Conspiracies* – 'Jesus, the Rebel?'
6. Jowett, George F., *The Drama of the Lost Disciples*, The Covenant Publishing Co. Ltd, p. 55
7. *Jesus Conspiracies* – 'Jesus, the Rebel?'
8. https://en.wikipedia.org/wiki/Ancient_Israelite_cuisine#Meat
9. http://www.oocities.org/abusamad/substi.html – Abu Samad, Nayeem Akhtar M.D.
10. Kelhoffer, James A., *Conceptions of 'Gospel' and Legitimacy in Early Christianity*, 2014, Mohr Siebeck, p. 80
11. Ehrman, Bart, *Lost Christianities*, 2005, OUP, pp. 185–7
12. Ehrman, Bart, *Lost Christianities*, 2005, OUP. pp. 187–8
13. Gardner, L., *The Magdalene Legacy*, 2007, Weiser Books, pp. 245
14. Jowett, George F., *The Drama of the Lost Disciples*, The Covenant Publishing Co. Ltd, p. 17
15. Gardner, L., *The Magdalene Legacy*, 2007, Weiser Books, p. 31
16. Gardner, L., *The Magdalene Legacy*, 2007, Weiser Books, pp. 193

Devoted
1. Hill Elder, Isabel, *Joseph of Arimathea*, 1999, Glastonbury Abbey Shop, p. 19
2. Gardner, L., *The Magdalene Legacy*, 2007, Weiser Books, p. 23

3. Hill Elder, Isabel, *Joseph of Arimathea*, 1999, Glastonbury Abbey Shop, p. 20; Jowett, George F., *The Drama of the Lost Disciples*, The Covenant Publishing Co. Ltd, pp. 31, 185
4. Hill Elder, Isabel, *Joseph of Arimathea*, 1999, Glastonbury Abbey Shop, p. 6–10
5. Jowett, George F., *The Drama of the Lost Disciples*, The Covenant Publishing Co. Ltd, p. 40
6. Hill Elder, Isabel, *Joseph of Arimathea*, 1999, Glastonbury Abbey Shop, p. 12
7. Jowett, George F., *The Drama of the Lost Disciples*, The Covenant Publishing Co. Ltd, p. 70
8. Gardner, L., *The Grail Enigma*, 2009, Harper Element, p. 245
9. Jowett, George F., *The Drama of the Lost Disciples*, The Covenant Publishing Co. Ltd, p. 70–77
10. Hill Elder, Isabel, *Joseph of Arimathea*, 1999, Glastonbury Abbey Shop, p. 13–14
11. Gardner, L., *The Magdalene Legacy*, 2007, Weiser Books, pp. 201–2
12. Gardner, L., *The Magdalene Legacy*, 2007, Weiser Books, p. 200
13. Hill Elder, Isabel, *Joseph of Arimathea*, 1999, Glastonbury Abbey Shop, p. 13–14
14. Jowett, George F., *The Drama of the Lost Disciples*, The Covenant Publishing Co. Ltd, pp. 173, 232
15. Jowett, George F, *The Drama of the Lost Disciples*, The Covenant Publishing Co. Ltd, Pg 173, 232 – 240

Enthusiast
1. Gardner, L., *The Grail Enigma*, 2009, Harper Element, p. 206

Evangelist
1. Acts 1:21–23
2. https://en.wikipedia.org/wiki/Zacchaeus
3. Acts 23:23, 25:1–13
4. https://en.wikipedia.org/wiki/Paul_the_Apostle
5. https://en.wikipedia.org/wiki/Ancient_Israelite_cuisine#Fish
6. Gardner, L., *The Magdalene Legacy*, 2007, Weiser Books, pp. 38–9
7. Gardner, L., *The Magdalene Legacy*, 2007, Weiser Books, pp. 135–6
8. https://en.wikipedia.org/wiki/Paul_the_Apostle

Besotted
1. Gardner, L., *The Magdalene Legacy*, 2007, Weiser Books, pp.8–9

2. Gardner, L., *The Magdalene Legacy*, 2007, Weiser Books, pp.12–13
3. *Jesus Conspiracies* – 'Jesus, The Rebel'
4. *Jesus Conspiracies* 'Mary Magdalene, The Mother of Christianity?', Gardner, L., *The Magdalene Legacy*, 2007, Weiser Books, p. 8
5. *Jesus Conspiracies* 'Mary Magdalene, The Mother of Christianity?',

Betrothed
1. Gardner, L., *The Grail Enigma*, 2009, Harper Element, pp. 105–6
2. Gardner, L., *The Magdalene Legacy*, 2007, Weiser Books, p. 60
3. Gardner, L., *The Grail Enigma*, 2009, Harper Element, p. 106
4. Gardner, L., *The Grail Enigma*, 2009, Harper Element, pp. 144, 155
5. Brodie, R., *The Healing Tones of Crystal Bowls*, 1996, Aroma Art Ltd, Vancouver, Canada, pp.82–3
6. Gardner, L., *The Grail Enigma*, 2009, Harper Element, p.84
7. Gardner, L., *The Magdalene Legacy*, 2007, Weiser Books, pp.161–3
8. Gardner, L., *The Grail Enigma*, 2009, Harper Element, pp. 31–2

Beloved
1. https://en.wikipedia.org/wiki/History_of_France
2. https://en.wikipedia.org/wiki/Aquitani
3. Gardner, L., *The Grail Enigma*, 2009, Harper Element, p. 171
4. Gardner, L., *The Magdalene Legacy*, 2007, Weiser Books, p. 176
5. Gardner, L., *The Magdalene Legacy*, 2007, Weiser Books, p. 25
6. Gardner, L., *The Magdalene Legacy*, 2007, Weiser Books, p. 59
7. Gardner, L., *The Grail Enigma*, 2009, Harper Element, pp.162–4
8. http://www.marymagdalenebooks.com/mary-magdalene-and-the-cathars
9. https://en.wikipedia.org/wiki/Catharism
10. Gardner, L., *The Magdalene Legacy*, 2007, Weiser Books, p. 198
11. Bridonneau, Y., *The Tomb of Mary Magdalene Saint Maximin la Sainte Baumeå, Christianity's Third Most Important Tomb*, 2006, Compagnie des Editions de la Lesse, Aix-en-Provence, France
12. Gardner, L., *The Magdalene Legacy*, 2007, Weiser Books, p. 160
13. Gardner, L., *The Grail Enigma*, 2009, Harper Element, pp. 111–44
14. Gardner, L., *The Magdalene Legacy*, 2007, Weiser Books, p. 136
15. Esteves, Junno Arocho, 6.10.2016, 'Pope Elevates Memorial of St. Mary Magdalene to Feast Day', Catholic News Service

http://www.catholicnews.com/services/englishnews/2016/po
pe-elevates-memorial-of-st-mary-magdalene-to-feast-day.cfm

16. Reidy, Tim, O'Connell, Gerard, August 2 2016, 'Vatican
Announces Commission on Women Deacons', America, The
National Catholic Review,
http://www.americamagazine.org/content/all-things/vatican-
francis-announces-commission-women-deacons

Devout

1. *Jesus Conspiracies*, 'Jesus, the Rebel?'
2. Gardner, L., *The Magdalene Legacy*, 2007, Weiser Books, p. 136
3. Gardner, L., *The Magdalene Legacy*, 2007, Weiser Books, p. 134
4. Gardner, L., *The Grail Enigma*, 2009, Harper Element, p. 251
5. Bridonneau, Y., *The Tomb of Mary Magdalene Saint Maximin la
Sainte Baumeâ, Christianity's Third Most Important Tomb*, 2006,
Compagnie des Editions de la Lesse, Aix-en-Provence, France
6. Jowett, George F., *The Drama of the Lost Disciples*, The Covenant
Publishing Co. Ltd, p. 44

Doubter

1. https://en.wikipedia.org/wiki/Thomas_the_Apostle, under
'Names and Etymologies'
2. http://www.crystalinks.com/poweranimals.html
3. https://en.wikipedia.org/wiki/Thomas_the_Apostle, under
'Names and Etymologies'
4. https://en.wikipedia.org/wiki/Thomas_the_Apostle, under
'Names and Etymologies'
6. Gardner, L., *The Grail Enigma*, 2009, Harper Element, pp. 32–
33
7. http://www.newworldencyclopedia.org/entry/Saint_Thomas
8. Gardner, L., *The Grail Enigma*, 2009, Harper Element, p. 81
9. Gardner, L., *The Grail Enigma*, 2009, Harper Element, p. 16
10. http://ldolphin.org/leprosy.html (R. K. Harrison, International
Standard Bible Encyclopedia, Eerdmans, Grand
Rapids,1986.http://www.marthomaorthodoxchurch.com/hist
ory.html, The Mar 11. Thoma Orthodox Church, 2014
11. http://www.newworldencyclopedia.org/entry/Saint_Thomas
12. http://www.prayerfoundation.org/how_apostles_died.htm

Forgotten

1. Gardner, L., *The Magdalene Legacy*, 2007, Weiser Books, p. 126

2. Churton, T., *The Mysteries of John the Baptist*, 2012, Inner Traditions, Vermont, p. 144

3. Churton, T., *The Mysteries of John the Baptist*, 2012, Inner Traditions, Vermont, p. 185

4. Gardner, L., *The Grail Enigma*, 2009, Harper Element, pp. 220, 243

Remembered

1. Gardner, L., *The Grail Enigma*, 2009, Harper Element, p. 251

2. Gardner, L., *The Grail Enigma*, 2009, Harper Element, p. 165

3. Wikipedia contributors, Wikipedia, the Free Encyclopedia, https://en.wikipedia.org/w/index.php?title=Aramaic_language&oldid=736847501

4. Gardner, L., *The Grail Enigma*, 2009, Harper Element, pp. 111–44

Substitute

1. http://www.gotquestions.org/Simon-of-Cyrene.html

2. *ibid.*

3. *ibid.*

4. Mark 15:21

5. http://www.answering-christianity.com/abdullah_smith/crucifixion_of_judas.htm

6. http://people.opposingviews.com/did-judas-iscariot-before-following-jesus-5530.html

7. http://www.answering-christianity.com/abdullah_smith/crucifixion_of_judas.htm

Hidden

1. Churton, T., *The Mysteries of John the Baptist*, 2012, Inner Traditions, Vermont, p. 214

2. Churton, T., *The Mysteries of John the Baptist*, 2012, Inner Traditions, Vermont, p. 133

3. Churton, T., *The Mysteries of John the Baptist*, 2012, Inner Traditions, Vermont, p. 126

4. Churton, T., *The Mysteries of John the Baptist*, 2012, Inner Traditions, Vermont, p. 136

5. Churton, T., *The Mysteries of John the Baptist*, 2012, Inner Traditions, Vermont, p. 143

6. Churton, T., *The Mysteries of John the Baptist*, 2012, Inner Traditions, Vermont, p. 144

7. Churton, T., *The Mysteries of John the Baptist*, 2012, Inner Traditions, Vermont, pp. 189–90
8. https://en.wikipedia.org/wiki/Herod_Antipas
9. Churton, T., *The Mysteries of John the Baptist*, 2012, Inner Traditions, Vermont, pp. 129–31
10. http://www.near-death.com/science/research/silver-cord.html, Near-Death Experiences and the Afterlife, 2016
11. Gardner, L., *The Grail Enigma*, 2009, Harper Element, p. 95
12. Churton, T., *The Mysteries of John the Baptist*, 2012, Inner Traditions, Vermont, p. 186

Consciousness
1. Gardner, L., *The Grail Enigma*, 2009, Harper Element, pp. 92–3
2. Gardner, L., *The Grail Enigma*, 2009, Harper Element, p. 104
3. Gardner, L., *The Grail Enigma*, 2009, Harper Element, pp. 63–8
4. Gardner, L., *The Grail Enigma*, 2009, Harper Element, p. 32

Conclusion
1. Robert L. Johnson http://www.deism.com/bibleorigins.htm
2. Jung, C.G., *The Archetypes and the Collective Unconscious*, translated by R.F.C. Hull, 1981, Bollingen Series, Princeton
3. Radin, D., 2009, *The Conscious Universe – The Scientific Truth of Psychic Phenomena*, Harper One

AUTHOR

Reena Kumarasingham is a therapist whose practice, *Divine Aspect*, has clients spanning Asia, Australia and Europe. She is a certified trainer and supervisor for the *Past Life Regression Academy* in the training of therapists in UK, Australia and USA. She has given talks internationally including the *World Congress of Regression Therapy* in Turkey and the *Past Life Regression Convention* in India. Reena is the author of the Radiant Light series, comprising of *Shrouded Truth*, *Illuminated Truth* and *Radiant Truth*. She also contributed two chapters on advanced regression therapy techniques to *Transforming the Eternal Soul*.

Website :   http://www.divineaspect.com
Facebook : http://www.facebook.com/reenakumarasingham
Twitter :   @DivineAspect

Connect with Reena

Divine Aspect

Divine Aspect's vision is for each individual to be totally empowered as you journey towards embracing and honouring your Authentic Selves, and to be supported as you move towards the New Vibration. For more information on how Reena helps clients embrace their 'I AM' to move into the New Consciousness through one to one therapy, training, books and meditations.

https:// www.divineaspect.com

Advanced Vibrational Technique in a New Plane

We are going though an intense shift in vibration, from the third dimension to a higher dimension. This shift has enabled us to access stronger more potent energies. Having access to these new energies gives us a different tool, in accordance to the new vibrational plane that we find ourselves in. We find ourselves having access to many new ways of Being.

Reena facilitates a seven-day training course that not only helps participants access and apply these high vibration energies, but also gives participants a taster of what it is to BE in the new consciousness. The course is highly practical, and includes lectures, interactive discussions, demonstrations and practice sessions.

https://www.divineaspect.com/vibration.htm
https://www.vibrationnewplane.com

Past Life Regression Academy

The Past Life Regression Academy specialises in Past Life Regression Therapy, Regression Therapy, Between Lives Spiritual Regression and Hypnosis training in Europe, Asia and the United States, as well as Soul Evolution workshops. Reena is a trainer for the Academy, specializing in teaching therapists Between Lives Spiritual Regression in the Australia, Singapore, UK and the US.

https://www.regressionacademy.com/life-between-lives-training.htm

https://www.divineaspect.com/workshops.htm

ILLUMINATED TRUTH

Book Two of the Radiant Light Series
coming out soon

Christianity two thousand years ago is very different to the Christianity that we are familiar with today.

Following on from *Shrouded Truth*, *Illuminated Truth* gives us an in depth look into the origins of the teachings of the main branches of Christianity in the Antiquities, through the past life regression of Paul the Evangelist, James, the Brother of Jesus, and Mary Magdalene, the Beloved of Jesus. They take us back on a journey of the rediscovery of three main branches of the teachings of Jesus in the antiquities. Through their memories and recollections, discover the original teachings of Christianity -Judeo Christianity, the lost esoteric wisdom of Christianity – Gnosticism, and how the Christianity that we are familiar with came about – Gentile Christianity.

Illuminated Truth gives us an insight into how these diverse teachings came about, what motivated these teachings, belief systems and philosophies to differ so wildly from one another, how the teachings were received, and what happened to them in the end, in the quest for orthodoxy. Backed by academic research and oral tradition, these regressions open our eyes to a complex and fascinating period in Christian Antiquities, and resurrect the rich wisdom and diverse practises that was once lost to us.

Journey with Paul, James and Mary Magdalene to the origins of their respective ministries, and discover their techniques and teachings for a holistic integrated look at

393

Christianity two thousand years ago, and it's evolution to what it is today.

CPSIA information can be obtained
at www.ICGtesting.com
Printed in the USA
LVHW052358261218
601761LV00009B/536